THE DYNAMIC WORKPLACE

Present Structure and Future Redesign

Seth Allcorn

Foreword by Michael Diamond

Westport, Connecticut
London

Library of Congress Cataloging-in-Publication Data

Allcorn, Seth.
  The dynamic workplace : present structure and future redesign /
Seth Allcorn : foreword by Michael Diamond.
     p. cm.
  Includes bibliographical references and index.
  ISBN 1–56720–619–0 (alk. paper)
  1. Office layout. 2. Work environment. 3. Work design. 4. Office management.
  5. Organizational behavior. I. Title.
HF5547.2 A43 2003
331.25—dc 21   2002030334

British Library Cataloguing in Publication Data is available.

Library of Congress Catalog Card Number: 2002030334
ISBN: 1–56720–619–0

First published in 2003

Praeger Publishers, 88 Post Road West, Westport, CT 06881
An imprint of Greenwood Publishing Group, Inc.
www.praeger.com

Printed in the United States of America

The paper used in this book complies with the
Permanent Paper Standard issued by the National
Information Standards Organization (Z39.48–1984).

10 9 8 7 6 5 4 3 2 1

Contents

Illustrations

Foreword

Seth Allcorn's most recent book, *The Dynamic Workplace: Present Structure and Future Redesign,* reflects the author's ambition to rise above the twenty-first century remnants of modern-day multi-sector Weberian bureaucracy. It is an ambitious goal stemming from wide-ranging observation and experience as an organizational analyst, consultant and executive manager. From his books and articles over the years, some of which we published together, you come to realize that Allcorn cares about restoring the humanity of the workplace as much as he does its functionality and structural adaptability. Furthermore, despite his persistent humanistic critique of hierarchy and bureaucracy he implicitly supports an element of structural functionalism, which evolves out of the strategic challenges of organizations and their leadership in adapting to complex environments. Hence, he is as much a pragmatist as he is a romantic and dialectician.

Early on in this book, Allcorn takes a historian's look back at organizations and organization theory from the beginning of the twentieth century. In so doing, he at least implicitly raises questions about human nature and the human condition as seen through the experience and intellect of theoreticians as diverse as Frederick W. Taylor and Mary Parker Follett, among others. Organizational writers generally agree that a paradigmatic shift took hold in the transition of Western organization and management thought from the scientific management of the early twentieth century to the human relations and organizational humanism movements of the 1930s through 1960s. And, while Allcorn recognizes and applauds this ideological movement, he finds it troubling as well. That is, it appears theory has not translated into practice at work.

In contrast with the emphasis on top-down control and the measured management of physical movements at work under scientific management, theoreticians of the human relations school came to see the workplace as composed of multidimensional, dynamic groups of human beings with unique needs and desires, formal and informal groups, and conscious and unconscious processes. It was a rather remarkable disparity with Taylor and his followers' earlier assumptions and attributions on human motivation. Nevertheless, Taylor's seemingly one-dimensional portrayal of workers as tools of management and his obsession with efficiency and subordinate control may seem stubbornly indicative of mainstream, techno-rational management thinking at the beginning of the twenty-first century. Unless I am mistaken, Allcorn observes that Taylorism is in fact "alive and well" in today's high tech, spiritless and thereby not so lively workplace.

In addition to his observations on the remnants of Taylorism and scientific management today, Allcorn spends a good deal of time wrestling with Weberian bureaucracy and its prominent structural attribute—hierarchy. It is here that Allcorn's argument gets interesting as well as paradoxical. It is evident that the author wants us to transcend Taylor's perpetual and trans-generational obsession with control in the management of people at work and its human consequences in sucking the life and spirit out of organizational experience. One can say that contemporary preoccupation with downsizing and reengineering has its origins in the philosophical foundations of scientific management. There may be a tinge of existentialism here, not that either Camus or Sartre is standing in for Allcorn's ego ideal or anything like that. Nevertheless, the author does demand the reader's willingness to embrace complexity and dynamic multidimensionality in understanding and transforming the workplace. Ultimately he views organizational dynamics as dialectical and thereby requiring managers not to control these dynamics but to contain and facilitate their diverse modalities and dimensions.

He begins with the idea that we need to accept both the objective and subjective realities of organizational life, which comprise three simultaneous operational dimensions:

1. organizational rationality;
2. organizational irrationality;
3. organizational spirituality.

The notion of organizational rationality signifying the formal structures, strategies, and realities of the task environment demands effective external adaptation and internal integration. These structures include hierarchy, divisions of labor, technical specialization, professionalism and impersonal norms, among other attributes many of his readers are fully aware of.

In addition to these elements of structural and technological rationalism, there is a simultaneous organizational irrationality, which demands our attention and a process for containment and creative exploitation. In so doing we require a depth of understanding, insight and most importantly, humility among leaders, consultants and students of organizations. Certainly a major premise for Allcorn is that we ought not try to control the presence of irrationality in the workplace, yet as noted above it demands our awareness. Moreover, the irrational side of organizational experience operates at multiple levels of analysis: intrapersonal, interpersonal, group and organizational. Thus, if we are to comprehend organizational dynamics, we have to come to understand the complexity of these interactive dimensions. We cannot escape nor deny, for example, the presence of human needs for aggression, affection, dependency and ideals at work. And rather than control and suppress human nature in the workplace, Allcorn demands that we accept, embrace and tap into this source of human energy and spirit.

Finally, his emphasis on spirituality certainly implies that workers demand human value from their professional careers and vocations, and he further assumes that they want to experience their worklives as meaningful, purposeful and productive. His previous book (2002), *Death of the Spirit in the American Workplace*, forcefully addresses these issues and I would direct the reader to this work for further elaboration on the subject. In sum, Allcorn's analysis of contemporary organizations has analytic depth, and his prescriptions for change are practical and moral. Yet, there are no easy answers or quick fixes.

In paying attention to the multidimensionality of organizational analysis, Allcorn strives for a particular balance and tension between bureaucratic, charismatic and chaotic dimensions of the workplace. Here, he seems to move beyond traditional forms of managerial control and toward containment and creative utilization of the contradictory dynamics of bureaucracy, charismatic leadership and the inevitability of chaos—tensions that comprise real work and passionate leadership in an unfettered structural context. Sound utopian, possibly, his presentation of a prototype, the "ring organization" model combines (what he calls) physical, potential and virtual workplaces into one nonhierarchic, dynamic organization.

Allcorn's vision for future organization goes beyond hybrid organization. Rather, it combines acknowledgment of technological advances in networking capabilities and increasing worker mobility with minimal structure for adaptability to constantly changing and complex environments. Most significantly, it recognizes the value of transitional and potential space for creativity, invention and innovation. His model of the "ring organization" transcends cumbersome hierarchy while maintaining accountability. In the final analysis, Allcorn formulates a new organization design that is intended to embrace complexity, free the spirit at work and process knowledge derived from inside and outside its permeable boundaries.

Michael Diamond

Preface

One's worklife is invariably filled with many experiences that lead to reflection and rumination, especially if that worklife is less than perfect. Executives, managers and employees must not only adjust to the constant presence of daily change, they must more often these days cope with the most expansive of all changes as operationalized by management phrases such as downsizing, restructuring and reengineering as well as merger and acquisition. Worklife can indeed be filled with many ducks nipping at one's legs and great white sharks tearing away massive chunks of one's well-being along with vast sections of one's workplace. How do we as organization leaders, members, consultants and researchers appreciate these workplace events and their accompanying complexity? How do we understand a workplace that is regrettably often filled to overflowing with distressing influences that make us feel anxious and defensive?

This book provides the reader a way to think about workplace events and in particular organizational politics or, using a more scholarly term, organizational dynamics. What it is like to live one's life at work is ultimately dominated by hard-to-understand complexity that can be demystified to a large extent if an insightful way of thinking about the workplace is used to examine it. This book introduces a dynamic theory of the workplace that contains elements firmly grounded in the workplace, where work can at times seem chaotic but also bureaucratic as well as autocratic. There are also, of course, those instances when employees feel joined together to accomplish meaningful work effectively and efficiently. Dynamic workplace theory represents an effort to draw upon the familiar while at the same time providing a sophisticated cognitive map for appreciating workplace experience in all of its diversity.

Dynamic workplace theory is an extension of earlier thinking on the part of myself and my colleague Michael Diamond (Diamond and Allcorn, 1987; Allcorn, 1989; Diamond, 1993). This earlier work and this book also owe much to a number of protracted experiential learning opportunities I attended sponsored by the A.K. Rice Institute. For those who know of these learning opportunities, little more need be said and for those unfamiliar with them, no amount of words can ultimately convey what often seems like a journey alongside Conrad into the darkness of intrapersonal, interpersonal and group dynamics. Additional learning also occurred when Michael, and another colleague, Bob Frank, and I teamed up to introduce experiential learning into graduate classes in public administration. It was certainly the case for myself that as a result of this work I came more fully to appreciate that these kinds of classroom experiences create anxieties that key-off psychological regression and defensiveness (Allcorn and Diamond, 1997). It also became equally clear that stressful workplace experiences promote regression to more primitive, hard-to-understand and unproductive interpersonal, group and organizational dynamics. The workplace, I learned, is not so rational a place to spend one's time. Dynamic workplace theory may then be understood to be the product of more than thirty years of study, writing, consultation and executive experience on my part. It represents my effort to understand the diversity and complexity of worklife.

It is my hope in writing down what I have learned that you the reader can use dynamic workplace theory as a jumping-off point for your own organizational research, reflection and understanding. I believe we can all appreciate that understanding workplace experience is a challenge regardless of the means used to study and analyze it. It is also the case that a perspective such as dynamic workplace theory provides a cognitive and affective anchor for gaining insight into workplace experience that may serve to minimize anxiety-filled personal experience and the possibility of regression that encourages reliance upon reality-altering psychological defenses.

Introduction

Modern-day organizations have a life of their own, or so it seems. In many ways each is unique while they also share much in common. As we begin the twenty-first century, those of us who work within organizations are all too often confronted with a vast array of organizational attributes, events, leaders, followers, departments, divisions, plans, performance expectations, and goals and objectives—complexity that is hard to understand in a meaningful way. We may feel overwhelmed by daily worklife when we really stop to think about it. This and stressful workplace events can make us feel anxious about others, the future and ourselves. What is really happening? Why? How will it affect me? The harder we examine our worklives and workplaces, the more is revealed. Layer upon layer of organizational and management hierarchy is found to be accompanied by the inevitable interpersonal tensions and conflicts as well as unpredictable outcomes that remind us of how bounded the assumption of workplace rationality really is.

Even the smallest organizations are filled with complexity that is not unlike the nature of their vast companions at the other end of the organizational size spectrum. A recent change in leadership in a retail organization with fewer than fifty employees revealed in a humbling way the complexity and unintended outcomes that change introduces into the workplace. It sometimes does truly seem to be the case that a butterfly flapping its wings in the Amazon might conceivably affect the nature of change in an organization. In this case, a new manager was hired to replace the owner. Some employees accepted the change without much comment while others became distressed, creating a feedback loop among themselves that led to ever stranger and harder to manage outcomes. One employee became personally disorganized and had to use powerful psychopharmacological substances to stay his anxiety and calm his self-experience. Others felt abandoned by their leader of many years. The sense of bonding, mentoring and familiarity with their leader, it was thought, would no longer be available. Yet another felt that he had been passed over for the management role and became enraged, threatening resignation and condemning the owner for the change and betrayal. Surely his out-of-control feelings were entirely the owner's fault, or so he seemed to think. He eventually left. Other employees fed the fires of discontent by selectively passing along confidential information about the operation of the business that made the owner appear to be greedy and out to get rich at their expense. The new manager was described as a hatchet man brought in to tighten things up and wring more work out of the employees. Fantasy upon fantasy was generated along with underlying reinforcing themes that fed the rumor mill and poisoned the well of interpersonal trust, respect and goodwill. I was reminded that the organizational dislocation created by making this single change in a small organization shared much in common with findings in my research into the downsizing of a large hospital (Allcorn et al., 1996). In this case the lives of employees were so severely disrupted that it was hard to tell who were the victims. Were the victims those terminated and put out of their misery, or those who remained to feel guilty about their personal survival and were forced to tolerate the awareness that they could be next despite their best efforts to be productive? These outcomes of organizational change underscore the hard-to-fathom complexity of the workplace that arises from the interaction of what is ultimately an unknowable universe of variables. In sum, it is truly hard to know one's workplace.

The ability to reach an understanding of our organizations and their dynamics inevitably devolves into editing out some data, making certain reasonable assumptions about how things work and sometimes just making it up or possibly trying to ignore it. Some employees will think, "Just leave me alone and let me do my job." For those who do try to understand how a large organization functions, there gradually develops a tacit and, for the most part out of awareness, cognitive model of how the organization works. This model, although consistently relied upon is, regrettably, not particularly open to inspection. It merely exists as a part of one's reality filter. A second possibility for those informed about management and organizational literature is the conscious selection of a way of thinking about organizational life—a model of organizational dynamics. This book is about this latter approach, the development of an explicit theoretical perspective or model that explains organizational dynamics by capturing much of the monumental complexity that exists within the workplace and placing it into a comprehendible context.

Dynamic workplace theory, as mentioned, is informed by my experience working as a manager and executive within perhaps the most complex organization form of all, the academic health sciences center. These centers are at, or nearly so, the pinnacle of organizational complexity and with it near unmanageability. Think for the moment of trying to balance the interests of twenty or more clinical and academic departments, a few research institutes, a huge outpatient facility with satellites, a large research hospital and perhaps a veterans' affairs hospital, schools of nursing and in some instances dentistry all residing within a university context and larger competitive health care delivery arena and society. The number of variables that must be considered in decision making can be overwhelming and, therefore, most often the outcomes are suboptimal. Dynamic workplace theory is, therefore, informed by a hard-won appreciation of just how complex the workplace can be.

The development and explication of dynamic workplace theory raised for me many tough questions about how we design and operate our organizations today. In particular, my work raised questions about the near universality of hierarchical and usually bureaucratic organizations. I have often wondered about whether there is some other way of creating an organization that would not only work but also conceivably work better than the bureaucratic hierarchy. Initially all of my thinking seemed to irresistibly return to hierarchy. It was as though I was stuck within a paradigm and simply could not get out of it, or as they say, "think outside of the box." After years of reflection and pondering I have developed a prototype nonhierarchical organization model to encourage critical thinking outside of the box. Ring organization design is described in this book as a counterpoint to hierarchical organizations. It is not my purpose in providing this prototype to advocate that this new form of organization be adopted or to prove beyond a reasonable doubt that it will work. Inevitably it is the case that some brave CEO must try it to see what will happen. Nonetheless, this new line of thinking about organizational design and operation introduces the reader to another way of understanding the complexity of the workplace, that of trying to find a better way of designing it.

In sum, this book presents readers a challenging way of understanding the workplace that encompasses much of its inherent and often unacknowledged complexity. It also provides a thought-provoking rethinking of organizational design that permits juxtaposing the new thinking with dynamic workplace theory for yet more learning.

This book is organized to provide readers summaries of the content as well as detailed discussions of dynamic workplace theory and its workings. In this regard, I appreciate that a detailed theoretical discussion is not to everyone's liking. The summaries provide a quick route through the basic points made in the book, in the hope if this route is taken the reader will take the time to read in greater detail those sections where the points made in the summaries seem to be counterintuitive. It is also often the case the prior content is not only merely summarized but also recast to provide additional insights for the reader who has read the detailed discussion. Regardless of one's reading proclivities, it is important to appreciate that a useful workplace theory must have sufficient complexity if it is to come close to providing a good cognitive map of the workplace. In sum, every effort has been made to balance readability with theoretical explication. This book is organized as follows.

Chapter 1 introduces a number of time-tested perspectives for examining the workplace, along with historical perspective. Much of what is of concern in the twenty-first century was of concern in the eighteenth and nineteenth centuries. This chapter serves to orient the reader to the many complexities of the workplace and some of the difficulties attached to any effort to develop a workplace model or theory about how things work.

Chapter 2 introduces dynamic workplace theory. A case example is provided to help the reader locate the basic elements of the theory relative to common workplace experiences. The workplace is found to be composed of four kinds of groups (chaotic, bureaucratic hierarchy, charismatically led, balanced) that contain specific kinds of workplace experiences as well as organizational dynamics. These groups, it is asserted, constitute the entire context within which we all labor on a daily basis. At the same time, these groups are familiar and, therefore, may not be thought of on a daily basis as existing at all. They essentially constitute the universally accepted nature of worklife, and consequently are taken for granted thereby going unnoticed and uninspected. Dynamic workplace theory is then faced with a challenge. It must make these accepted, and for the most part out of awareness, aspects of worklife observable and subject to inspection by organization members.

Chapter 3 begins the process of "peeling the onion." Dynamic workplace theory is thoroughly inspected in terms of its basic elements (the four types of group and organizational experience) and its dynamic nature. Discussed is how change occurs within and among the groups. In particular, what makes this theory of the workplace dynamic is the deeply embedded tensions, conflicts and imbalances that lie within each of the types of workplace experience. Change within the theory is a constant potential, the direction of which is indeterminate at any given moment.

Chapter 4 continues the peeling process by inspecting the transitional spaces that exist between the four groups. Organizational change does not occur as though a switch is flipped and one moment there is only darkness and the next light. If a lightbulb is filmed at high speed one can observe the process of the filament becoming heated to glowing, thereby creating light. Organizational change is much like the metaphor of the light. Even though it is tempting to think of organizational change in much the same way as flipping a switch and turning on a light, it is, in fact, a process filled with many discernible steps that exist on a time continuum. Planning and implementing organizational change is, in my experience, a demanding endeavor for any executive or consultant to undertake, as is illustrated by the above organizational change vignette. It is, therefore, essential to inspect dynamic workplace theory for its contribution to understanding how change occurs. A shift from one of the four types of group process and experience to another contains much that must be understood in order to appreciate the psychosocial elements of dynamic workplace theory.

Chapter 5 explores the nature of the implicit underlying stability contained within each of the four types of work experience. Each of the four types of workplace experience described in dynamic workplace theory contains elements that encourage it to be maintained over time. Change to another of the experiences, it may be felt, is too threatening. The familiar may be lost. What will happen? Fear regarding even the contemplation of change often leads to the thought that change is too hard to achieve and that it is better to try to improve upon the current group or organization dynamic. Each of the four types of workplace experience is evaluated for this underlying stability that encourages organization members to maintain the experience, however unsatisfactory it may become over time. As noted in chapter 4, organizational change is often problematic, especially when it is perceived as fundamentally changing the nature of what may have become familiar organizational experience and working relationships. When problems are encountered in making change it is natural to retreat back to what has worked in the past. Why fix it if it is not broken? is a question that may be asked. "Don't we just need to tune things up a bit?"

Chapter 6 explores the contribution of dynamic workplace theory for executives, managers and consultants who strive to improve the workplace and its performance. Dynamic workplace theory draws upon aspects of workplace experience that are not hard to locate. What is important about the theory is that it provides an integrated perspective for understanding these types of experience relative to each other. In this regard the theory offers executives, managers, supervisors, employees, students of organizational dynamics and consultants not only a way of seeing the workplace from a new perspective but also a way of working and managing within the workplace. In sum, this chapter explores the contribution the theory makes to managing and working within our modern-day organizations as well as consulting to them.

Chapter 7 commences a process of introducing a new nonhierarchical perspective for organizational design. The industrial revolution yielded what has become a nearly universal form of organization design, that of the bureaucratic hierarchy. This chapter presents the larger historical context for attempting to think outside of the box created by what must be considered to be a thought-limiting organizational paradigm. This historical perspective is especially sobering as we contemplate the future of organizational design and management. Have things really changed so little over the centuries?

Chapter 8 introduces an entirely new and nonhierarchical concept for designing organizational structure that minimizes compulsive reliance upon bureaucratic control. Ring organization does away with the traditional notion of a formal and often rigid command and control structure where positions are arrayed in a traditional organization chart, from the most powerful and important at the top to the least important and powerful at the bottom. Ring organization design presents the reader with a new way of thinking about organizational design. It also demonstrates how difficult it is to envision a new workable workplace design when the only perspective available for assessing its efficacy is experience acquired within traditional bureaucratic hierarchies.

Chapter 9 steps back from the discussion of dynamic workplace theory and ring organization design to inspect both theoretical perspectives for their veracity. Each perspective introduces the reader to new ideas and ways of understanding and integrating workplace experience. In particular, ring organization design points to the exceptional difficulties involved with envisioning any kind of organization that does not have at its core a command and control structure—a bureaucratic hierarchy. This chapter inspects dynamic workplace theory and

ring organization design for important omissions, internal inconsistencies and
conflicts with other perspectives. Is the theory and ring design ultimately useful in the workplace? This chapter concludes by comparing the two perspectives
relative to each other. Are the elements of dynamic workplace theory applicable
to the proposed ring organization design?

Chapter 10 brings the book to an end by examining what the nature of the
crossover may be when dynamic workplace theory is used to inform how we
manage and operate our contemporary organization form, the bureaucratic hierarchy. The dynamic and ultimately uncontrollable nature of the theory when
combined with the uncontrollable nature of an organization's task environment
directs our attention to the necessity of designing into our organizations a
dynamic adaptiveness that improves long-term survivability. This chapter
introduces the notion of organizational plasticity as an integral part of re-
envisioning how our contemporary organizations work. The chapter concludes
with the perhaps obvious observation that what is learned from dynamic workplace theory also informs how we live our lives outside of work.

PROVISOS

Language is an important part of any theoretical discussion. For my purposes
here I will often speak of group and organization dynamics by using only the
word "group" or "organization," depending on the context. However, when either of the words is used, the other applies just as well.

One of the central elements to this book is exploring not so much the concrete aspects of the workplace but rather the harder to quantify and understand
psychological and social aspects of worklife that most often become the dominant influence in achieving outstanding organizational performance. The human
side of the enterprise is, in my experience, the most difficult part to understand
and manage. Dynamic workplace theory is, therefore, most of all a perspective
for understanding the psychosocial side of the workplace. However, it may also
be readily understood that many of the concrete aspects of the workplace become the tools of the human side of the enterprise in carrying out less than
thoughtful and rational human motivations.

This appreciation introduces an additional proviso. Organizations are most
often thought of as having a concrete presence and are spoken of in a reified
manner. The organization, it may be asserted, has a certain attribute, or that "it"
laid off employees. However, other than their physical properties, some of which
may not exist at all in the virtual organizations of tomorrow, organizations are
created every day their members come to work. In this regard the primary substance of an organization is the experience of its members and it is this experience that is emphasized in this book. Employees experience their workplace in
many different ways, ranging from caring and nurturing to threatening and
alienating. Traditional bureaucratic hierarchies are, it is suggested here, concep-

tual constructs that exist within the hearts and minds of their members (Czander, 1993). They introduce a context for experience of the workplace that, in turn, dominates their ability to succeed. Experience of organizational life is emphasized throughout this book.

Last and already mentioned earlier, the book presents a theoretical perspective that is then thoroughly analyzed in terms of its workplace applicability and dynamics. It is my view that many ideas about how the workplace functions are not carefully enough thought through for all of their many implications if they are to be successfully adopted for use in the workplace. Equally important, by taking the time to try to explain the dynamics of the model, the reader is hopefully encouraged to inspect his or her implicit out-of-awareness model(s) of how the workplace works in just as much detail. In this regard the book introduces consciousness-raising about implicit and tacit workplace theories and models that are in operation all of the time, but not at a level of formal awareness and, therefore, not open to inspection and learning.

In conclusion, this book presents the reader many challenging perspectives that must be thought about and inspected for their utility based on one's firsthand experience of worklife. In a sense, only you the reader can validate or invalidate the contributions this book makes toward understanding your work experience.

Chapter 1

Know Thy Workplace

Groups are organized for different purposes, but all units are alike in one respect: they are intended to be useful to members, nonmembers, or both. If groups are to serve a specific function, it follows that the purposes of groups shift as the desires of those who have a stake in the group change— different wishes or interests cause new requirements.

(Zander, 1985, p. 33)

Thus organizations are composed of interdependent groups having different immediate goals, different ways of working, different formal training, even different personality types within them. These differences make for different styles of functioning within them.

(Levinson, 1972, p. 3)

It is relatively recent that theorists have suggested that organization structure may be designed and developed through a set of motivations that may be other than rational. . . . These theorists suggest that organization structures are created to reflect unconscious fantasies associated with the wishes and needs of executives. These unconscious fantasies may be associated with the wish for power, idealization, order, security, and domination, as well as fear of loss and castration.

(Czander, 1993, p. 103)

The workplace, regardless of whether it is a small fifty-employee retail store or a global enterprise employing hundreds of thousands of workers, is filled with a hard-to-know complexity that we most often pretend is not there in order to function in our jobs. The vastness of workplace attributes overwhelms efforts to enumerate them, much less understand them as a dynamic whole where their unlimited interactions further multiply the vastness to unimaginable proportions. This appreciation amounts to a humbling additional proviso for this book and you the reader. There is no way all of this can be addressed for what it is. We are rather reduced to locating ways of thinking about this complexity that do not do a gross injustice to the true nature of the workplace. At the same time the cognitive maps that we use must provide us reasonably good insights that permit us to come to some understanding of the workplace and how it relates to us and how we relate to it. This chapter provides an overview and historical perspective of the evolving complexity of the workplace and the development of cognitive maps, models and theories for understanding it. I begin the discussion with a review of several serviceable perspectives of the workplace that I have found to be of use as an executive and as a management consultant. The reader is reminded that a fast path through the chapter is provided in the form of summaries.

THE THREE SIDES TO ORGANIZATIONAL LIFE

One way to think about the workplace is that it contains rational elements that exist alongside and in tension with irrational and spiritual elements (Allcorn, 2002). Each is informed by the other where their contrasts delineate their differences. The three sides to organizational life are, for the most part, three independent perspectives that ultimately exist simultaneously and are always available to organization members even though one may reach a temporary ascendancy. Let us begin with the familiar notion that the workplace and work are logically and rationally designed to achieve efficiency and effectiveness.

The Rational Side of Organization Life

The amount that has been written about trying to create a more logical, efficient and effective workplace is staggering. A watershed was passed at the beginning of the twentieth century with the work of Frederick W. Taylor, who advocated a much more logical and scientific approach to managing work to achieve better organizational performance. Taylor (1947) writes: "The body of this paper will make it clear that, to work according to scientific laws, the management must take over and perform much of the work which is now left to the men; almost every act of the workman should be preceded by one or more preparatory acts of the management which enable him to do his work better and quicker than he otherwise could. And each man should be taught by and receive the most friendly help from those who are over him, instead of being, at the one extreme, driven or coerced by his bosses, and at the other left to his own unaided devices" (p. 26).

Taylor (1947) further elaborated his perspective by writing: "It is true that with scientific management the workman is not allowed to use whatever implements and methods he sees fit in the daily practice of his work. Every encouragement, however, should be given him to suggest improvements, both in methods and in implements. . . . And whenever the new method is found to be markedly superior to the old, it should be adopted as the standard for the whole establishment" (p. 128). Today this basic concept is often referred to as best practices, total quality management, or continuous improvement, and it is a precursor to the Japanese model for improving organizational performance. Little has changed from management considerations raised a century or more ago.

Taylor's work and the thoughtful labors of countless others have all served to make the workplace in most instances more efficient and cost-effective by achieving ever-greater control and predictability. The organizational ideal is to have the workplace run like a clock (Morgan, 1986; Schwartz, 1990). Fayol (1949) for example writes: "To co-ordinate is to harmonize all the activities of a concern so as to facilitate its working, and its success. In a well coordinated enterprise the following facts are to be observed—1. Each department works in harmony with the rest. . . . 2. In each department divisions and sub-divisions are precisely informed as to the share they must take in the communal task and the reciprocal aid they are to afford one another. The working schedule of the various departments and sub-divisions thereof is constantly attuned to circumstances" (pp. 103–4). He also adds: "In an undertaking, control consists in verifying whether everything occurs in conformity with the plan adopted, the instructions issued and principles established" (p. 107). Problems in achieving organizational efficiency and effectiveness to maximize performance and profitability have been and still are seen in large part as engineering and control problems.

If we skip ahead 75–100 years from Taylor's scientific management we are confronted with much the same thinking today. Starting a decade or more ago and continuing to this day there are many rationalistic efforts to reengineer, restructure, rightsize, and quality-assure our organizations. It is often the case that a certain organization structure or the exact size of a reduction in force is delivered into the workplace by the analysis of numbers that may not be further questioned. During the last decade of the twentieth century almost everyone in the American workforce was downsized or restructured or knows others who were. It is, in fact, a pervasive commonality among those who work at all levels of organizations, so much so that one might suggest that our organizations seem to share a common culture (Allcorn et al., 1996).

In Sum

The pursuit of a rationally designed workplace that runs like a highly efficient and well-oiled machine has been the holy grail of executives, managers and management thinkers not only during the twentieth century but, indeed, for millennia. In some ways no stone has been left unturned or at least uninspected in the pursuit of the profit created by efforts to make the workplace into a scientific and over-engineered enterprise. All of the work of Taylor and his legions of colleagues in the pursuit of the rational workplace, however, overlooked a quality to the workplace that is not so rational and indeed might be considered at times irrational—human nature.

The Irrational Side of Organizational Life

The irrational side of the workplace has had much light shed on it during the twentieth century. If Taylor ignited the fires of scientific management, Elton Mayo introduced the confounding variable of human nature as an outcome of his early efforts to further extend the precepts of scientific management into the workplace. It is certainly the case that the reengineering of the corporation would have been informed by his work. Mayo (1945) writes,

But for the individual worker the problem is really much more serious. He has suffered a profound loss of security and certainty in his actual living and in the background of his thinking. For all of us the feeling of security and certainty derives always from assured membership of a group. If this is lost, no monetary gain, no job guarantee, can be sufficient compensation. Where groups change ceaselessly as jobs and mechanical processes change, the individual inevitably experiences a sense of void, of emptiness, where his fathers knew the joy of comradeship and security. And in such situations, his anxieties—many, no doubt irrational or ill-founded—increase and he becomes more difficult both to fellow workers and to supervisors. (p. 76)

Mayo's analysis of work extended to trying to find the best possible way to control employee workplace experience in order to maximize productivity. Employees in his famous lighting experiment just did not, however, behave as predicted. Management could not, it seemed, perfectly engineer the workplace to create a setting where every aspect of human nature was controlled. Indeed, far from it. Many others have looked into the inner life of organizations. An explosion of psychoanalytically informed inquiry that started during the last quarter of the twentieth century has been contributed to by many voices, including the author's. Two of the earliest authors who advocated this line of inquiry are Abraham Zaleznik and Harry Levinson. An early example of this inquiry is represented by Abraham Zaleznik's 1966 examination of the nature of leadership. He writes:

I should like to try to lift the veil somewhat on the nature of conflicts in exercising leadership. The two points I want to develop are: 1. The main source of the dilemmas leaders face is found within themselves, in their own inner conflicts. 2. Dealing more intelligently with knotty decisions and the inevitable conflicts of interest existing among men in organizations presupposes that executives, at least the successful ones, are able to put their own houses in order. It presupposes that the executive is able to resolve or manage his inner conflicts so that his actions are strongly grounded in reality, so that he does not find himself constantly making and then undoing decisions to the service of his own mixed feelings and to the disservice and confusion of his subordinates. (p. 31)

Harry Levinson (1968) further underscores the importance of a carefully modulated leadership style within the workplace and the difficulty in achieving this by noting: "The conception of personality developed by psychoanalytic theory has two implicit assumptions. It assumes that personality is a genetic phenomenon, evolving continuously from a changing physical matrix and shaped from experience" (pp. 23–24). He further notes: "This conception assumes, further, that personality is a dynamic phenomenon—that it is a result of many different forces and seeks to maintain its equilibrium" (p. 24). He concludes: "These assumptions about personality underlie two propositions. First, people bring to their jobs attitudes, expectations, and modes of behavior that have evolved from their life experiences. Second, as they work, they are continually trying to maintain their personality equilibrium" (p. 24). The workplace, it may be safely concluded, is filled by human nature that many times defeats the best engineered controls.

In Sum

The comforting aspect of the rather more concrete aspects of the rational workplace must yield to the uncomfortable and even distressing nature of individual, interpersonal, group and organizational dynamics that introduce extraordinarily difficult to grasp nuances and complexity. It is not possible here to more than briefly touch upon the issues raised by the irrational side of the workplace. However, discussed below is the subject of organizational dynamics that includes inspection of intrapersonal, interpersonal, group and organizational dynamics of a psychological nature.

The Spiritual Side of Organizational Life

A more recent line of inquiry arises out of the monumental organizational devastation wrought by Michael Hammer and James Champy's (1993) advocacy of reengineering the corporation and the many consultants cashing in on this management fad. It is noteworthy that in a recent book Hammer acknowledges he had it wrong. Nonetheless, in much the same way Taylor reengineered work, Hammer and Champy suggest that organizations can be created in much the same way. This toxic mix of quasi-scientific thinking ended up creating an unpalatable stew of management fads and consulting companies that irresistibly diminished the quality of organizational life (Micklethwait, J. and Woolridge, A., 1996). This diminishment and alienation from oneself, one's work and the workplace is further underscored by Robert De Board (1978), who writes:

One common effect all organizations seem able to produce is the promotion of non-human objectives above people, so that the human spirit is sacrificed to such sterile aims as profit and technology. One answer is to retire to the hills, grow organic foods, and live in a house powered by wind and sun. However, I would argue that modern society is too complex and too interdependent to develop this way. The answer, perhaps, lies in developing organizations that produce wealth and which at the same time, enable the people working in them to maintain and develop their humanity. How this will happen is uncertain. (p. vii)

Employees find themselves treated as organizational fat that can be eradicated at any time, liposuctioned via the hygienic notion of outplacement. Organizations are flattened and otherwise hammered into shape. Employees become expendable even at the highest levels. These trends are more than distressing, they are disheartening and personally disorganizing. Organizations are having their social fabric ripped apart. Employees are faced with possible career annihilation and the inability to support their families. They are metaphorically packed into cattle cars and hauled out of the organizations that they have often served with a lifetime of loyal work. In the end one can think of dislocations of this magnitude and depravity as destroying the spirit within the workplace as well as the human spirit (Allcorn, 2002 and Allcorn, S., et al., 1996).

Overlooked in this milieu of organizational destruction has been the much earlier work of Roethlisberger, Dickson and Wright (1939) who caution, "This resistance (to change) was expressed whenever changes were introduced too rapidly or without sufficient consideration of their social implications; in other words, whenever the workers were being asked to adjust themselves to new methods or systems which seemed to them to deprive their work of its customary social significance" (p. 567). The same authors also remind us, "But the relation of the individual employee to the company is not a closed system. All the values of the individual cannot be accounted for by the social organization of the company. The meaning a person assigns to his position depends on whether or not the position is allowing him to fulfill the social demands he is making of his work. The ultimate significance of his work is not defined so much by his relation to the company as by his relation to the wider social reality" (p. 375).

Mary Parker Follett, who wrote in the first quarter of the twentieth century, if consulted today, would no doubt caution against management fads such as downsizing, restructuring and reengineering. She writes:

There are leaders who do not appeal to man's complacency but to all their best impulses, their greatest capacities, their deepest desires. I think it was Emerson who told us of those who supply us with new powers out of the recesses of the spirit and urge us to new and unattempted performance. This is far more than imitating your leader. In this conception of Emerson's, what you receive from your leader does not come from him, but from the "recesses of the spirit." Whoever connects me with the hidden springs of all life, whoever increases the sense of life in me, he is my leader. (Metcalf and Urwick, 1941, p. 294)

Indeed as we begin the 21st century one wonders why, if methods such as downsizing and reengineering the corporation metaphorically cut the heart out of an organization and diminish the spirit of employees in America, warnings of other contemporary management writers have been disregarded. Vaill (1989) reminds us that, "A culture is a system of attitudes, actions, and artifacts that endures over time and that operates to produce among its members a relatively unique common psychology" (p. 147). He goes on to note, "True culture change is systemic change at a deep psychological level involving attitudes, actions, and artifacts that have developed over substantial periods of time" (Vaill, 1989, pp. 149–50). This appreciation seems to provide an important warning for the advocates of downsizing and reengineering. Abrupt and sweeping change can destroy the culture and with it the soul of an organization.

Another organization theorist, Bergquist (1993), notes, "Greater attention must be given to organizational culture and to creating a strong feeling of solidarity; otherwise, organizations will increasingly be experienced as fragmented and inconsistent" (p. 42). And more profoundly he suggests, "The culture of an organization provides the glue that holds the organization's diverse elements together and creates a sense of continuity among those working in and leading the organization" (p. 47). These considerations speak to the importance of the spiritual nature of the workplace. Creating organizational change that destroys the spiritual side of the workplace and the spirituality of employees may well plant the seeds of failure requiring yet another round of destructive organizational change (Allcorn, 2002). I now turn to another complex dimension for examining the workplace, that of the psychological and social side of the workplace, and the accompanying organizational dynamics.

In Sum

A new consideration that adds to the complexity of understanding the workplace is the spiritual side of human nature and work. Organizations that ignore this deeper side of organizations and their members do so at great peril. An organization with a downtrodden spirit is not unlike a person whose spirit is similarly downtrodden. The individual may feel listless, depressed, alienated from self and others and de-energized. One must wonder why leaders would want to create an organization with similar attributes.

EXPLORING ORGANIZATIONAL DYNAMICS

The above three sides of organizational life provide us a vision of what amounts to a familiar complexity that is at the minimum intuitively known. We are usually very aware of these aspects of our worklives. The three ways of understanding work experience can be further explained by using what is likely a less familiar perspective that merges psychological and sociological (psychosocial) perspectives of the workplace. The following discussion is intended only to highlight the importance of these perspectives, as much has been written in depth on all of these layers of organizational awareness. Despite the brevity, the reader will take away a more complete appreciation of the true complexity that is the workplace.

The Intrapersonal Realm

The intrapersonal realm is that part of us that is internal. It is what goes on in our minds whether it is conscious or unconscious. Our lives are in large part dominated by what we think and feel and subsequently act out. There is, in effect, a blooming buzzing confusion that is with us every minute. It is in a sense who we are and is so omnipresent as to often escape any form of direct inspection. Why do we seem to warm up to one of two people we just met and not the other? Why might we resent being criticized by a supervisor or cringe at receiving a direct order? Why might feelings of anger be acted on by one individual in a self- and other-destructive manner and not acted on by another person experiencing the same situation? These questions are intended to draw the reader's attention to much of what we simply take for granted. There is a vast realm of conscious and unconscious process that takes place within us that influences our behavior. The intrapersonal realm amounts to a black box with much going on in it that is at the same time out of awareness.

This realm includes much of what is written about individual psychology, and can become the focal point of therapy if thoughts and feelings grow to be out of bounds thereby introducing personal dysfunction. Individuals starting from infancy may be exposed to life experience that is nurturing or along a range toward less than satisfactorily nurturing, culminating in highly pathological relationships with caretaking others. The degree of dysfunction that lies within this context deeply imprints the infant, child and young adult with a range of self-experience. This experience may be satisfying and secure, thereby promoting self-esteem, or much less so, thereby promoting exceptional personal fragility and hard to tolerate and regulate anxiety-ridden self-experience. These childhood trends are then transferred to some degree into the balance of one's life experience, thereby making life fulfilling or much less so. These intrapsychic dynamics enter directly into the workplace filling it with hard to understand psychologically defensive tendencies that may make the person an unpredictable employee (Allcorn and Diamond, 1997). Reflection upon oneself and one's experience within the workplace is very likely all that is needed to validate the importance of intrapsychic dynamics.

In Sum

Individual psychology offers to those trying to understand the workplace a hard to comprehend complexity and diversity that have led to many different insights into human nature within the workplace. This complexity defies efforts to directly and even indirectly manage or reengineer it, thereby squarely confronting those who aspire to lead others with an extraordinary challenge.

The Interpersonal Realm

If the intrapersonal realm is complex then one need only think a moment to imagine how complex the interpersonal world is. Intrapersonal dynamics are, much of the time, directed toward others or energized by the actions of others relative to us. The interpersonal world is filled with many dynamics that have been explored in many different ways. Others starting at infancy become the focal points for many intrapersonal dynamics that leak out into relating to others, who may at first only be known in a fragmented and tentative way often described as part object relations (Ogden, 1989). This primitive side of life arises when a person such as the mother of the infant is experienced by the infant as good at one moment by offering nurturance and bad at another time by withholding nurturance. Early object relations are described as "part" in that the good mother is known to be different from the bad mother. There are two mothers in this example. As the infant develops he or she gradually comes to appreciate that there is but one mother with both good and bad attributes. This much more integrated understanding is described as "whole" object relations that introduce the depressive state. The infant is no longer in control of his or her objects and more importantly, objects (others) can have two or more conflicting attributes. The good mother and the bad mother are, in effect, lost to the mother as a unified person. However, part object relations are always accessible and may reappear if stressful conditions induce psychological regression.

Interpersonal dynamics implicitly incorporate the intrapsychic world thereby filling relationships with others with many hard to understand elements, tensions and hidden agendas. For example, a child who experienced considerable physical and psychological abuse at the hands of his or her mother may very well be highly sensitized to other women who have attributes that remind the person of his or her mother. This interpersonal dynamic may be fuelled by splitting and projection thereby creating an "all bad" other. This tendency may be further generalized to include anyone's behavior including male behavior that reminds the person of his or her mother's painful behavior. The result is that distressing self-experience from the past is transferred onto the present, creating the proverbial "hot button." The response becomes disproportionate to the circumstance. Other aspects of interpersonal dynamics that may be encountered in the workplace are the pursuit of fulfilling excessive dependency needs or needs to withdraw from relating to others altogether.

In Sum

Individual psychology combines with the interpersonal world to create a middle ground or potential space between individuals who aspire to relate to each other that is filled with many hard to know and understand individual and interpersonal dynamics. As a result we are left with extremely hard to manage workplace dynamics that defy management when psychological "hot buttons" create explosive interpersonal relations.

The Group Realm

Group dynamics have also been subjected to an exceptional amount of analysis and theorizing by academics and consultants (Bion, 1961 and Colman and Bexton, 1975). The group realm introduces yet another level of complexity that transcends the individual and interpersonal worlds. We are once again reminded by Mary Parker Follett (Metcalf and Urwick, 1941) that the importance of understanding group dynamics in the workplace is nothing new; only an ongoing and hard to master challenge. She writes: "The leader in scientifically managed plants tends not to persuade men to follow *his* will. He shows them what it is necessary for them to do in order to meet *their responsibility*, a responsibility that has been explicitly defined to them" (p. 282). She continues: "If the best leader takes all the means in his power to develop leadership among his subordinates and gives them opportunity to exercise it, he has then, his supreme task, to unite all the different degrees and different types of leadership that come to the surface in the ramifications of a modern business. Since power is now beginning to be thought of by many not as inhering in one person but as the combined capacities of a group, we are beginning to think of the leader not as the man who is able to assert his individual will and get others to follow him, but as the one who knows how to relate the different wills in a group so that they will have driving force" (p. 282).

The workplace, while filled with individuals, is composed of groups where one individual may be a member of more than one group and most often is. Group leaders are faced with the challenge of not commanding group members but rather drawing them into a mutually acceptable context where leadership and followership occur. It is equally important to appreciate that groups are periodically filled with many hard to understand individual, interpersonal and subgroup interactions that often confound the efforts of the best managers and consultants to understand, much less manage. Also to be considered is that groups interact with each other, which directs our attention to the organizational realm.

In Sum

Group dynamics have long been considered an important element within the workplace that requires inspection, study and analysis in order to be effectively incorporated into the workplace. Groups may take many forms such as informal groups, task and work groups, teams, departments and divisions. They usually share in common a group culture—who we are and how we understand what is going on within the workplace. This culture governs group dynamics and interaction with other groups. A great deal more could be said about groups and group dynamics. Regrettably, this brief overview will have to suffice for the moment. Much of the balance of this book is devoted to delving into group dynamics in the workplace.

The Organizational Realm

Organizational dynamics might be thought of as the sum total of individual, interpersonal and group dynamics mixed with a healthy dose of reality testing relative to the task environment of the organization. Good reality testing is essential in order to keep competitors from eating your sandwich for lunch. The complexity at this level is once again increased.

Our hierarchical organizations are constructed of many horizontal layers and vertical divisions that introduce communication and coordination discontinuities as a result of organizational fragmentation. Communication, for example, up and down an organizational hierarchy is notoriously inaccurate and fraught with interpretations and reinterpretations that may serve as "spin" to protect one's domain from another's oversight. Similarly, communication may be found simply to not occur between divisions and operating sections (organizational silos or smokestacks) that represent specialties with their own language such as legal services, finance and marketing.

There are many other organizational attributes that contribute to the complexity. Leaders throughout an organization may pursue their work and fulfill their responsibilities by using many different leadership styles, some of which are adaptive and some less so. Organizational history is also often a factor where old grudges may linger and misunderstandings predominate. Organization culture is yet another aspect of organizational dynamics that can serve in many ways to make the organization more effective or less so (Diamond, 1993). There is indeed much to comprehend about the organization realm. The challenge is to do so without introducing too many distortions.

Consultants, researchers, executives and employees are, at the organizational level of analysis, faced with so many possible data points that it can seem impossible to locate what is important. This complexity makes it essential to try to encompass as much as possible what is happening within an organization in any model-building effort. It is also essential to be able to locate those elements and trends that are most pronounced at any moment in time. In this regard there is perhaps no better argument for the support of the use of explicit organization models than when trying to understand organizational dynamics, especially if insights are to be shared with others.

In Sum

The organizational realm of analysis is inclusive of the complexity of the other realms while adding many of its own complex elements. Understanding and changing organizational dynamics at the organization level can be infinitely challenging as a result of the combination of intrapersonal, interpersonal and group dynamics.

The Societal Realm

All organizations exist within a larger context that I shall limit consideration of to a society as compared with the world or universe, although both apply. Our organizations are influenced by larger social trends and conversely they influence society. Within the United States there are many often conflicting social values and mores that enter directly into the workplace. For example, during the later portion of the twentieth century the rise in nontraditional families where divorce has created many working mothers has introduced into the workplace many demands to support this social trend. Issues such as health care insurance, childcare and working hours that flex with childcare needs have all influenced how employers design jobs and company benefit plans. A closely related social trend has been feminism, where the women who do enter the workforce are expected to be treated equally in terms of both compensation and career advancement. Certainly areas such as sexual harassment have dramatically affected male/female working relationships. Other areas where the social and political nature of our nation influences the workplace are legislation and administrative policies whereby many aspects of the workplace come under federal and state regulation. Areas such as equal opportunity, employment law, immigration, occupational safety and conserving the environment have all heavily impacted the workplace. Not to be overlooked are the many other contributions our society makes to the workplace such as monetary policy that limits inflation, constantly improving transportation systems and infrastructure and the fostering of international trade.

The influences are bidirectional, as evidenced by the many aspects of the workplace and business community that positively and negatively affect our society. On the positive side are jobs and economic prosperity, new products and services that improve our lives and contributions to our communities in the form of donations to charities. On the negative side are such things as plant closings, downsizings and layoffs, destruction of the environment and interest in making a profit sometimes at the expense of customers such as is often said to be the case with health maintenance organizations (HMOs). All of this complexity resident within the workplace is hard to comprehend without some type of cognitive map or theory of the workplace. This appreciation leads to considering exactly why these orienting and sense-making tools are necessary.

In Sum

Social influences are major contributors to workplace dynamics as are workplace dynamics to society. Appreciating this much greater level of complexity is important in order to understand what exactly is going on in the workplace and why.

WHY DO WE NEED A THEORY OR MODEL OF THE WORKPLACE?

The foregoing overview of some of the complexities of the workplace should be sobering to every reader. Our organizations and how they operate can, upon close inspection, seem to be infinitely complex and in final analysis defy ready management and efforts to change them. Executives, employees, consultants and researchers, it will hopefully be appreciated by now, need to have a clear and explicit model of how organizations work that permits them to locate the most important data points while also creating a framework for their understanding and discussion with others. In sum, one needs a theoretical perspective or model to facilitate knowing the workplace in an integrated and systemic way.

Placing Things into Perspective

The discussion thus far has underscored many important workplace attributes that must be attended to if organizational life is to be understood. Many of these are commonly accepted aspects of the workplace that are seldom questioned or indeed open to being questioned. Such things as the organization, arrangement of work, tools and equipment used, facility, goals, production schedules, raw materials, products, sales and desired profit levels do not really seem to be open to being questioned most of the time by organization members. In this regard it may be noted that Taylor's admonitions have been heeded. These attributes of worklife may only be questioned at great personal risk. In particular, leadership styles, planning and decision making, while often the subject of much organizational conversation, are, at the same time, not available for open discussion. Authority may not be questioned. Nonetheless, in order for organizations to become and remain successful, there must exist opportunities for change fostered by somehow finding safe ways to question what is going on and why. Therefore, the ability to locate the most important organizational elements and place them into a larger context where they may be examined and discussed with objectivity is essential if change is to be achieved.

In Sum

A theory or model of the workplace offers a way of looking at the workplace and seeing new patterns and connections between all of these attributes and, most importantly, between individuals and within work groups. By making the model explicit it also becomes open to discussion and validation or revision. This openness is essential in terms of coming to an understanding of what is going on in the workplace, what I have come to describe as "negotiated organizational reality."

Sorting Out Organizational Experience

The workplace as described is a vast assortment of different kinds of data sets. Putting aside for the moment all of the more concrete aspects of the workplace that can be measured by efficiency experts, we are confronted with even greater complexity when we examine the wonderful and frustrating complexity that human nature introduces into the workplace. The use of an explicit model or theory of the workplace that demystifies human nature by locating it within a comprehensive organizational and operations perspective is essential in terms of facilitating an open discussion of the intrapersonal, interpersonal, group and organizational dynamics that are dominated by what people think, feel and do. Indeed, without such a model into which may be placed many of these usually undiscussable dynamics, change may not be contemplated. It is often just too dangerous to approach others about leadership and followership styles as well as interpersonal relations and group process.

Dynamic workplace theory proposed here offers to do several important things in terms of locating the important aspects of organizational experience and creating a context in which they may be discussed. First, the theory helps to create meaning in terms of how all the experience of organization life may be brought together. Patterns can be found in what seems like confusing and overwhelming experience. The theoretical approach described in chapter 2 helps to create meaning where none may be observed to exist at the moment. A second and closely related outcome of having a model or theory of organizational dynamics is that it serves to allay anxiety. There is something comforting about having in hand a useful way of understanding what is going on. In particular it must be appreciated that the more anxious consultants, executives and employees become, the less likely they are able to think objectively about events and appreciate their feelings and those of others that contribute to the distressing workplace experience of the moment.

In Sum

The ability to understand the complexity of worklife and the ability to discuss it with others with an eye on changing those aspects that are dysfunctional is dependent upon having a shared context that permits joining together to do this work. Dynamic workplace theory offers the promise of providing this context for organization members.

NOTES ON ORGANIZATIONAL MODEL BUILDING

The workplace has thus far been described as a humbling place for even the brightest of researchers and theorists to understand even though they have the luxury of time to do their work, as compared with employees who have little time available to them to reflect upon and analyze workplace events and attributes (Jaques, 1989, 1990 and Kilmann and Kilmann, 1994). Outstanding academics and consultants have provided many organizational perspectives and models. Each provides a framework that helps the observer of organizational life to see the patterns in all of the detail and complexity. Things might be thought of as coming into focus. In this regard, there are two aspects to all of this theorizing and model building that must be mentioned in order to appreciate dynamic workplace theory presented in this book.

Start with Theory and Apply to the Workplace

This is a time-tested approach. A famous example is Einstein's theory of relativity, which has been subjected to testing ever since its conception. This approach is at least in part if not in large part unencumbered by the realities of the universe, which may be the case in some management books. Many wonderful points of view, theories and models have been created. Some have advocated rationally engineering the workplace to create the perfectly operating machine (Weber, 1947 and Jaques, 1990). Others have pointed out that science and engineering overlook the fact that human nature is also a dominant influence in the workplace, at least for now (Baum, 1987; Czander, 1993; Diamond, 1993; Kets de Vries, 1984 and Schwartz, 1990).

These theories and models offer the reader many thought-provoking perspectives on what makes the workplace tick. And it is certainly the case there are a great many points of view that focus on but one or a few aspects of the workplace (Allcorn, 1997; Diamond, 1984; Kernberg, 1979 and Schein, 1985). Almost any kind of theory can be ingeniously adapted to the workplace to explain how it works or some of its parts operate. The uppermost question is, however, does the theory seem to fit the reality of the workplace? It is certainly the case that some do and some don't and some fit to some extent some of the time. As a creator of a few of these perspectives I am always humbled by the problem of trying to determine the efficacy of the approach advocated. I am equally taxed to avoid introducing observer bias that creates self-fulfilling prophecies where magically the theoretical perspective is observed to be at work regardless of data to the contrary.

In Sum

Creating a theory of the workplace that may in part be borrowed from other fields can offer many new insights that are at least initially only loosely connected to the workplace. At the same time these efforts are problematic in that they may do a poor job of explaining actual workplace experience or guiding work and decision making. They may also encourage biased observation that encourages proving the theory rather than disproving it or qualifying its utility.

Start with the Workplace and Build the Theory

This is also a time-tested approach. Newton, while sitting under a tree, watched an apple fall and he wondered why. When one looks about within the workplace there are many organizational attributes, artifacts, events, trends, goals and leadership styles, to list but a few elements of the workplace, that provoke the question why. As one observes more facets to the phenomenon under study, there may emerge the appearance of causality thereby leading to hypotheses and conclusions as to why things happen as they do. This strategy for building organizational theory also confronts some limitations. One important limitation is that there are limits to how much can be observed or probed, especially if one wants to keep one's job. There are, therefore, limits to how much data can be collected. Perfect data is not available, much less perfect information and knowledge. A second related aspect to this is that experiments to test the efficacy of one's organization theory or model are not possible unless you are the boss and perhaps not even then. It is reasonable to conclude that it is hard to test one's insights against reality. A third important limitation, as already mentioned, is that as a theory develops it often introduces observer bias in favor of supporting the theory. Last, it is also the case that elements of workplaces vary across organizations thereby introducing the likelihood that a good theory developed to account for worklife in one organization may not generalize to other organizations.

The theory described in this book arises in this manner, from firsthand experience in the workplace, therefore, making its elements familiar to anyone with work experience in a large organization. The model may be understood to be backward engineered from work experience to explain what can be observed at work. In this regard the reader must critically examine it for its veracity based on the above theory-building provisos.

In Sum

Workplace theories may be developed as intellectual exercises that may or may not fit well with the workplace or provide useful guidance for leaders and organization members. Workplace theories and models may also be developed after a careful observation of what is going on in the workplace. How much data can be collected and processed as well as observed impartially limits this approach to theory building. The resulting work may also not necessarily apply well to other organizations. Dynamic workplace theory has its origins in this latter type of model building. It represents an effort to better understand what is observed to be going on in the workplace.

IN CONCLUSION

This chapter has introduced the reader to much of the nature of the complexity of organizational life that leads directly to the problematic nature of ultimately understanding it with any clarity. Rationality, irrationality and spirituality are interspersed with individual, interpersonal, group and organizational dynamics that are in turn interactive with the larger society. This complexity serves to underscore the necessity for those who would lead and study organizations having a model or theory of organizational life and experience. Whether we can acknowledge it or not, every member of an organization has developed an implicit and usually unarticulated theory about how things work. These tacit theories represent one of the confounding problems that leaders, consultants and researchers must confront to more completely appreciate organizational dynamics. The knowledge-creating limitations of these tacit organization theories are often only directly addressed by the use of an explicit model that when articulated introduces objectivity to organizational experience as well as promotes its testing against the tacit models that lie within every employee. Also discussed have been some of the problematic aspects of building any form of explicit theory or model of organizational life. This appreciation must be kept in mind as we turn to a detailed explanation of dynamic workplace theory.

Chapter 2

Dynamic Workplace Theory

One of the major perplexities confronting those who want to understand groups and to work with them effectively is how to explain the great differences in "groupness" that distinguish groups from one another. Why is it that the attendance of one group is so irregular as to result in its slow death while the attendance of another group with similar activities and leadership remains high? What makes a group "healthy" so that its members work harder, make more sacrifices for the group, more readily extol its virtues, seem happier together, interact more often, and agree with one another more readily than do the members of a dying organization?
(Cartwright and Zander, 1960, p. 69)

Dynamic workplace theory focuses attention not on the concrete aspects of organizations such as physical plant, production lines, marketing and profit, but rather on the more subtle and harder to understand side of the workplace—groups and their dynamics. The workplace is readily understood to be composed of task groups, teams, departments and divisions. How all of the many kinds of groups function and relate to each other in large part determines the viability of the organization. The reader is again reminded that the words "group" and "organization" are, for the balance of the book, used in an interchangeable manner. It is important to appreciate at the outset that, while groups and organizations have readily apparent physical parameters, they also represent unique experiential and cultural settings that evoke one kind of experience over another. This chapter begins with a case example that presents the context onto which dynamic workplace theory may be overlaid to help locate insight and meaning in what may otherwise be a complex and overwhelming experience of the psychological and social aspects of the workplace.

CASE EXAMPLE: GROUPS AT WORK

Working as a manager in a large organization can be a confusing and frustrating experience. During a workweek any one of us might wonder whether it is worth it. Trying to get a handle on why we feel this way usually leads to thinking over the major organizational influences we contend with. An example is Sarah, who is a member of WDL's pest control production team.

The Making of a Better Mouse Trap

Sarah is worrying about who is leading the organization. The inability to get timely and adequate decisions from on high has led to a number of production crises. No one seems to care. Work experience is somewhat chaotic. No one seems to be in charge. Risk taking to surface problems and making decisions is avoided. Issues are not confronted. No one wants to be fingered as the messenger of the bad news or go unheard if the risk of speaking up is accepted.

This had not been the case for Sarah when she was a member of a product development project. It seemed at first that the leaderless culture of the organization had been imported into the group. No one assumed responsibility, including the manager assigned to lead the group. After weeks of aimless and ineffective work, news arrived that a similar team in a competing organization was about to come up with a product similar to the one being worked on by her team. The realization that losing out was imminent had a sobering effect. At first there was an unrestrained attack on top management's inactivity and incompetence. Eventually feelings of fear, confusion and frustration led to the willingness to take some major risks. This led to the drafting of a new member into the team, Bill, to replace top management's "plant." Management provisionally accepted the decision and their man was withdrawn. Bill was expected to lead the group in beating out the competing company. Flattered and amazed by his sudden selection, he was, nonetheless, willing to rise to the occasion. He proceeded to provide clear direction that got things moving along rapidly even though not everyone was buying in.

Just when the project team was beginning to make progress, Sarah was reassigned to the production section responsible for tooling up to make the new product. For Sarah, her new job became an instant replay of her experience with the product development team. The manager in charge of the section provided little leadership. He was absent most of the time from meetings, and eventually indicated his willingness to hand over leadership of the group to one of its members. The group's members responded by developing a meticulous selection process beginning with defining the future leader's position, power and authority. A position description was developed. Rules of order for conducting meetings were adopted. Interested members of the group were interviewed as to how they would act if selected to be the leader. This bureaucratic process was, for Sarah, a marked contrast to the knee-jerk reaction of the product development group. The process was slow and painstaking and eventually led to the selection of a leader everyone felt comfortable with, but no one was too sure would be able to lead the group in meeting its deadlines.

Within a few months Sarah was surprised to learn that Bill had been replaced as leader of the product development group in what had been a dramatic shift of support. Bill was "dethroned" by a coalition of group members who had gone unheard and had been systematically excluded from major decision making. Bill and key members of his development team were to be reassigned.

Meanwhile the production group's work ground on. Deadlines were missed. Work was arduous. Nonetheless, the many rules that the group had developed were followed. Regular progress and deviation reports had to be prepared. The acknowledgement that the group was not going to meet the deadlines led to the realization that more expedient means were needed. What was needed, many thought, was a more active and directive leader and less bureaucratic red tape. Coincidental with this perceived need was Bill's availability. His experience with the product's development and his take-charge and in some instances take-no-prisoners charismatic leadership style made him a natural to take over the leadership of the group. In contrast to everything the group had done up to this point, Bill was recruited and appointed the team leader in one meeting. Bill and his colleagues from the development team quickly energized the group. Meeting the deadlines now seemed possible.

Sarah was puzzled by what had happened. It was not too long before it was rumored Bill was being considered for an influential top spot. Despite the fact his leadership style was also eventually rejected by the production group, he made it to the top. Sarah's frustration and skepticism with how the company was being managed continued to grow. Why was there so much trouble with organizing groups, selecting suitable leadership and getting work done? Why was it always necessary to change the structure and leadership of the groups when major problems and threats were encountered?

In Sum

Managing individual and group behavior in organizations requires understanding the psychological and social aspects of organizational life. Complex interpersonal and group dynamics require conceptual frames of reference to understand them. One conceptual framework Sarah could have used is dynamic workplace theory that, as will be observed, offers managers a useful way to think about what is going on around them. The theory assumes group behavior, while arising from a core of individual psychological processes, can be understood on a group-as-a-whole basis.

DYNAMIC WORKPLACE THEORY'S TYPOLOGY OF GROUP EXPERIENCE

The typology of workplace experience that comprises the core element of the theory identifies groups and group experiences that are familiar to anyone who has worked in small or large organizations. They would be familiar to Sarah. The three psychologically defensive groups to be discussed are the chaotic group, the bureaucratic group, and the charismatic leadership group (see Figure 1). Each group offers its members a different psychological defensive solution to the same problem, anxiety arising from distressing experience of group membership and the workplace. In contrast, the balanced group experience minimizes psychologically defensiveness where, to a much greater extent, free will exists, personal responsibility is embraced and intentionality becomes a pervasive aspect of group culture and experience.

These four groups exist within a mutually dynamic context where each contributes to knowing and understanding the others while simultaneously threatening their existence. Change and stability in the theory, as discussed here and

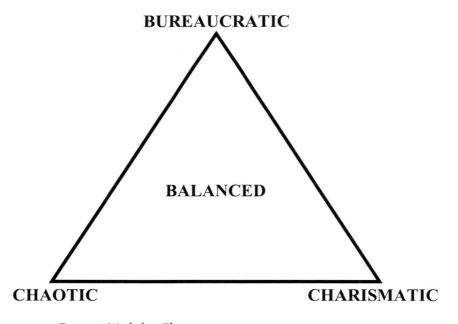

Figure 1. Dynamic Workplace Elements

to a greater extent in chapters 3–5, is driven by collective trends in individual needs for security and self-esteem and by threats to group existence arising from within the larger organization or the arena in which the organization seeks competitive advantage. The following discussion explains each of the types of workplace experience and the chapter concludes with a discussion of the theory's deeply embedded dynamic nature.

Chaotic Group Experience

The chaotic group presents its members with the most primitive workplace experience of the four groups, thereby provoking the most psychologically defensive response of the three psychologically defensive group experiences. The following discussion points out the many interactive aspects of this experience that tend to be mutually supportive thereby creating a reinforcing circularity.

The chaotic group acts "as if" there is a lack of effective leadership within the group (organization) and that there is no clear agenda or task for the group to work on although some members may occasionally point out that these are present at least to some degree. Direction may be only minimally provided or not followed if offered. Phrases like "too many bulls in the china shop" and "herding a group of cats" express experience in this chaotic setting. Group members appear to be uncertain as to what to do and how to act. This lack of direction and purpose leads to the experience of the group as fragmented and lacking cohesion. This outcome makes most of its members feel anxious about their experience of the group. The group essentially acts as though "doing nothing" is an option. There does not appear to be any compelling reason to accomplish work within this experiential context as time seems to have stopped and external events are not taking place.

Participation in this group, despite all of the personal autonomy it provides, eventually becomes unrewarding for most of its members. In particular many of the needs of individual members to feel good about themselves and their participation in the group are diminished or absent. Their wish to feel secure relative to each other and their leader is frustrated by the chaotic fragmentation. These experiences of self, others, the formal group leader and the group are stressful. It is not uncommon for some group members to feel that their participation in the group is actually threatening and dangerous to their well-being. At times almost anything seems possible, even interpersonal violence where someone is picked out by the group for ritualized aggression.

These experiences frequently lead to a lack of member self-individuation. Everyone just wants to blend in. This usually takes the form of avoiding participation such as performing work or offering information or direction. In fact there are many indications that self-individuation not only is experienced as personally dangerous but also is actively suppressed by some group members. Those who do speak up to offer direction often seem to be speaking into a vacuum where their words go unheard by most group members. Their efforts, in a sense, fall upon deaf ears. In this context, if a group member or perhaps the nominal leader of the group persists in trying to provide direction, the individual may ultimately find him- or herself the focus of the group's anxieties, fears, frustrations and anger. As a result those who offer direction find themselves being interviewed by group members as to their intentions, motivations and experience. They may be quizzed about all aspects of their point of view, and their leadership challenged by a few who also aspire to lead the group. Why is he or she advocating this point of view? Why does he or she feel empowered to do this? What credentials does he or she have to make such an assertion? In general anyone observing these group dynamics including its members is discouraged from self-individuation that attracts attention to one's self. It just seems too dangerous.

These group dynamics predictably lead group members to experience themselves as cut off from themselves, their skills, their work, and from each other. These threatening and frustrating elements of group experience frequently evoke hostility that is expressed in many directions and many different forms. Hostility may then be directed toward fellow group members who are hiding out in the group by not saying anything (avoiding self-individuation). Not contributing, therefore, becomes dangerous. The group as a whole may also be attacked for being incompetent to do anything. The nominal group leader may be criticized and challenged for not doing anything to allay anxiety arising from distressing group experience. Even those outside of the group who are thought to be responsible for creating the group and assigning it work may be attacked.

The group's hostility may take many forms ranging from passive to active aggression. Passive aggression usually takes the form of not supporting others, indifference to the group's dynamics and the undermining of the efforts of others who try to make contributions aimed at getting the group back on track. Active aggression usually takes the form of intense questioning of anyone who has something to say, and may include verbal attacks and public character assassinations. Despite the perceived presence of aggression or the distinct possibility that someone is about to be attacked, when hostility does emerge, it is most often paradoxically contained and suppressed by other group members. It is just too unpleasant and threatening to be tolerated and simply makes the group experience too distressing and anxiety ridden. No one really wants to see someone, figuratively speaking, destroyed by the group. The mere threat of personal destruction, it is hoped, will contain self-individuation and the possibility an effective leader might emerge to threaten individual autonomy.

The circular reinforcing nature of chaotic group experience may, at this point, be observed to have been established. Group members behave in an aimless, perhaps joking or escapist manner to relieve anxiety. This further reduces the group's productivity, adding to the threat the group may not succeed. Group members are not supportive of each other and are combative regarding each other's needs for security and self-esteem. Group members are all in the same boat and it may be easier to go down together than face each other and the situation. The group may gradually lose touch with important aspects of its task environment as members of the group withdraw from accomplishing assigned work.

Alienation, anxiety and hostility abound. This chaotic, uncertain and threatening group experience may also be inspected from a depth psychology perspective. In psychological terms, experience of this nature promotes primitive forms of aggression. Oral sadistic and incorporative hunger for objects (interpersonal connectedness) creates anxiety over safety. Group members paradoxically feel that they need others while simultaneously fearing that they will consume their friends as well as be consumed by them. As a result there gradually emerges a great hunger for relatedness that is at the same time threatening to everyone.

One outcome of these group dynamics is that group members seek safety by psychologically and sometimes physically dropping out of the group. Members may withdraw from active participation while denying their feelings of frustration, aggression and fears that group members may devour them. Paradoxically, the greater their desire (hunger) for interpersonal relatedness within the group, the greater the likelihood others will feel unbalanced by the threat of being devoured by those in need. This experience results in an increasing interpersonal defensiveness to avoid being used by others to meet their affiliation needs to feel connected and good about themselves.

Groups that contain these conditions accomplish little work. The unacknowledged primary task becomes one of personal survival that is made all the more difficult as members withdraw from each other and active participation in the group. Few opportunities for interpersonal support exist at a time when supporting each other is most needed. Members often experience themselves as neither in nor out of the group, and may express considerable ambivalence about the group and their participation in it. Most members seem to be unable to commit to group participation while at the same time they are unable to separate from the group at the risk of annihilation by the group or a superior who assigned them to work in the group.

As a result, group and self-experience contains within it a reinforcing circularity. To be found in the group is what seems like an inability to learn from experience that forecloses the possibility of changing to another type of group experience that promises to resolve bad feelings and lack of productivity. As discussed in chapters 3 and 4, change, in the case of these group dynamics only seems possible when a mutually acceptable and willing leader is identified in a time frame when the group contains within it a readiness to follow a leader such as Bill. In this regard group experience is so distressing that threatening and painful reservations about allowing a leader to self-differentiate are overcome. As will be discussed in chapter 4, a fight/flight mechanism leads to a readiness to change. This occurs when fleeing from the current group experience becomes paramount or, conversely, fighting back against it or external events is felt to be necessary to insure personal and group survival.

In Sum

Members of the chaotic group may feel:

(1) fear regarding the perceived consequences of being heard or acting,

(2) helpless as others are observed to be attacked by the group's members,

(3) much more secure by going unnoticed within the group,

(4) the group has lost its purpose and direction and

(5) frustrated that nothing seems to help restore the group's ability to perform work.

These feelings that are held by many group members lead them to shrink away from interacting with others and from participating in the group. At the same time, individual survival is also threatened by poor group performance that may, if felt by many group members, create a context for change where a leader is identified to lead the group in a new direction. This new direction will be toward one of the other two psychologically defensive groups or perhaps toward the more psychologically balanced group where group experience contains interpersonal trust and cooperation.

Bureaucratic Group Experience

In contrast to the chaotic group where effective leadership is for the most part absent, participants in the bureaucratized group control their anxieties by creating a socially defensive system aimed at eliminating adverse group experience and containing anxiety. The result is the familiar hierarchical organization structure and accompanying policies and procedures, rules and regulations that regulate work and member interactions. Bureaucratic hierarchies provide for nonthreatening leadership where the leader's power and authority are carefully circumscribed and preferably exercised in an impersonal manner. The leader must, in effect, play by the rules of the organization or risk rejection and even termination.

The bureaucratized group controls the action of its members by creating rigid routines, impersonal professional interactions, carefully defined authority and routinized leadership. Working relationships are preferably role-to-role interactions. Communication, interactions and decision making must follow prescribed protocols that maintain the integrity of the chain of command where progressively more decision-making authority lies with ever higher positions within the management hierarchy. Many layers of command and control exist, as well as specialized departments and divisions that may not be allowed to interact directly across organizational boundaries. These outcomes introduce vertical and horizontal organizational fragmentation. It is, therefore, fairly easy to conclude that within an organizational context such as this, meaningful interpersonal relationships are, for the most part, discouraged in favor of promoting a mechanistic professionalism devoid of feelings, passion and personal interests and motivations.

These organizational attributes, it is hoped, will provide group members the comforting illusion of stability, predictability, equality and dependability. Personal autonomy that abounds in the chaotic group experience is discouraged. Control of feelings, beliefs and actions is the primary task. Productivity paradoxically may be of secondary importance. However, unlike chaotic groups that produce little other than anxiety and an occasional but uncoordinated flare of creativity, bureaucratized groups are able to accomplish work by following the policies and procedures. Readers will no doubt possess the deepest familiarity with this kind of group and organizational experience and further elaboration of its attributes is not necessary.

Reliance upon the bureaucratic hierarchical approach to designing organizations and groups is not without its difficulties and dysfunctions. Many have noted that bureaucracies have difficulty in learning from experience and adjusting to new circumstances, and they encourage dependence on the part of their members (Blau and Meyer, 1956; Jacoby, 1977 and Merton et al., 1952). This solution to controlling group process, however, also often fails to provide its members a permanent solution to controlling their anxiety. Feelings of oppression and alienation readily emerge that threaten security and control. Self-individuation remains undesirable as was the case in the chaotic group. These experiences are especially likely to occur among those who are most apt to self-differentiate either by offering new ideas or perhaps outperforming others (Allcorn, 1991). Czander (1993) also points out that while the espoused practice appears to be one of professional objectivity, actual experience is different. "Rewards and punishments are used as motivational instruments and are supposed to be based on 'objective' evaluations of performance. However, this process is rarely objective; instead it is political, which precipitates conflict and adversarial relations between superior and subordinate" (p. 119). Problems such as these readily lead to a greater reliance upon bureaucratic control in the belief if "we just do it right (according to the policies and procedures), everything will be all right" and by extension our anxious feelings will be allayed.

Bureaucratic hierarchical organization contains many elements that are either the fulfillment of psychologically defensive tendencies or conversely nurture their persistence. This structure is, in part, the outcome of the pervasive pursuit of control over inner experience. Control presents a paradox. It alleviates anxiety on the part of management and employees and it encourages anxiety on the part of those who must submit to the control. Within this context there is never enough control within the hands of management and there may never be too little control relative to those who must submit (Czander, 1993). As mentioned, deviation and self-individuation is ideally to be avoided in favor of maintaining rigorous order. Czander (1993) notes:

The structure assumes regulatory authority over the subordinate only when the subordinate assumes a submissive position. The regulators' authority takes over the superego functions, such as conscious ideals, morality, equality, self-observation, and the reality testing ego. The regulatory authority is external; it is embedded in the structure and is, under certain conditions, incorporated by employees over time through participation in organizational activities, rituals, myths, ceremonies and tasks. (p. 12)

Herein lies the psychological significance of the bureaucratic hierarchy. Employees experience the liberating abandonment of personal responsibility for their thoughts, feelings and actions and simultaneously must defend themselves against their distressing experience of submission and self-annihilation where praise and rewards are, it is hoped, sufficient to compensate for these losses of self-integrity to the system of control. These and other tensions inherent within this type of workplace experience may well lead to feelings that things could be better.

A desire for change as further discussed in chapters 3 and 4 may develop within this group experiential context if operating problems are persistent and the group or organization gradually becomes distressingly dysfunctional. There may develop feelings that the group is unable to survive within its operating environment that is filled with competitors. In this case sufficient threat and shared pain and anxiety that is no longer thought to be adequately controlled by the bureaucratic hierarchy lead to identifying a leader to save the group by providing new direction and a way of working together. The leader will take the group in the direction of one of the other types of group experiences and away from the bureaucratic hierarchy and red tape that is felt to be the problem. The person identified as the potential leader must, therefore, be prepared to lead by deviating from the comforting familiarity of the bureaucratic hierarchy.

In Sum

Bureaucratic group experience encourages members to feel:

(1) fearful of speaking out and initiating action where everything seems to be prescribed,

(2) helpless in the face of overwhelming control and the careful monitoring of behavior,

(3) safe only if they follow all the rules and regulations,

(4) that they have lost their sense of purpose and ideals when confronted with what seems like a monolithic organization and

(5) frustrated that little seems possible in terms of changing how the organization functions even when change appears to be necessary.

When change does seem unavoidable there develops a fight/flight emotion-filled dynamic. A leader is located who is prepared to lead the group in a new direction and a sufficient number of the group's members are ready to be led in that direction—toward one of the other two psychologically defensive groups or to the more psychologically balanced group experience.

Charismatic Group Experience

The charismatic group approaches the problem of controlling experience by identifying an all-good, all-powerful charismatic leader whose omnipotence, it is hoped, will save the group's members from their fears and anxieties and each other. The result is a group or an organization that is controlled and dominated by its leader. The leader provides direction to and rewards for followers although he or she is also willing to punish members for defying or challenging his or her direction and need for control. Questioning authority is not desirable and once again self-differentiation not approved of by the leader is not encouraged.

The leader's power over organization members, it is hoped, permits him or her to maintain control of everyone and internal and external events, thereby minimizing the distressing experience of excessive anxiety that organization members seek to avoid. Problems that do occur are generally interpreted as the leader still not having enough power and control or that group or organization members are not sufficiently supportive of their leader by being loyal, hard-working and submissive. The group culture is ideally one of unquestioningly following every instruction issued and maintaining absolute faith in the leader's judgement.

Charismatic leaders become bigger than life as group members gradually and unconsciously divest themselves of their own personal authority and responsibility as well as their skills, knowledge and abilities. The psychological tendency of projecting one's good parts onto the leader is supported by the leader who identifies with the idealized projections and actively encourages followers to seek roles of subordinancy and dependency. The leader, it is thought, is all-knowing and powerful (paternalistic or materialistic) and may, in fact, control information flows. This outcome is, of course, comforting to many organization members who come to feel that they will be taken care of if they are sufficiently loyal, supportive and compliant. As a result, they feel less anxious about their presence in the group or organization by not feeling responsible for themselves, each other, the group or organization, the direction of work or how work is performed. They enjoy basking in the warm glow created by their leader.

The leader, however, may also use this leadership opportunity to fulfill his or her narcissistic needs to feel powerful and admired. He or she may locate zealous admirers within the group and elevate them to important roles close to him or her. Observation of many charismatic leaders has led me to understand that there is a perverse leader/follower dynamic at work here. The leader, by assuming responsibility for just about everything, ends up placing him- or herself under immense pressure to perform and fulfill the expectations and fantasies followers hold for him or her. It is also the case for many of these leaders that they tacitly understand no amount of power and authority is sufficient to provide the absolute control of anxiety followers desire. As a result, the pressure to meet follower expectations contains a debilitating quality. The leader's suffering, therefore, can be thought of as being ameliorated by the devoted service of some followers who love, adore, care and sacrifice for and otherwise service their leader.

Yet another aspect of this group dynamic is that the grandiose view of the leader held by many followers promotes grandiose self-experience on the part of the leader that may lead to him or her feeling overly powerful and admired. The leader unconsciously identifies with the many follower projections. This self-experience leads to feeling that rules of fair play and civility do not apply to him or her. The leader may think nothing of humiliating a follower or perhaps seeking sexual favors that may be more than readily supplied by some followers who are flattered by the attention and consciously or unconsciously aspire to unite with their leader. The leader may also arbitrarily make and break rules and even laws of the larger society. The combination of the excessive performance pressure combined with the grandiosity tends to make the charismatic leader bigger than life. The creation of a band of loyal, unquestioning followers (sycophants) is a natural outcome of these leader/follower dynamics that further reinforces the grandiosity by constantly providing the leader narcissistic supplies.

Yet another likely outcome of the experience of charismatic leadership is that the leader politicizes his or her leadership by avoiding making tough decisions that may alienate some followers and create enemies. Additionally, the leader, who strives to conserve his or her position, power and role and accompanying follower admiration, cannot risk making too many wrong decisions that call into question his or her omnipotence. As a result a paradox develops in which the leader is at once seemingly all-powerful and at the same time powerless relative to the group.

Examples of the charismatic group experience are numerous. Many captains of industry who are much applauded for their turn-arounds and high P/E ratios are overrepresented within this group of leaders. Many politicians attract exceptionally loyal followers and are many times thought of as charismatic. Similarly, many religious figures are charismatic leaders of their loyal flock of sheep. It is also important to note that charismatic group experience is one that can be exceptionally productive. These groups can, often through considerable personal sacrifice on the part of their members, achieve great feats that reinforce the charismatic qualities of the leader and group cohesion. An athletic team led by a charismatic coach or captain may achieve unexpectedly good performance. A charismatic leader who makes good use of his or her unusually powerful position may resurrect a down-and-out organization.

In this regard, the charismatic leader is able to make rapid changes in the direction and operation of the group or organization to take advantage of opportunities (opportunism). Group members for the most part do not seriously question or resist rapid and at times contradictory changes, thereby making the organization fast on its collective feet. This outcome is a highly desirable attribute assuming the organization is moving in the right direction. However, at the same time, the group is vulnerable to being led in the wrong direction as is illustrated by Enron, WorldCom, and Andersen, the group suicide at Jonestown and other equally horrendous recent events such as the Waco deaths. Additionally, rampant opportunism can lead to isolated successes at the expense of fulfilling a larger more unified vision for the organization that promises to secure future competitiveness.

It is inevitable, however, that the charismatic leader cannot sustain his or her "god-like" presence in the group. Eventually the leader is found to have feet of clay. Mistakes are made. Group and organizational performance is not uniformly even. These realizations evoke fear on the part of the leader that he or she will not succeed in the task of protecting group members from each other and from bad feelings arising from group membership. Ultimately, aggression from some of the more frustrated and left-out group members or a superior may lead to the symbolic murder of the leader. A new leader may renew the cycle of charismatic group life or lead the group to an alternate group form as a part of overall group dissatisfaction with charismatic leadership.

In Sum

Group members who follow a charismatic leader may feel:

(1) fear when contemplating any idea or action that may be contrary to the leader's vision,

(2) helpless in the face of the leader's firm convictions that will not likely be changed even when influence is used,

(3) unsafe and insecure relative to the leader who may become at any moment dissatisfied with one's performance,

(4) a loss of personal efficacy and purpose where these attributes are threatening to the leader and

(5) frustrated when the group cannot seem to solve problems that stem from the leader's direction, style and control.

The charismatic leader can, however, avoid for only so long the recognition of his or her feet of clay. This recognition leads to anxiety on the part of followers, who express their discontent via criticism, more frequent questioning of instructions and perhaps even the location of an anti-leader to countervail the power of their charismatic leader. This new leader, given supportive circumstances, is permitted by group members to lead them in a new direction possibly away from the now questionable model of the charismatic group leader.

Balanced Group Experience

The balanced group experience, in contrast to the three psychologically defensive group experiences, is relatively free of the regressive need for its members to defend themselves from the experience of excessive anxiety and potential aggression within the group. Group members are less anxious about themselves, each other and group process and performance. Group members are reflective since they are less preoccupied with personal survival and coping with their fears and anxieties. They are able to examine their own thoughts, feelings and behavior and participate in the group's work with intentionality.

An observer of this group discerns that group members have a variety of feelings that are accepted by others and the group as a whole. Others who also share the same experience of the group and accompanying feelings frequently validate these feelings. Additionally, the group is thoughtful and flexible in its thinking. Divergent ideas are explored for their merit and applicability. Balanced group experience is, therefore, one where thinking and feeling are accepted in a nondefensive manner and used by the group to its best advantage.

The distinguishing characteristic of this group is its ability to deal openly with group fantasies, unconscious motivations, personal needs and psychologically defensive behavior. One of the central elements to achieving these outcomes is the ability to acknowledge conflicts when they develop. In this regard the only "bad" conflict is the conflict that is not open to discussion and resolution. Conflicts and similar group dynamics most often have embedded within them fantasies about group process, unconscious motivations regarding group participation and unacknowledged personal needs that members are trying to fulfill through group participation. All of these individual, interpersonal and group dynamics represent potentially disruptive hidden agendas when worked by some group members relative to others. For example, a group member who constantly seeks approval from others to shore up low self-esteem may consistently act in ways to receive the approval even though this behavior does not contribute to group success. Others may come to feel that they are being used to shore up the person's self-esteem. Similarly an individual who invariably and usually out of immediate awareness feels that he or she must triumph over others in order to secure self-esteem is equally dysfunctional to group dynamics. His or her excessively competitive nature tends to drive away the contributions others can make to the group's performance. Instances such as these are open to inspection by group members who feel that it is safe enough to speak to individual, interpersonal and group dynamics. As a result, there is little reason for the members of this group to flee from participation or resort to the sanctuary of psychological defenses. The more open and trusting group culture provides for a much greater degree of interpersonal connectedness. Undiscussible hidden interpersonal agendas do not exist to any great extent and when thought to exist, they are open to meaningful discussion.

The balanced group experience may, however, not be able to sustain its balanced culture and become drawn into change toward one or more of the three psychologically defensive groups. This is especially likely when the right combination of leadership and group stress occurs. The reader is reminded that contained within the balanced group are all the potentially regressive and psychologically defensive tendencies of the other groups. Chapters 3 and 4 discuss the nature of this potentiality in detail. It suffices at this point to note the obvious about group dynamics. Groups can spontaneously embark on a course of thinking, feeling and action that is inconsistent with being open with each other. As discussed below, there always exists the potential for a retreat from this hard-earned sense of organizational balance. It is this potential within each of the four types of groups that makes the theory dynamic.

In Sum

Members of the balanced group experience will feel:

(1) eager to comment on the group's work and offer different points of view,
(2) considerable self-worth and efficacy rather than helplessness,
(3) safe and secure within the group and relative to each other,
(4) that they have a real sense of purpose in their work where their efforts are acknowledged by other group members and
(5) any sense of frustration with the group's work is open to discussion.

Experience within this group context is for the most part positive and exciting. Group cohesion and spirit hold the group together as it works on its tasks. At the same time the other three psychologically defensive groups continue to exist as a latent potential that may become a force within the group should it encounter stressful operating conditions. A potential leader who advocates change may speak to this distress and promise a way out. These considerations underscore the dynamic nature of workplace theory.

THE DYNAMIC NATURE OF THE THEORY

The dynamic nature of this theoretical perspective has thus far been mentioned and discussed. It is, however, important to further explicate the underlying aspects of the theory's dynamics. Dynamic workplace theory is dynamic because of the latent potential of the other three types of groups to emerge to displace the group experience of the moment. In effect, all four types of experience coexist all of the time where one may predominate but the others may emerge. The group and organizational context depicted is, therefore, one of dynamic tension among the four kinds of group and organizational experiences. Participants in the group experience of the moment and, it may be added, the potential members of the remaining types of group experience share or may come to share a group valence or sentience. Each type of group experience elicits thoughts, feelings and behavior that are consistent with its underlying dynamics whether they are psychologically and socially defensive or one of more balance and intentionality. In this regard, loss of the current group experience is threatened when a sufficient number of its members come to feel that unresolved problems exist and change is needed. However, the painful experience of distress and anxiety must be sufficient in order to provide the risk-taking motivation to support change. "No pain, no change." It is equally important to appreciate that, at this juncture, sufficiently distressing experience fuels a fight/flight group dynamic that comes to be led by an individual who speaks to the changing sentiments of the group or organization.

The critical components of group and organization change are, therefore, twofold. A group member must become available to either lead the group in renewed efforts to get control of the group's current process or lead change to another type of group experience. At the same time, there must be present a readiness among group members to follow a leader who promises to make things better. In sum, there must be a leader and followers. As indicated by the theory, given the presence of these change dynamics, the direction of change is problematic. In particular, during the early stages of change a number of potential leaders may speak to different directions that promise to allay anxiety and solve operating problems. It is from this certainty of uncertainty that the challenge of managing groups arises. Exploring these facets of the theory's dynamic nature is the subject of the remainder of this chapter.

Constant Dynamic Tension

Thus far the four kinds of group experience have been discussed and a case example provided of how this experience actually occurs within the workplace. It is not difficult to come to the conclusion that the four types of group experience are very different and implicitly contain many elements in opposition to the others. In this regard each represents a potential direction for change in group and organizational culture where the three psychologically defensive group experiences may be thought of as points on a triangle and at the center of the triangle is the balanced group experience (see Figure 1). So long as one form of group or organizational experience is in ascendancy, the others remain as potential directions for change. It is within the constant presence of this potentiality that the workplace remains in a dynamic state where forces for change are pitted against forces of stability. The following discussion of change dynamics, uncertainty and the balance point of group experience further articulates the dynamic nature of the model.

Change Dynamics

Groups are filled, as mentioned, with many hard to locate and understand intrapersonal and interpersonal dynamics as well as influences from outside the group or organization. Three of these influences that are especially pertinent to understanding the theory's dynamic nature are fight/flight, leadership and group sentience.

Fight/flight group experiences are something that everyone has experienced. These are primitive responses to problems and threats to oneself and to groups. A fundamental example of these dynamics lies within the animal kingdom where an animal may stand its ground and fight another animal that is attacking it or flee to fight or flee another day. These responses to what is happening around us are equally present within each of us. Fight and flight are two often unthinking responses to a stressful situation that are hardwired into our brains.

We have all had the occasion to have to choose between standing our ground in a stressful situation or giving up and retreating. Groups also exhibit the same behavior, which is often facilitated by the location of a leader and the development of a sufficiently shared group experience (sentience) that provides the emotional fuel to either fight back or flee the situation. Within dynamic workplace theory, these tendencies provide the psychological and group energy that is tapped to create change. Crudely speaking, when individual, group and organizational survival is on the line, almost anything is possible as a result of the release of these fight/flight tendencies that may occur on a battlefield or in a corporate boardroom.

In Sum

Group and organizational change is many times fueled by primitive individual, interpersonal, group and organizational dynamics. In the case of the dynamic workplace theory the deeply ingrained genetically based fight/flight response provides the raw energy that is harnessed for group and organizational change.

Leadership, as noted, is one of the key ingredients for changing group direction. In this case the leader need not be the formal group leader and many times is not. Initially the leadership shown is subtle and basically tests the situation as to whether a change in a direction might be entertained by group members. This testing is frequently a response to an awareness of the presence of a threat, feelings of distress and the emergence of a fight/flight dynamic and its accompanying energy that create a tension that destabilizes the prevailing group or organization experiential context. As a result, the potential for a transitional state arises in the minds of group members.

Equally important is that the potential leader develops his or her unique experience of the situation. The person may, for example, feel that the chaos of group experience needs order and strict discipline applied to it in the form of following rules of order and adopting more predictable methods—the bureaucratic response. Similarly, the experience of the group as unable to get anything done because of "red tape" may support the notion that what is needed is an effective leader who will lead the group out of its current situation—the charismatic response. It is also certainly the case that sentiment may arise for a more balanced, open and trusting work group setting where everyone feels valued. There may, as mentioned, be individuals within a group that speak to several of these directions for change at different times or in competition relative to each other.

The sentiment of the group is tested on occasion by these potential leaders articulating a point of view consistent with a direction for change. Perhaps the person might say, "Wouldn't we be more likely to get on with the work if we had more structure and developed a system for decision making?" Or another might say, "Don't we need to have a clear direction set for us and someone located to get us there?" Regardless of what is said, the underlying dynamic is whether what is said resonates with a sufficiently pervasive underlying group sentiment that is distressed with the current state of affairs and identifies the direction spoken to as a way out of the current distressing state of affairs. It is also noteworthy that the direction offered by these leaders is also in many ways consistent with their personality or character. Some individuals consistently and even compulsively choose to try to lead in a charismatic manner. Others prefer the control provided by a more bureaucratic approach to worklife. There is then a convergence between personality variables, the situation, the leader's experience and the group's experience of the moment.

Sentence Groups

Potential group leaders are able to read the situation and float trial balloons. When group members feel sufficiently anxious about what is going on, a potential leader who articulates a direction that is generally thought will alleviate everyone's distressing experience will be followed many times without further reflection.

Sentience groups are omnipresent within organizations. Sentience groups frequently spontaneously form around a set of commonly shared feelings and experience. They are filled with shared personal agendas, feelings and experience. For example, a group of upper and middle management executives that meets for a weekend planning retreat may have sentience groups formed up around how upper management has treated middle management and vice versa. The same outcome might occur between management and union employees participating in the retreat. Members of the various sentience groups quickly recognize each other based on the sentiments expressed. A participant that speaks to unilateral decision making by top management that is disconnected from the realities of the workplace will immediately resonate with those who have had similar experiences. These same individuals will identify top management as a group sharing similar thoughts, feelings and experiences relative to the rest of their organization. Sentience groups are, therefore, constantly being formed and abandoned as conditions change and they are often filled with strong emotions and motivations that can promote polarization. It should also be clear sentience groups readily form up around the four kinds of group experience, as everyone in the workplace has firsthand experience with each type of group experience.

In Sum

Groups and organizations often contain subgroups that may be thought of as having their own axe to grind. These groups contain members who share thoughts, feelings and experience that lead them to see the workplace in much the same way. These are sentience groups that are frequently challenging to manage.

The Uncertainty Principle of Group Dynamics

If one thing can be said about group dynamics within groups and relative to groups within organizations, it is that many times what happens as a result of these dynamics is unpredictable and can not be guessed prior to its occurrence. Almost like the popping of popcorn, group dynamics often just seem to pop on and off in a chaotic manner although there may be a hard to detect underlying coherence to what is happening as represented by dynamic workplace theory. The ability to sustain one kind of group experience across time is problematic and the tendency to want to change to another type of group experience is always present. Equally unlikely is predicting which of the other types of group experience may ultimately evolve regardless of when the change occurs.

In Sum

Groups have a life of their own. Even the best-led group can develop hard to predict dynamics that are subsequently hard to manage. Group experience has at its core unpredictability arising from individual and interpersonal variables. This underlying fragility to group stability and the quality of group life is a major contributor to members becoming anxious, psychologically defensive and more intensely interested in controlling their experience.

Balanced Experience and Stability

Yet another implicit aspect of dynamic workplace theory is the balancing of these dynamic forces as represented by the emergence of the balanced group experience. This balance point (see Figure 1) that is discussed in greater detail in chapter 5 contains within it a stability where the other three types of psychologically defensive group experience cancel each other out. Much like centrifugal and centripetal forces in nature where one seeks to fling an object outward and the other draw it inward, balance between the two forces creates a stable orbit, as is the case of the planets around the sun, or the moon around the earth. The comparison of these natural forces to group dynamics is straightforward. When group dynamics are balanced, the three psychologically defensive groups continue to exist as a latent potential but for the moment are neutralized by each other. The chaotic experience becomes one of creativity and exploring the possibilities where new ideas and experiments are openly considered. Organizational life may well be a bit messy but not evoke a sense of being out of control or threatening. Formal group and organizational structure exists but is not depended on to regulate anxiety through strict control. Rather, in this case, features of bureaucratic hierarchical structure provide a sufficient anchoring of process to permit organization members to both be creative and try new things without a sense of losing control over their group process and organization. Some structure is liberating and facilitating so long as it does not become rigidly depended upon to regulate experience via excessive control. Last, leaders with admired skills, knowledge and styles of doing things are present at different times within groups and organizations. These leaders are not compulsively relied upon to control adverse experience of organizational life. Rather, they may encourage chaotic and messy creativity and support organizational operating protocols, but in a balanced fashion. They also avoid the narcissistic pitfalls leadership roles tend to promote. These leaders do not encourage others to see them as grandiose and all-powerful, and do not see themselves that way either. It is also the case, as discussed in chapter 5, that each of the psychologically defensive groups contains elements that promote stability of the defensive group experience. This appreciation is underscored by acknowledging the exceptional stability achieved by bureaucratic hierarchies that often continue to persist despite the gravest of operating dysfunctions and losses of original purpose.

In Sum

The dynamic workplace model provides for the presence of a more thoughtful and intentional work group experience where a balance is struck between chaos, the rigidities of bureaucracy and the idiosyncrasies of charismatic leadership. The balance point creates a transcendence of the psychologically defensive nature of these group experiences where their underlying basic tendencies and assumptions are moderated and combined in such a way as to countervail each other. However, their pathological nature always remains available to group members at times when balance may be lost under stressful conditions. Similarly, each of the psychologically defensive groups can find balance that creates stability (see chapter 5) that may only be challenged when group or organizational failure is perceived to be imminent.

IN CONCLUSION

Individual and group behavior in organizations create a complex setting that is difficult to understand and even more difficult to manage. Dynamic workplace theory incorporates the diversity that this experience possesses. More specifically, the theory not only explains how opposing personal, interpersonal, group and organizational trends energize group and organizational dynamics, it places these trends in dynamic tension one with the other to account for the indeterminacy of worklife. Organizational life and experience are filled with dynamic tensions that may, at any time, shift in one direction or another in an effort to control workplace anxiety. Managers, therefore, need conceptual maps to understand and appreciate intrapersonal, interpersonal, group and organizational dynamics. Dynamic workplace theory provides one such map. The following chapters explore to a much greater extent the intricacies of this theoretical perspective.

Chapter 3

The Elemental Forces of Dynamic Workplace Theory

In the last analysis, each person works for himself, unless some kind of pressure forces him in another direction. What psychoanalysis helps to reveal are those processes which occur within every individual and which determine how each person will act. It shows how psychological pressures, especially anxiety, can neutralize productive effort and drain away human energy. It shows the ways in which people affect and relate to each other in groups, and the ways in which leaders are created.

(De Board, 1978, p. viii)

Dynamic workplace theory enters the workplace by aiding us in observing what is there and making sense of it. The model and its dynamics were described. Starting with this chapter, the elements and dynamic nature of the model are more thoroughly explored for their contribution to understanding our workplace experiences within groups and organizations. Understanding the workplace, as has been pointed out, is a challenging endeavor that must come to grips with a vast array of elements and dynamics while also avoiding cognitive overloading. A realistic theoretical perspective that offers insight into this complexity must intuitively make sense while also locating important aspects of workplace experience and placing them into a context where they can be understood individually and relative to each other. This chapter is devoted to a thorough discussion of the four group and organizational experiences. Chaotic, bureaucratic, charismatic and balanced group experiences offer organization members, consultants and researchers a rich milieu for examination. There are many facets to each of these types of experience that must be elaborated. This work commences with chaotic work experience following a brief mention of workplace psychodynamics.

A WORD ON WORKPLACE PSYCHODYNAMICS

Not discussed to any great extent thus far is the contribution depth psychology makes to understanding the workplace. The usefulness of using psychoanalytically informed perspectives has been explained and justified by others and this intellectual ground shall not be covered here. Skeptical readers are encouraged to do additional reading to assure themselves that the theoretical content is not "pop" psychobabble. There are a number of accessible books on the subject (Allcorn and Diamond, 1997; Czander, 1993; De Board, 1978 and Gabriel, 1999).

Individual, interpersonal, group and organizational dynamics, as alluded to in chapter 2, can be understood to be driven in large part by the thoughts and feelings that lie within each organization member and leader. It is, therefore, worthwhile to explore what a psychodynamic perspective contributes to understanding these individually based psychodynamics and dynamic workplace theory. I approach this task by providing a discussion of a number of theoretical points of view.

To start, it is important to appreciate that the central dilemma for organization members arises out of the need to find a balance between independence (personal identity and self-esteem) and group membership (a sense of belonging and affiliation) without becoming overly anxious about maintaining the balance between them (Diamond, 1993). Persistent or extreme imbalances between maintaining self-integrity and group membership evoke distressing self, other, group and organizational experiences. This experience fundamentally arises from separation and attachment anxieties. No one wants to feel taken over, dominated, and forced to submit to the will of another (the leader) or others (the group). At the same time there also exists a fear of being left alone to make one's way in the organizational wilderness.

These drivers of individual, interpersonal, group and organizational dynamics have their origin in infancy. The infant is initially preoccupied with the quality of attachment to caretaking others, and as an adult we may likewise find ourselves dominated or ignored and avoided. Feelings of self-annihilation as a result of being taken over or abandoned are the underlying interior and interpersonal threat. These are distressing experiences that promote defensive psychological regression. Regression leads to an ever heavier reliance upon psychological defenses such as denial, splitting and projection associated with Freud's oral stage of development, and reaction-formation, isolation and undoing associated with Freud's anal stage of development (Diamond, 1993). It is also the case that other theoretical perspectives may be used, and they are incorporated into the discussion of the four kinds of group experience.

In Sum

The psychological side of organizational life has a profound influence upon interpersonal, group and organizational dynamics. In particular, a substantial psychological tension and threat exists relative to one's workplace attachment that may be overwhelmingly controlling or isolating and abandoning. There can be too much or too little attachment that spawns psychologically defensive regression that is best understood from a psychodynamic perspective.

CHAOTIC WORK EXPERIENCE

There are many occasions where group and organization experience can seem to be chaotic and contain a sense of confusion, dread, fear, threat and distressing personality clashes that include not-so-hidden struggles for power and ascendancy. The old phrase "too many bulls in the china shop" was no doubt intended to capture some of the fundamental nature of this kind of experience. In this case there are "too many chiefs and not enough Indians," to borrow not so necessarily politically correct terminology. A few key individuals may be willing to do whatever seems necessary to protect their turf, expand their decision-making authority, improve their reputations and resumes, and advance their careers. In these cases the good of the group and organization is compromised by the pursuit of self-interest.

Many other group members may also add to the chaotic workplace experience by actively or passively aggressing leaders by not following instructions, rules and regulations. Getting quality-controlled work done on time and cost-effectively may take a back seat to interpersonal rivalries driven by personality and character attributes that are resistant to or outright opposed to authority. Group and organizational well-being is again compromised by these highly energized individual, interpersonal and group dynamics.

Stacey (1992) writes: "Chaos in a business organization takes the form of contradiction: the simultaneous presence of opposing ways of behaving. It is evidenced, for example, by managers who operate budgetary forms of control to keep the organization stable, while at the same time engaging in amplifying forms of political activity in which they try to undermine the status quo. Chaos in its scientific sense takes the form of conflict, as when an organization experiences the clash of countercultures, the tensions of political activity, the contention and dialogue through which managers handle ambiguous strategic decisions" (p. 68). He continues: "Chaotic dynamics are evidenced by escalating small changes and self-reinforcing circles, in the manner in which managers deal with events and actions that have long-term consequences" (p. 68).

Stacey is concerned about managing the unknowable that is a constant problem in organizations. No one can consistently predict what will happen, when and in what manner. It is similarly the case that no amount of protracted effort to master reality will entirely succeed.

It is certainly the case that much of what is potentially chaotic in the group or organization may be ritualized and institutionalized over time. A good example is the management versus union mentality where ritualized combat often seems more important than striving for organizational success. It is also the case that employees who are union or nonunion may contribute their fair share to the tensions. Other forms of ritualized group and organizational combat take the form of different disciplines that are usually organized into their own departments that may use language that is not understood by others. To this may be added unfamiliar thinking and analytical processes that tend to make other groups with different experience and expertise and approaches to problem solving and decision making anxious. One need only think of the implicit tension between automobile designers and automobile engineers, or financial analysts who compute the cost benefit in making a product recall versus marketing that wants to portray the company as socially responsible by caring about its customers and their well-being. Everyone may not be on the same page.

A great many more kinds and types of examples of potentially chaotic group and organizational experience could be provided. However, the reader, who is familiar with working in groups and large organizations, should have no difficulty thinking of many similar experiences that permit an in-depth understanding of what it means to experience chaotic organizational experience. It is, however, also important to appreciate that the most chaotic of workplaces contains other dimensions that may escape immediate awareness and understanding. The chaos may, in some ways, be understood to be one surface of the organization or group. Work experience may seem chaotic but yet there may also be a sense of a multilayered underlying structure that holds the group or organization together. Mathematicians who work with chaos theory and nonlinear feedback systems are quick to point out that, while at one level things may appear to be chaotic, there is a deeper or superordinate structure that organizes the chaos and permits understanding it. Organizations may then be understood to contain bounded instability (Stacey, 1992).

In Sum

Chaos presents organization members with an exceptional amount of anxiety-promoting ambiguity and uncertainty that is further aggravated by hard to understand, individual, interpersonal, group and organizational dynamics. It is the juxtaposition of the vagaries of operating businesses or large public organizations with these organizational dynamics that humbles the best efforts of executives, consultants and researchers to fully comprehend them, much less effectively and consistently manage them. Group and organization leaders, charismatic or not, are faced in many ways with an insurmountable problem. Nonetheless, when in doubt they must proceed. The utility of dynamic workplace theory arises out of this need to be able to function within this hard to know chaotic context of bounded instability.

The Underlying Order of Chaos—Bounded Instability

No matter how chaotic work experience becomes, it is most often the case that the members of a work group do not suddenly flee the work group or abandon their jobs when worklife becomes chaotic. At least intuitively the most chaotic of workplace experiences is understood to possess an organizing principle that holds things together; that bounds the instability. For example, one arena where chaos is often spoken of is in a combat situation. One's awareness is filled with thousands of rounds of small arms fire in all directions, small and large explosions, wounded and dead, smoke and dust, confused communications, gaps in the chain of command and perhaps above all paralyzing fear. Nonetheless the soldiers forge ahead to take the beachhead or mountaintop or regroup to create a defensive parameter in a firefight. These are extreme examples that have less life-threatening organizational counterparts. Individual, group and organizational survival can, however, also be felt to be at stake regarding maintaining one's employment and keeping the organization competitive. The point to be made here is that regardless of how chaotic and out of control workplace experience may seem, at some level there is an underlying structure that holds things together regardless of whether the organizational battlefield is filled with bullets or the aggressive actions of others and competitors.

Dynamic workplace theory represents one way of thinking about this larger underlying framework. In this regard all bureaucratic hierarchical structure is not entirely or permanently lost and one or more charismatic individuals may be able to provide leadership under the worst of conditions. Group members may easily have their attention directed to these other types of workplace experience if the distressing experience of anxiety contained within the chaotic experience is sufficient to encourage group members to feel that almost anything is better than how things are. This self, other, group and organizational experience or sentience lays the foundation for a readiness to change and the emergence of one or more leaders who offer hope and new direction, which is further discussed in chapter 4. Chaotic experience and the readiness to accept change also contain important underlying psychodynamics that provide additional insight.

The Psychodynamics of Chaotic Work Experience

The predominant mode of experience within the chaotic group is annihilation anxiety arising from both an absence of self-differentiation and loss of self and abandonment by other members of the group or organization. Everyone has retreated or, as Horney (1950) notes, resigned by withdrawing into psychological foxholes to avoid the potential of being consumed by others and destroyed by the group for self-differentiation. Life within these psychic foxholes, however, also threatens self-annihilation as a result of feeling almost entirely disconnected from the group. Organization members are stuck between a rock and a hard place. Anxiety about membership in the group is hard to manage thereby provoking regression and the use of psychological defenses that hold the promise of helping the individual effectively cope with the anxiety. These defenses include denial and the splitting-off of experience that is associated with the oral stage of development where a hunger for relations with others (objects) is manifest. In this case, pressing personal needs for affiliation are disowned and located in others who are then experienced as possessing aggressive oral incorporative motives relative to one's self. "Good" self-experience is retained and "bad" experience denied, split off and projected onto others, creating pathological certainty regarding their perverse motivations. This dynamic encourages organization members to see others and events in black-and-white terms that polarize thoughts and feelings thereby once again reinforcing the experience of the chaotic group as personally dangerous.

These intrapersonal, interpersonal, group and organizational dynamics contain primitive psychological defenses that may also paradoxically be observed to further accentuate the presence of anxiety relative to oneself. This outcome may include hard to know and articulate fantasies about being consumed by others to meet their needs. The presence of many denied and split-off thoughts and feelings of an aggressive oral incorporative nature makes the chaotic group one that is dangerous to try to lead, as this requires attracting attention to oneself (self-differentiation) that can promote being consumed by group members.

These perceived tendencies on the part of others are reinforced by their very real need for affiliation. They behave in a way that encourages the projection of these needs onto them. Others are then with great certainty understood to be out to use them to meet their own needs to feel better about themselves. Within a context such as this, withdrawal from interpersonal relations may seem to be the only way out. Withdrawal, however, paradoxically reinforces one's own needs to feel connected to others while simultaneously frustrating the same need on the part of others. It is then no wonder that chaotic group experience is so threatening, self-perpetuating and unfulfilling.

In Sum

Chaotic group experience is filled with many anxiety-ridden threats to personal survival that originate from within and without. This threatening interpersonal and group landscape finds organization members steadfastly retreating from relating to each other to avoid their malevolent intentions aimed at consuming others to meet their affiliation needs (emotional cannibalism). This retreat may be thought of as employees entering organizational foxholes that provide a comforting autistic organizational artifact where a boundary can be potentially created and defended to avoid annihilation (Ogden, 1989).

The experience of chaos within groups and organizations, therefore, has a circular quality to it. On the one hand the experience promotes anxiety and regression to psychological defensiveness that, in turn, contributes to the individual withdrawal and losses of connection to others that further the sense of fragmentation and disconnectedness. Even though there is a circular reinforcing quality to this experience there inevitably develops enough anxiety that implies an underlying awareness that this cannot go on forever. Group and organizational survival will eventually be threatened. Lying within this awareness is the possibility of change to another type of group experience (see chapter 4). The direction of this change may be toward the comforting and regulated bureaucratic work experience.

BUREAUCRATIC WORK EXPERIENCE

The bureaucratic hierarchy is by far the most abundant organization form as we start the new millennium. It is something everyone is intimately familiar with from having to deal with them as a client, customer or employee. They are everywhere all of the time and it is hard to envision a world without them, or indeed any other kind of organization form that will work as well (chapter 8 presents a thought experiment for creating a nonhierarchical and bureaucratic organization). The superabundance of the bureaucratic hierarchical organization form merits a brief "time-out" to establish a historical context for its ascendancy to a position of dominance in organizational design.

As we start the twenty-first century, the omnipresence of an organizational form developed during the eighteenth and nineteenth centuries and further perfected in the twentieth century points to the hard to deny fact that little progress has been made in creating new theoretical models that transcend the bureaucratic hierarchical organizational design paradigm. Before proceeding, revisiting the industrial revolution and its contribution to the rise of the bureaucratic hierarchy is informative. Daniel Wren (1979) writes:

Starting in the mid 1700s and eventually aided by James Watt's perfection of the steam engine during the last quarter of the century, the 1800s witnessed the ever growing impact of industrialization. The Industrial Revolution created a new cultural environment and a revised set of problems for management. People's needs were becoming more complex as they sought to adjust to life in the city and to the new rigor of the factory. Organizations were being reshaped by the demands for heavy infusions of capital, by the division of labor, and by the need for economical, predictable performance. Organizations needed to innovate and compete in a market economy and this created pressures for growth and the economies to be obtained from large-scale production and distribution. Economic theory recognized that the entrepreneur-manager performed a distinct role in combining the traditional three factors of production in the ever-growing factory system. With size came the need for managers, the need for a capable, disciplined, trained, motivated work force, and the need for rationalizing the planning, organizing, and controlling of operations in the early enterprise. (p. 69)

Wren's encapsulation of the basis for the creation of the bureaucratic hierarchy allows us to appreciate that we continue to try to perfect it. When it comes to organizational design one needs to look no further than Elliott Jaques (1989, 1990), who is of the firm belief that the bureaucratic hierarchy's only problem is that it still lacks complete perfection, and Hammer and Champy (1993), who assert that bureaucracy is a glue that holds organizations together.

This brief historical overview despite its brevity provides a powerful testament to the dominance of the bureaucratic hierarchy. It is, therefore, only appropriate to have it as one of the central elements to any theory that accounts for workplace experience. We are all familiar with the hierarchical nature of our organizations where positions are arrayed in vertical columns downward from the chief executive officer or owner to positions that possess almost no power, authority or discretion as to how to perform work. It is also the case that the bureaucratic hierarchy is a response to specialization that may take many forms. The columns of an organization chart are composed of the specialties such as finance, human resource management, marketing, planning, sales, legal, information systems and operations, to list but some of the possibilities. Each area of specialization possesses its own language, way of thinking about the workplace and unique knowledge base and ethics that make it a profession. Our organizations are, therefore, divided into layers of power and authority and columns of specialization. Above all this seems logical when you stop to think about it.

Nonetheless this logical form of organization is notoriously filled with dysfunctions that detract from performance and introduce uncertainty, losses of predictability and personal safety and even chaotic experiences and instances where routinized leadership is temporarily abandoned for charismatic leadership. These dysfunctions arise from the layers and columns where instructions, information and communications become distorted as they move up and down the organization through the hierarchical layers where each layer filters information. A performance problem in one work team in one department within one division may gradually have the information about the analysis of the problem modified as it moves upward through the filtering layers. Eventually awareness of the problem at the top of the organization may be entirely lost. Yet another example of organizational dysfunction is illustrated by one specialized division knowing that a product will be changed in the near future and a second division proceeding to purchase improved equipment to produce the current product design that will ultimately be incompatible with the new design. Considerable waste and inefficiency is built into these commonplace workplace dynamics. The logical organization design does not always work so logically.

The Role of Human Nature in Defeating Logical Organization

During the last quarter of the twentieth century there developed a growing interest in the paradoxical nature of the presumably rational bureaucratic hierarchy where workplace reality many times does not appear to be operating in any kind of logical manner. Those who have studied this aspect of organizational reality have come to appreciate that severe organizational dysfunction is introduced into the rational workplace by the irrational side of human nature (Blau and Meyer, 1956). This irrationality, it is also thought, is encouraged by the features of the bureaucratic hierarchy. In this regard bureaucratic hierarchy contains within it elements that destabilize it thereby encouraging change. To more fully appreciate this aspect of worklife, the psychodynamic workplace must be inspected.

The Psychodynamics of Bureaucratic Work Experience

There are two important aspects of this discussion. The first are the psychodynamic origins of the bureaucratic hierarchy and the second the circular reinforcing quality of the interaction of this organization design with human nature.

The Psychodynamics of Bureaucratic Hierarchy

Czander (1993) and Diamond (1993) point out a discomforting but important perspective of organizational life. They and others describe an organizational context where unconscious and most often undiscussible human motivations exercise their influence in the adoption of an organization's design and subsequent operation. Bureaucratic hierarchies, they point out, contain many elements that arise out of individual and socially defensive psychodynamics. In particular, organizational membership raises control and dominance and submission issues that first arise in infancy and continue throughout life. It is, therefore, not much of a leap of faith to understand that how organizations are conceived and operated is heavily influenced by the kinds of individual propensities that we all share, thereby creating a shared but unconscious socially defensive response. The form, substance and operation of our organizations may then be seen to be in large part the long shadow cast by human needs.

Reinforcing Circularity

The bureaucratic solution to workplace anxiety encourages psychological defensiveness that may be observed to help maintain it. It is the underlying defensive nature of bureaucracy that introduces the dysfunctions associated with bureaucracy, such as organizational rigidity and compromised adaptiveness, as well as heavy reliance upon policies and procedures to maintain control that stifle work and creativity.

The bureaucratic solution to workplace anxiety that arises out of threats to self serves to, in turn, create shared social defenses in response to the demand for obedience and submission to impersonal authority, and for the finely tuned structuring of work. Fear of interpersonal and group aggression and personal annihilation are, in contrast to chaotic experience, not coped with by withdrawal, unilateral interpersonal defenses and resignation. Rather the response is more proactive where depersonalization and the creation of a controlling social structure are relied upon to regulate self and other experience to sustain personal identity (Diamond, 1993 and Kernberg, 1979). Self-effacing personal submission becomes the norm (Horney, 1950). This reliance on control is closely related to Freud's anal stage of human development. Work becomes ritualized and leadership institutionalized and routinized. Paranoia arising from membership and accompanying persecutory anxiety is sufficiently mediated so as to sustain individual, group and organizational functionality. Interpersonal fears of aggression and being taken over or consumed by others or the leader is sufficiently allayed. However, when stresses and strains arise in the workplace, the pursuit of control of these fears and anxieties can lead to obsessive focus on their socially defensive nature, stifling creativity and adaptiveness that may paradoxically provide the way out of the stressful situation. Shame, guilt and losses of personal responsibility may emerge as features of organizational control as may splitting and projection that frequently serves to locate an enemy without (Baum, 1987, 1990). In this regard there develops a destructive feedback loop that introduces and perpetuates distressing workplace experience, as was the case for chaotic work experience. It is, therefore, not hard to see that the bureaucratic socially defensive system carries within it the seeds of its own destruction. Undeniable problems that threaten personal, group and organizational survival may exist. These threats, when acknowledged, can lead to the development of a fight/flight culture that energizes change to one of the other types of groups. Chapter 4 discusses this potential for change.

In Sum

The bureaucratic hierarchy is so commonplace as to be taken for granted as the only meaningful organization form. At the same time it contains within it horizontal and vertical fragmentation and socially defensive reliance upon control that introduces potentially serious losses of organizational performance that may, like the chaotic group experience, be perceived as threatening individual, group and organizational survival. The group or organization may not fail, but it may fail to succeed, especially in those cases where competing organizations do not present much of a threat, as is the case for governmental entities and large public and private universities. However, when the sense of collective threat is sufficient and enough group or organization members feel that change is necessary, the door is opened to change and the acquisition of another type of workplace experience such as one led by a charismatic leader.

CHARISMATIC LEADERSHIP AND WORK EXPERIENCE

Charismatic leaders are those that intentionally or at the minimum unintentionally focus attention upon themselves. They have an engaging and well-articulated and very often expansive vision about the type of work that should be accomplished and how (Horney, 1950). They are more than willing to provide direction as to how organization members should relate to each other and them. These leaders seem to take up a lot of organizational space. They further add to their visibility by introducing a constellation of paradoxes into the workplace that come to at least intuitively be known to others and, in the end, can only be resolved by them. For example, the leader may espouse popular notions such as empowerment and self-managing teams while simultaneously closely monitoring every decision and the work of employees and groups. The notion of empowering employees is not new. Mary Parker Follett observed: "The best type of leader today does not want men who are subservient to him, those who render him a passive obedience. He is trying to develop men exactly the opposite of this, men themselves with mastery, and such men will give his own leadership worth and power" (Metcalf and Urwick, 1941, p. 267). However, contrary to this advice, the charismatic leader often intervenes to take control of decision making and work processes at any time he or she perceives a variance between his or her not always fully explained and often perfectionist expectations and reality. Employees fairly quickly figure out that, while the leader espouses a philosophy consistent with Follett's point of view, the reality is that the leader is going to try to control just about everything. Micromanagement may abound.

The Origins of Charismatic Leaders within Groups and Organizations

Groups and organizations can come to be dominated by a charismatic leader by any number of means. One common example is that the governing board hires a charismatic leader to turn the organization around. Another source of charismatic leaders arises when top management identifies within their ranks a few individuals with charismatic qualities who are moved about within the organization to shape things up. Follett describes a third common way charismatic leaders emerge. She writes: "My only thesis in this paper is that in the more progressively managed business—I realize that they are greatly in the minority—in these we see a tendency, only a tendency but one which seems to me very encouraging, for the control of a particular situation to go to the man with the largest knowledge of that situation, to him who can grasp and organize its essential elements, who understands its total significance, who can see it through—who can see length as well as breadth—rather than to one with merely a dominating personality or in virtue of his official position" (Metcalf and Urwick, 1941, p. 281). Bennis (1989) also notes: "Leadership can be felt throughout an organization. It gives pace and energy to the work and empowers the work force" (p. 22). These authors point out the possibility that charismatic leaders may arise anywhere within an organization. Charismatic leaders need not necessarily be executives and managers when their talents and skills emerge to take charge of a situation.

Charismatic leaders are eager to identify themselves as leaders, and often attract attention to themselves that encourages others to see them as potential leaders. They will often speak of grand visions, criticize current leaders, and provide an inspirational message that attracts others to them. They are also often adept at relating to people one-on-one. They are interpersonally charming and seductive. They are busy networkers who gradually build up relationships that promise to support them personally and their career. These networked others may eventually become the much needed loyal followers every charismatic leader requires.

When provided an opportunity to lead, charismatic leaders seize it even if it is a marginal opportunity. These individuals are sufficiently arrogant to believe that they can accomplish just about anything. As a result any leadership opportunity is felt to provide an opportunity for career advancement and may be used in such a way as to expand personal authority and responsibility beyond the original scope of the leadership opportunity. Those in the way are often disposed of by any means available. Resistance to their leadership is felt to be a personal offense and a threat that is often countered by highly motivated vindictive triumph (Horney, 1950). This individual is willing to escalate interpersonal rivalry and conflict to uncomfortable levels where it is felt winning is everything and defeat amounts to personal destruction. Rivals will frequently retreat in the face of excessively energized and personalized aggression. This highly motivated individual is no person to mess with, which directs our attention to the psychodynamics of charismatic leadership.

The Psychodynamics of Charismatic Work Experience

Charismatic leaders are in large part the outcome of group dynamics. He or she is often the right person in the right place at the right time. Charismatically based group and organizational dynamics locate as a primary defense against group membership anxiety an individual who it is hoped will provide the control needed to allay anxiety about losses of self, personal identity and integrity and consumption by others seeking to fulfill pressing personal needs. The leader responds to the leadership opportunity by encouraging group and organization members to split off those aspects of themselves that are effective and project them onto their leader. At the same time, organization members implicitly retain those parts of themselves that are fearful, helpless, anxious and ineffective. This creates a black-and-white world where the leader is idealized as being "good" and group members despise themselves as "bad." It is certainly the case in the military that embattled soldiers hope that their leaders possess a god-like perfection regarding their planning and decision making. And, by analogy, so it is the case in charismatically led groups and organizations. Group and organization members are encouraged to and may willingly volunteer idealization of their leader who, it is hoped, is omnipotent. Fantasy life, therefore, creates a leader who is ultimately much bigger than life.

The charismatic leader may also be inspected from a psychodynamic perspective. He or she may be thought of as responding to the leadership opportunity with an expansive solution to his or her anxiety (Horney, 1950). This individual's narcissism is encouraged to expand to unhealthy proportions where he or she comes to feel in some ways god-like. This results in the development of many grand and inspiring visions for the future. The details are, however, left to others to figure out. Perfectionism becomes an awe-inspiring instrument in the hands of this leader, who may appear at any time or place to criticize and sometimes momentarily intervene to create change in a grand flurry of work and audacity. Organization members also know from the rumor mill, organizational history and mythology that no one will survive crossing swords with their leader. The leader's power, control and authority assure eventual domination and the eradication of naysayers. His or her excessive pride will be defended at any cost.

This leader is, however, inevitably not omnipotent, omniscient or omnipresent. The leader ultimately will fail to perfectly control all distressing aspects of work experience. He or she may also contribute to this process by creating a small loyal in-group and a much larger out-group that contains members who are cut off to some degree from affiliating with their leader. Loyal followers jealously guard their special relationship with their leader by actively limiting the ability of others to communicate and meet with him or her, thereby accentuating this dynamic.

Failure to overcome every problem and the splitting of the group and organization become the feet of clay that the charismatic leader is doomed to develop. Anxieties and interpersonal and inter-group conflict are not entirely controlled by the leader, who may also come to feel overwhelmed by his or her experience of responsibility. This promotes splitting and projection on his or her part where aggressive, sadistic and incompetent aspects of self are located within his or her followers. Loyal followers may be seen to be incompetent, helpless and dependent and not meriting respect. At the same time, out-group members are invested with aggressive and sadistic qualities that the leader understands are directed at him or her. This reinforces to some extent his or her rejection of out-group members.

It is, therefore, apparent that charismatic experience contains, like the other workplace experiences, the seeds of its own destruction. Fight/flight dynamics will eventually emerge to energize a search for a new and improved leader or possibly a new kind of group experience and approach to work and leadership. Change may dramatically occur when the leader is suddenly killed off by the governing board.

In Sum

Charismatic group experience contains the hope of allaying member anxiety about personal survival by investing all power, authority and control in one individual who, like the perfect parental figure, it is fantasized, will provide even attention for all "family" members. As the charismatic leader emerges group members invest magnificent personal qualities in their leader that concurrently limit their experience of themselves as being effective and meriting respect and admiration. This process accentuates the difference between the leader and his or her followers, who tend to progressively see themselves as fearful, weak and needing to be taken care of (the flock). However, the most effective leader, when invested with these fantasies, expectations and qualities, with few exceptions, must ultimately fail to meet them. Operating problems and threats to individual, group and organizational well-being develop. Additionally, those attracted to charismatic roles seek to develop a band of loyal and admiring followers to bolster their self-experience and compensate for deeply felt narcissistic deficits. This process serves to split the group and organization into an in-group and out-group where in-group members are many times ruthlessly exploited and out-group members are held in suspicion and frequently undermined and attacked. These dynamics lead to disillusionment with the leader, dissent within the organization and the gradual emergence of aggressive and destructive tendencies directed at the leader. Given time, these dynamics lead to the distressing experience of open conflict and threatening losses of organizational cohesion and performance. The only solution may be to replace the leader with a more perfect leader, or perhaps a change to another type of group and organization experience with greater balance may work.

BALANCED WORK EXPERIENCE

The balanced group experience provides balance in several important ways. First, there exists a balance in the presence of the other three psychologically and socially defensive workplace experiences. The underlying tendencies of these three group experiences are balanced relative to each other. The qualities of the three defensive experiences that promote work are accessible while the anxiety-promoting and psychologically defensive nature of the groups is minimized. Chaos, bureaucratic order and charismatic leadership are all present but in their constructive forms. The negative side of these groups is ameliorated by the anxiety-avoiding nature of the balanced group experience. Chapter 4 speaks to the notion that a dynamic tension exists between each of these types of workplace experience.

Balanced work experience is, however, more than the absence of psychological and social defensiveness. It represents a positive force in its own right and contains elements of experience that encourage members to hold on to the experience. This positive force arises out of the basic human motivations to achieve self-integration, self-esteem, true self and authentic self-other relations. This striving for self-efficacy and self-actualization becomes a driving force in the development and maintenance of the balanced workplace experience.

Constructive Chaos

Organizational and individual creativity contains many chaotic elements. Senge (1990) builds upon this notion: "That means building an organization where it is safe for people to create visions, where inquiry and commitment to the truth are the norm, and where challenging the status quo is expected—

especially when the status quo includes obscuring aspects of current reality that people seek to avoid" (p. 172). Groups that are set the task of solving operating problems will most often generate the best solution only after a thorough brainstorming of the possibilities where the ideas generated are analyzed in a constructive manner for their likely contribution to solving the problem. To be avoided for the most part is envy-driven interpersonal competition to generate the idea the group will adopt (often referred to as a risky shift in thinking).

Organizations that are able to adapt quickly to take advantage of unanticipated opportunities and respond to unexpected operating problems are many times also thought of as a bit messy, as they seem to be more often in the midst of change rather than in a static state. Organizational dynamic adaptiveness and plasticity are discussed in chapter 10. Anyone observing these kinds of adaptive group and organizational dynamics readily perceives that there is an element of chaos when members search for solutions and ways of taking advantage of opportunities. At the same time they do not entirely disregard how the group or organization is functioning or the long-term organizational vision. Participation in these settings is exhilarating as many kinds of change are contemplated and some tried out. Change can be exciting if properly conceived, planned and managed. It need not necessarily encounter resistance.

Constructive Bureaucratic Hierarchical Order

Groups and organizations benefit from structures that provide for planned and voluntary coordination of work. In large complex organizations this is especially necessary. Assembly lines and production and delivery schedules are examples where in the near-term some of the rigidities that accompany bureaucratic hierarchical order are not only adaptive but also essential. However, as noted, it is also necessary for these periods of stability to be overlaid with a constant rate of change. In a sense it is not unlike drawing a circle out of a large number of straight lines.

Organizational creativity and adaptiveness lead to interim periods of stability where new ideas are embraced, modified and adapted to the realities of the workplace and the actions of competitors. Likewise, organizational change is good up to a point where a common thread of cooperation and direction is compromised. I encountered an organization that when closely inspected had a completely failed billing system that no one actually understood had failed. On an invoice-by-invoice basis the amount billed rarely matched the amount of product delivered. It was also the case that the customers, who in this case received blood transfusions, were not usually prepared to check the billing against what they received. Therefore, over- and underbilling was not spotted. As a result of this two-way compensating error the total amount billed did come close to what was produced. When the executive in charge was confronted with the error rates his response was simple. The system had been changed a year or so ago and was about to be changed again. Therefore, correcting the problem now was not necessary and would be too costly to contemplate. Organizational change can indeed be a detriment to organizational performance if not properly managed. Intervening periods of controlled stability assure proper performance before more change is contemplated.

Constructive Charismatic Leadership

Groups and organizations are often blessed with many individuals who spontaneously and in a highly effective manner offer outstanding leadership for a finite period of time. An interdisciplinary group that is working on a production problem will periodically benefit from the leadership of many of its members who possess different skill sets, history, insights and ways of thinking about the problem (Metcalf and Urwick, 1941). At the same time these individuals will have their leadership and contribution welcomed by other members of the group who can see the contribution that is offered by the individual. These leaders do a good job without feeling that they need everyone's approval or that they have to take over the group. Conversely, group members do not feel overly dependent upon the leadership of any one individual. Leadership becomes more of a process than a person.

The Psychodynamics of Balanced Group Experience

Work experience within the balanced group is less stressful than the other three defensive group dynamics. Less anxiety and psychological regression and dependency upon defenses are encountered. This anxiety-minimizing sense of balance is illustrated by the earlier discussion of the constructive sides of chaos, bureaucracy and charisma. These basic elements of groups do not become overdetermined defenses against each other and anxiety over membership. Terms such as work group, task group, collaboration, collegiality and intentionality apply to the balanced group experience. It contains within it the ability to openly inspect interpersonal and group dynamics for their contribution to group performance or, conversely, their contribution to performance problems. This inspection or reflective process implies that a firm basis of interpersonal trust and respect exists where feelings of being set upon, bullied or intimidated by others are avoided. Natural psychological processes such as projection and transference are minimized and their pathological qualities are open to inspection. The psychodynamics of the moment contribute to the positive experience of others, group, the organization and worklife in general.

In Sum

The balanced group experience is one where the positive qualities of chaos (creativity), bureaucracy (optimal structure) and charisma (optimal leadership) are present. The negative outcomes of these psychologically and socially defensive groups cancel each other out as each contains elements antithetical to the others. In final analysis the accessing of the positive qualities and the negation of the negative qualities of the three defensive experiences is at work within the balanced group experience. Anxiety associated with creativity, change and achievement, while present, is not experienced as threatening. The group is able to work effectively on task and call into question individual, interpersonal and group dynamics that negatively affect performance without provoking defensiveness that encourages psychological regression and reliance upon defensive routines to avoid the distressing experience of anxiety.

THE NOTION OF GROUP AND ORGANIZATIONAL CULTURE

The four types of group experience and accompanying dynamics may be thought of as transitional organization cultures. Organization culture as described by Schein (1985) contains a number of important elements. He writes: "To summarize, at any of these structural levels, I will mean by 'culture': *a pattern of basic assumptions—invented, discovered, or developed by a given group as it learns to cope with its problems of external adaptation and internal integration—that has worked well enough to be considered valid and, therefore, to be taught to new members as the correct way to perceive, think, and feel in relation to those problems"* (p. 9). This definition of organizational culture adds yet another perspective to understanding the four types of group experience where each is understood to constitute a culture.

Each type of group experience is a way to cope with regression-inducing anxiety when external adaptation problems and internal integration difficulties are encountered. Each type of experience contains a unique culture of thoughts and feelings that have many predictable outcomes. The groups are, therefore, a context for thinking, feeling and doing that exist along a range of adaptation and integration. The notion of culture also explains why these types of group experience are so resilient and hard to ultimately change. Much more is being changed than an organization chart and reporting relationships. The imposition of rules and regulations written on paper may have little influence upon a chaotic or charismatic culture. Achieving change is, therefore, always problematic and very likely only achievable where a consensus develops that failures at external adaptation and internal integration threaten group or organizational survival. The hard to detect stabilizing nature of culture must, therefore, be appreciated to understand the powerful dynamics implicit within each type of group experience.

In Sum

The notion of organization culture adds an additional perspective for understanding the four types of group experience. Organizational culture provides members an overarching context for interpreting events for oneself, others, groups and the organization. Culture, much like the types of group experience resident within dynamic workplace theory, serves to narrow experience by focusing attention upon certain elements of workplace experience in a specific way. Culture, therefore, becomes a filter for experience that creates meaning, learning and action. The four types of group experience discussed here also serve the same function.

IN CONCLUSION

This chapter has elaborated on the four types of group and organizational experience that constitute the elemental forces of dynamic workplace theory. Each of the three psychologically and socially defensive types of workplace experience contains within them considerable complexity and a unique mix of defensive processes that, it is hoped, will mediate the distressing experience of anxiety relative to the thoughts, feelings and actions of others relative to oneself. This chapter has emphasized that each of the defensive group and organizational experiences contain flaws that, rather than allaying anxiety, may exacerbate it. This inevitability leads to distress, scapegoating, blaming rituals and a fight/flight mechanism that energizes change to another type of group experience that promises to better allay member anxiety. Also discussed is the significance of a balance among the three types of psychologically and socially defensive group experiences where the positive sides of these groups are meaningfully accessed while their counterproductive aspects temporarily cancel each other out. I now turn from the discussion of the four kinds of group and organizational experience to the causes, means, methods and nature of change from one type of group experience to another. Dynamic workplace theory implicitly contains the notion that organizational change is a potentiality that exists in the conceptual space that lies between the four types of workplace experience.

Chapter 4

Transitional Organizational Space

When we address ourselves to the meaning of events and the motives of actions, we find that the mundane disappears, and that even apparently ordinary events arise for reasons that are not evident. The distinctions between the rational and the irrational may become a bit blurred. Actions that appear on the surface to make perfectly good sense can turn out to serve ends that have little to do with organizational efficiency and rationality. Such actions may in the end turn out to be better understood by reference to motives that some organizational members may not openly acknowledge or may prefer not to understand. The idea of stability fares no better, for we find that underneath the appearance of stability and order, an appearance often cultivated with great care by organizational leaders, lie tensions, conflict and flux, always threatening to change the order of things.

(Gabriel, 1999, p. 1)

Dynamic workplace theory's four workplace experiences introduce more sophistication and complexity than might at first be appreciated. One way to examine the dynamic workplace is to explore the potential organizational space between the four types of experience. The dynamic tension that exists within the theory among the experiences encourages an inspection of the nature of the conceptual space between them. This inspection is necessary in order to appreciate how the potential for change symbolized by the space affects the existence of the four types of experience as well as contributes to the direction of change. In particular, the space between can be understood to be composed of transitional space and time. It is the case that one form of group experience does not cease at one moment and another begin as though a light switch was flipped, although when a group or organization is under extreme pressure the change may be rapid, as may occur with the implantation of a new turnaround CEO. The transitional space and time that reside within the theory create a context for discussing the migration from one type of workplace experience to another. In a sense the potential organizational space between the four types of experience represents temporary groups that facilitate change.

This chapter examines the four types of group and organizational experience in a two-by-two process that explains how they influence each other. To start, it must be appreciated that these influences contribute to the unpredictability of organizational life, if not in the short-term most certainly in the long-term. Discussion of the six possible group interactions and the nature of the transitional space and time begins with the interaction of chaotic work experience with the other three types of experience. Before continuing it must be noted that it is not my intention to explore every possible facet of transitional workplace experience. The discussion will focus on conveying the substance of the experience to avoid creating an overwhelming amount of detailed discussion that will inevitably fall short of covering all or even most possibilities. Also to be appreciated is that the nature of the experience of the change process is different depending on the direction of the change.

The reader is reminded of the basic elements involved with group and organizational change highlighted in chapters 2 and 3. Group sentience and one or more potential leaders who speak to a desired direction of change are the basic ingredients of change. Dissatisfaction with the current state of affairs creates a tension within organization members that, if heightened by continuing problems and focused by a new leader, creates fight/flight dynamics that energize the change process. Therefore, the following discussion of the transitional spaces between the group types is filled with sentience, leaders and fight/flight dynamics. Also to be considered is the psychodynamic nature of the transitional space. This is discussed first. The reader is again reminded that summaries are provided to fast-track reading.

THE PSYCHODYNAMICS OF TRANSITIONAL SPACE

The dynamic nature of the workplace is in large part the outcome of psychodynamics. Psychodynamics are an implicit part of individuals, interpersonal relations and membership in groups and organizations. There are many aspects of these psychodynamics that are psychologically and socially defensive at their core (Allcorn and Diamond, 1997). The discussion of these psychodynamics is limited here to pointing out some of the more important aspects of the psychologically and socially defensive nature of the workplace as they relate to a discussion of the transitional organizational space and time.

The context of transitional space, time and organizational change arises out of the distressing experience of anxiety where organization members progress through a period of change in a direction that it is hoped will provide just the right type and amount of control to make worklife less stressful and anxiety ridden. Psychological defensiveness arising from the distress precedes change and is temporarily accentuated during the period of change where uncertainty about what will happen to "me" reaches its peak. The psychodynamics of this transitional space have been explored by a number of authors (Czander, 1993; Diamond, 1993; Greenberg and Mitchell, 1983 and Winnicott, 1965). For our purposes here, a brief inspection of some of these dynamics leads to an appreciation of the more psychologically primitive side of the nature of transitional organizational space and time.

I shall approach this discussion by relying on object relations (Greenberg and Mitchell, 1983 and Ogden, 1989). Human experience may include no, part and full object relations (relationships with others) and accompanying psychodynamics such as denial, splitting and projection. To begin, anxiety held by many as to how things are going and where the group or organization is headed fuels denial, splitting and projection that create polarized experience of the group and external world. Large numbers of employees may deny their limitations and vulnerabilities and feel that even they could do better than their leaders. Feelings of incompetence that they have denied are split off from self-experience and projected onto others who are usually visible leaders of the group or organization. Unconscious internal life becomes externalized when these leaders are then openly criticized and treated as though they possessed the full measure of these disposed of feelings of incompetence. They are seen as the source of the problem with almost absolute certainty on the part of many. The employees come to know themselves as good, effective people who deserve better leaders. Projection, therefore, creates a black-and-white world with little middle ground. It must also be noted that those receiving the projections very often present personal attributes and behavior that are not unlike the projected content. They, in a sense, invite projections of a certain type. Also to be considered is that organization members may split off their competence and locate it in their superiors. And it is certainly the case that those in charge split and project in much the same way. Denial, splitting and projection, therefore, create a complex and rich organizational surface to inspect from a psychodynamically informed perspective.

The process of denial, splitting and projection, while perhaps temporarily comforting to individuals, contributes to the anxiety-ridden aspects of the moment. Polarized points of view emerge fueled by undiscussable certainty regarding how things are and who is responsible. Object relatedness takes on a more primitive quality where self and others are experienced as part objects. Others are seen to possess some qualities and attributes and not others. Leaders may be seen as primarily all bad, impersonal, ineffective and the source of the distressing organizational performance and experience. Some groups within an organization may also be seen this way. At the same time others will not see themselves this way at all. Experience, as mentioned, becomes split apart, black-and-white and polarized. There develops a growing problem with accurate reality testing as others are blamed for the distressing experience of anxiety. These dynamics are accentuated by the experience of transitional space where change from one type of familiar if not unsatisfactory group experience toward another that promises to solve the problem is encountered. The following pairings of work experience permit exploring the nature of the transitional space between the types of workplace experience.

In Sum

One's experience of organizational life can become distressing and anxiety ridden as a result of unresolved operating problems and conflict. Change seems to be needed but the question arises, who will lead it and to where? Unresolved anxiety fuels individual recourse to psychodynamically defensive behavior that, when shared by others, leads to socially defensive outcomes. Organizational life gradually becomes filled with black-and-white images where those in charge may be seen to be the source of the problems. However, change presents organization members with the proverbial problem of jumping from the frying pan into the fire. Change, as represented by many uncertainties and a notion such as transitional space and time, presents organization members with a context that may be more anxiety ridden than their current experience. Therefore, organizational change contains many problematic and even chaotic elements. Transitional space and time hold the hope of salvation as well as fulfill the fantasy of the monster under the bed.

CHAOTIC VERSUS BUREAUCRATIC WORK EXPERIENCE

The combination of chaotic and bureaucratic work experience provides individuals, groups and organization members dramatically different expectations for and experience of the workplace. The dynamic tension between these two modes of workplace experience is profound. A nihilistic, chaotic anarchy may be advocated to tear away the bureaucratic restraints that confine workers and stifle effective and timely decision making. The organization and its leader(s), it is thought by many, are the problem and this leader must go. Conversely, chaotic work experience can become so distressing to many as to be experienced as completely out of control where personal, group and organizational survival is severely threatened from within. The drive for change may, therefore, become highly energized as the mutual terror that resides in one group experience leads to flight toward another group experience that promises delivery from the anxiety. A willingness to fight those who resist the direction of change is also present.

Change from Chaotic to Bureaucratic Experience

The fundamental nature of this transitional space is that there is a flight from distressing chaotic experience combined with a willingness to confront (fight) others within the group or organization. Group and organization members are sufficiently motivated by their anxiety-ridden chaotic experience to speak to a desire for structure and order to gain control over the chaos. Those who continue to actively contribute to the chaos and oppose the emerging desire to gain some sense of control must be overcome. Initially there may exist a combative relationship with organization members who prefer the highly individualized and unaccountable aspects of the chaotic experience. They feel less distressed by the presence of chaos and its threat to group and organizational survival. These individuals speak to issues of personal autonomy, creativity and tolerance of ambiguity while suggesting that bureaucratic control will be overwhelming, filled with red tape and more unacceptable than the chaos. In contrast, many of those feeling the most distressed by the chaos steadfastly pursue by every means available establishing dependable and rational order. They are willing to support anyone who volunteers leadership that promises to achieve this desired outcome.

Experience of the Transitional Space

A moment should be taken to highlight the nature of this transitional space. This space contains a great deal of fluidity. Much effort is expended in trying out new ways of organizing and controlling work via traditional bureaucratic means such as policies, procedures, rules, regulations and expectations of compliance and accountability. Considerable effort is also focused on locating a leader who is "safe enough" in the sense that he or she is willing to submit to the will of the group, thereby routinizing his or her leadership and providing organization members predictable uses of position-based power and authority. This type of leadership does not favor unilateral decision making in preference to the leader being controlled by the group via expectations of participation in decision making and inclusion in planning and designing work. Every aspect of the leader's thoughts, feelings and actions is ideally open to inspection. What are often thought to be admirable participative leadership qualities become pathologized by the need for control on the part of organization members.

Group members are, therefore, preoccupied with allaying individual, interpersonal and group membership anxiety by attempting to create rational controls for all aspects of worklife. This is compellingly seductive to many who prefer order and discipline or conversely do not possess a well-developed tolerance of ambiguity. However, this transitional space contains some of its own chaos as experimentation proceeds to locate what will work. This very often leads to premature closure where what has been developed is good enough and, even though it is deficient, it is accepted. This dynamic may account for why bureaucracies are so often inherently ineffective but at the same time rigidly relied upon by organization members. This transitional space and the process of change that it encompasses, therefore, contain a quality not unlike organization members venturing forth across a great sea in a rickety ship to discover a promised land. There is, in effect, "good news" and "bad news" associated with crossing the transitional space and time.

Gradually those advocating chaos become fewer in number and less motivated as a result of having been shut down by the majority of group members or perhaps having been ejected out of the organization for not being team players. Thoughts and feelings become ever more focused on allaying anxiety by developing order, creating protocols that progressively become more comprehensive and rigorously constructed and enforced, leading to a rule-bound culture and a carefully selected leader who believes in the routinized nature of the leadership style supported by the group.

Change from Bureaucratic to Chaotic Experience

Many of the above group dynamics are similar. In this case organization members gradually come to feel that all of the red tape and structure associated with bureaucracy, when combined with routinized leaders who seldom offer new ideas or take reasonable risks, is stifling and threatens organizational survival.

Some organization members may have been reduced to thinking of themselves as survivors focused on conserving their position and its power and authority. Up until now organization members have not felt overly threatened by the leader's power, as he or she does not command much respect. However, when organizational performance lags and there gradually develops a sense of being threatened by competitors, a desire arises to shake things up. Opposition to change can, however, be expected to arise as organization members begin to see that the structure and red tape are a problem and that the way out appears to be a need to start breaking the rules and tearing up the red tape. Gradually many organization members become excited about the possibilities change holds for them and they become receptive to embracing the possibilities chaos offers. Chaos can be experienced as something new, refreshing and promising renewal and may be welcomed as compared with the continuing maintenance of the bureaucratic hierarchy's preoccupation with control and order. I recall a strange moment while in the navy in the late '60s. My ship had been performing much the same duty for many months. Every day was the same. One morning I awoke to find our ship no longer in the Gulf of Tonkin but at sea. This was not a part of the plan. A brief scan of the sea revealed a great many ships sailing in a vast armada that I learned was headed north to surround North Korea after a surveillance plane had been shot down. Action, war and the accompanying chaos seemed preferable over the boring duty. There was something exciting about the novelty of the moment. This recollection is provided to underscore some of the feeling state that may emerge when the boring predictability of bureaucracy is confronted. Anything might be better, and chaos contains an exciting quality that stands in marked contrast to the oppressive and predictable routine of bureaucratic experience.

Experience of the Transitional Space

Once again a moment should be taken to explore the nature of this transitional space. This space contains fluidity as experimentation begins. This might be described as "unfreezing" the organization. However, in this case ever more experimentation, conflicting points of view, unresolved conflict, the rise and fall of many temporary leaders who challenge each other and the presence of a perverse sense of personal and group autonomy serve to pull the organization and the experience of work in many directions. Decisions and plans should be made but are not, or only minimally so, and then they may not be followed or they may be constantly changed. There gradually arises a descent into organizational madness where ideas and innovations seem to randomly pop on and off. When something does happen the outcome is not useful. The overwhelming experience of the space is that it is leaderless, structureless and wasteful. When the hope of hanging onto the predictability of bureaucratic process is lost, chaos has arrived. Crossing this transitional space is, therefore, one filled with exciting risk taking on the part of some and a shrinking away by many into their psychological foxholes to shelter themselves from the excessive buffeting and distressing anxiety of the loss of control.

In Sum

The change from chaos to bureaucracy amounts to a desire to allay individual, interpersonal and group membership anxiety by creating a predictable and controlled workplace. Chaotic work experience has become too distressing for most organization members, who become the constituents of change (a sentience group). In contrast, the very nature of the often overly rigid and compulsively complied with controls of bureaucracy accompanied by unimaginative and frequently marginally effective leaders can be experienced as confining, stifling and lacking sufficient creativity to consistently adapt to changes in the marketplace. Things just seem stuck. Once again, many may feel limited and threatened by poor organizational performance. This distressing state of affairs has to be changed to get rid of the red tape. In the end organizational members become ever more committed to taking the slippery slope that leads to the chaos of minimal control and the emergence of distressing personal and group autonomy and with it unpredictability.

CHAOTIC VERSUS CHARISMATIC WORK EXPERIENCE

A change from chaotic work experience to the leadership provided by a charismatic leader creates profound effects much like a change to bureaucracy. In this case a person emerges who possesses many of the attributes associated with charismatic leaders, such as: good interpersonal and verbal skills, a flattering and seductive interpersonal relatedness, a firm vision and the drive to achieve it, a willingness to discipline those who stray from the path and the development of a loyal band of admiring followers. This leader not only promises to provide clear direction and guide organization members in their work, he or she most importantly promises to contain all the chaotic experience and establish anxiety-allaying organizational predictability. The leader is expected to command and control the organization and its members to create order. Followership is more than expected, it becomes a patriotic duty or obligation.

In contrast, a change from charismatic work experience to chaos signals a great deal of displeasure with the leader who has failed to sufficiently contain the experience of anxiety that in part arises out of the quality of interpersonal relatedness with the leader. The leader may have become arrogant and disrespectful of others and pitted one individual or group against another. The development of an in-group and the obligatory out-group often splits and polarizes organizational experience, creating a sense of foreboding when it comes to the relations between in- and out-group members. Things can get out of control and the leader may not always be willing to intervene.

Change from Chaotic to Charismatic Experience

Chaotic experience, once it becomes sufficiently distressing, leads group members to feel that the only way out of the chaos is to locate a leader who will magically deliver the group from the chaos. Chaotic experience eventually creates a sentience group that is mobilized to make a change. In this case the notion of locating a leader and getting the person to act promises to minimize the personal responsibility of this group's members. It also avoids the threat of failure or shifts it to the leader, who must then confront those who are comfortable with the chaotic experience. The group's expectations are made clear once a willing leader is located. The leader must then work hard to fulfill them or face being metaphorically annihilated by the group. Those supporting the leader gradually become larger in number and progressively more supportive and submissive as the leader begins to provide clear direction that is thought to be effective. Gradually the leader assumes more and more control that is accompanied by the development of excessive power, authority and control. Remaining opponents are subordinated, isolated or perhaps "outplaced."

Experience of the Transitional Space

This space is marked by the persistent efforts of one or more individuals to provide direction even though initially the efforts are not well received and may be opposed by other would-be leaders. However, in a Darwinian sense, there gradually emerges a winner among those striving to achieve a leadership role. This individual has gradually mobilized many to believe that he or she can get control of the situation and make things happen. Once again there emerges an experimentation to locate what works. In this case the leader rapidly moves the experimentation along based on his or her needs to look good (powerful and effective) and quickly gain control to assure personal survival. He or she cannot resemble a routinized leader. As time passes a few are identified as loyal supporters, and resisters are ruthlessly dealt with to firm up control of the organizational agenda. Gradually, and at the same time almost miraculously, the chaos is left behind. The leader, having succeeded, gradually becomes mythologized, worshipped and perceived as bigger than life.

Change from Charismatic to Chaotic Experience

Charismatic leaders are often eventually seduced by others and by their growing expansive self-image into believing they should rule. The outcome is that they become tyrannical. They may be dismissive of followers as well as recklessly inattentive of the task environment. Competitors and enemies within who may be aligned to oppose this individual are recklessly maligned and labeled as unworthy and incompetent. The leader must assure everyone that his or her vision is the right one and that he or she will continue to save organization members from themselves. The organization gradually becomes split between those who assume subservient roles relative to the leader and those who retain some autonomy. The in-group and out-groups often end up conducting mortal combat relative to each other. Trends such as arrogance, tyranny, sabatoge, recklessness and the search for loyal followers eventually combine to motivate a sufficient number of organization members to feel threatened by this experience so as to want to be rid of their leader. The removal of the leader is, however, filled with personal threat and the possibility of sudden organizational death or banishment if, in the end, the leader is not removed. These fears and anxieties about taking action relative to the leader promote chaotic experience. Organization members are faced with hard to resolve conflict relative to maintaining the charismatic leader in his or her role or being punished by the leader in the event of a failure to change the leader.

Experience of the Transitional Space

The experience of this space is filled with the proverbial flesh-eating dinosaur that may eat them alive if they are not careful in going about imposing extinction. This is by far the dominant experience of this transitional space. One or more would-be anti-leaders may emerge only to be "taken out" by their all-powerful leader. Appeals to higher authorities may be made only at great personal risk. The leader's superior, the governing board and even the press may be employed for this purpose. Nonetheless the messenger may inevitably be slaughtered by the leader and ritualistically consumed by his or her loyal band of followers. These dynamics, however, often only serve to further mobilize out-group members. Efforts to undermine and expose the leader's methods and feet of clay increase and the leader is eventually disposed of by the infliction of a thousand small injuries. Having accomplished this feat, organization members are strongly predisposed to want to avoid the recreation of this primordial scene. Effective leadership that threatens to reawaken the beast is at least temporarily rejected and along with it the direction and methods of the former leader. Many voices arise within the organization that point to many unheeded directions. Everyone begins to do his or her own thing. Chaos has arrived.

In Sum

Chaotic work experience can be depended upon to eventually mobilize the feeling on the part of many that change is needed, and now. The sense of immediacy reinforced by the distressing experience of anxiety lead to the anointment of one individual with admirable leadership abilities to take over and whip the organization into shape. This leader who provides vision, direction and firm control provides deliverance from the chaos. Opposition to his or her direction is not readily tolerated. Gradually the leader becomes ever more powerful and controlling. Control is further assured by the development of a loyal group of followers who keep him or her informed of what is being felt, thought and done within the organization. However, when excessive and at the same time imperfect control is combined with the creation of in-group and out-group dynamics that split the organization and pit individuals and groups against each other for the leader's attention, the accompanying disturbing organizational experiences signal a need for change. Getting rid of the leader gradually emerges as important for a large number of organization members who are willing to, in some instances, risk sacrificing themselves and their careers to make a change. Having ousted the leader, organization members are at least for the moment turned off by people seeking leadership roles. A growing lack of direction and control gradually leads to the emergence of chaotic workplace experience. Everyone is enabled to seemingly do just about anything that he or she wants to do.

CHAOTIC VERSUS BALANCED WORK EXPERIENCE

A change from chaotic work experience to a workplace where the compulsive reliance upon the other two types of defensive group experience is mediated creates a balanced experience of the workplace. There exists a greater sense of comfort with the unpredictable aspects of worklife. In this case a person may emerge who possesses many of the above-mentioned attributes associated with charismatic leaders. However, this leader does not promote adoration and strive to acquire excessive control. Followers do not expect their leader to be entirely responsible for managing the organization. A shared sense of personal responsibility for managing the organization arises. The negative side of the three defensive group experiences is as a result minimized while their inherent strengths are reinforced.

In contrast, a change from balanced work experience to chaos arises when the organization is placed under excessive stress such as the need to respond to a business recession or a hostile takeover. The best of organizational cultures cannot allay anxiety under the worst of conditions. Increases in organizational stress and the accompanying distressing experience of anxiety lead to the emergence of confusion and a distrust of management. Organization members may ask, "How did we get into this situation?" Given sufficient stress and anxiety, conflicting voices emerge that lead to the formation of sentience groups formed around the different points of view. Gradually inter-subgroup conflict breaks out as to which course of action promises to deliver the organization from its current stressful situation. Organizational dynamics such as these, if not openly and effectively addressed, encourage ever greater fragmentation that increases rather than decreases the stress. Formal leaders, when faced with these circular and reinforcing organizational dynamics, may become confused, uncertain and ineffective thereby presenting organization members with the specter of a leadership vacuum. Under these conditions, chaotic workplace experience emerges as control of the situation seems to slip away.

Change from Chaotic to Balanced Work Experience

This change amounts to a major shift in organizational experience. Chaotic experience contains an absence of control (bureaucratic order) and leadership (charismatic leadership in particular). Things seem to be out of control and no one is able to provide effective leadership. The presence of chaos makes it equally likely that any of the other three types of group experience are an option even though intuitively it may seem a big jump to change from chaos to the intentionality and reflectivity of balanced work experience. However, upon closer inspection, it is less of a radical change than might be initially thought. In particular, movement toward the balanced group experience represents a rejection of the other two alternatives where the problems and pitfalls associated with bureaucracy and charismatic leadership are appreciated by most organization members. These outcomes, it is generally felt, must be avoided. This leaves the organization with but one real choice. Group and organization members must pull themselves together to take charge of the situation without recreating these undesirable outcomes. There gradually arises a shift to and acceptance of more leadership that promises order even though some chaotic experience associated with creativity (the skunk works) is retained. Those leading this change effort focus on promoting group and organizational well-being rather than themselves. Those offering the leadership are not interested in pursuing control, power and status. Notions such as coaching and developing others are welcomed as everyone, it is tacitly understood, has something to contribute to organizational success.

Experience of the Transitional Space

This organizational space is filled with a desire to do better and simultaneously avoid creating or recreating other types of group experience that are felt to be just as undesirable as the chaotic context of the moment. Many may speak at different times to the threats and problems of becoming overreliant upon a single leader upon whom everyone becomes dependent. Those who speak to a desire for a strong commanding leader are not attended to by most group members, who prefer to focus on what they can do as individuals to help get things under control. At the same time others in the organization are just as intent on avoiding an experience filled with the confining red tape of bureaucracy. In fact the presence of chaotic organizational experience is often an explicit if not tacit rejection of a charismatic leader and the stifling and overly controlling experience of bureaucracy. No one wants to have to submit to an all-powerful leader or feel overly controlled by policies, procedures, rules and regulations. Therefore, group experience and sentience essentially require moving in the direction of a more balanced organizational experience, as challenging as it may seem.

Change from Balanced Work to Chaotic Experience

Balanced work experience contains leadership and order while at the same time tapping the creative potential of chaos. Conversely, small losses of leadership and order can translate into organizational experience gravitating toward chaos. There may be occasional dips into this experience as messy creative and adaptive processes temporarily take over group and organizational dynamics. Opportunism can become the norm where planning and analysis and achieving an overarching direction are compromised. Too many different ideas and directions can end up being pursued at one time, thereby suboptimizing group and organizational performance. In other cases, operating problems may not be sufficiently addressed on a timely basis. In general, one's experience of organizational life is that things are beginning to slide a bit. The change toward chaos is subtle and gradual. One or more effective leaders may leave or be promoted to take a position elsewhere in the organization resulting in a leadership vacuum. There may be instances where a manager or supervisor overcompensates by attempting to micromanage work thereby making workers anxious about their personal autonomy and value. These same leaders, upon receiving negative feedback and resistance to their control, may, rather than reflect on their leadership style and what is going on around them, respond by trying to achieve more control and stifle dissent. Despite their best efforts organizational balance continues to be gradually lost as more chaotic elements emerge. At some point on this change continuum many in the organization begin to appreciate that much of what is going on seems to be out of control. There are too many voices and directions and too little leadership to make a difference.

Experience of the Transitional Space

This organizational space may be thought of as being filled with a sense of loss and even mourning. The gradual descent into chaos is distressing to many organization members who have come to feel intensely frustrated over losses of effective intentional leaders and thoughtful liberating levels of organizational control. A collective sense of failure and threat emerges as awareness of a loss of direction and a growing number of highly noticeable and often costly mistakes and missed opportunities increases. Many may reminisce about better times in the past that are recalled very often with idealized quality that did not really exist (Gabriel, 1993). Many who were once hard-working organization members gradually withdraw their enthusiasm and effort, thereby creating small but nonetheless cumulative losses of productivity. At the same time effective leaders are not located to restore performance, and frequent turnover in the management ranks may develop. The most effective people become fed up with the situation and find positions within other organizations. The brain drain is on. This dynamic may be accompanied by other spiritually destructive events such as downsizings and restructurings where the hope of restoring organizational performance hangs on finding just the right mix of organizational variables (Allcorn et al., 1996). Strangely enough one downsizing and restructuring is followed by another and yet another (Allcorn, 2002). Management cannot seem to find the answer. The best employees have voluntarily left, been incentivized to retire or accepted outplacement. Organizational chaos has arrived.

In Sum

Chaotic work experience tends to eventually mobilize feelings in a large number of organization members that change is needed, and now. The sense of threat-filled immediacy is, however, accompanied by a sense of caution. Attention must be directed to avoiding jumping from the frying pan into the fire. In this case there arises a sufficiently coherent group sentience that seizing upon a charismatic leader or trying to get control by creating bureaucracy are not desirable. This appreciation is many times reinforced by past distressing experiences of these two alternatives. In this case, deliverance from chaos is achieved by a more carefully thought-through dynamic where there first arises considerable self-empowerment and acceptance of personal responsibility for doing something to save the situation. Leadership by those who offer it is accepted. At the same time followers avoid becoming overly dependent on the leader, who does not encourage dependency. Care is also taken to not become overly dependent on organizational attributes associated with bureaucracy. Some is accepted as enabling control and coordination of work while every effort is made to avoid excessive reliance upon controlling work through impersonal means. Increases in the assumption of personal responsibility and growing intentionality promote reflective group and organizational processes that gradually establish a balanced experience where creative chaos, intentional leadership, and sufficient organization structure promote organizational effectiveness.

Loss of the balanced organizational experience arises out of slow and hard to detect shifts in leadership, group and organizational process and through a growing awareness of a loss of operating effectiveness that threatens long-term survival. Effective leaders are lost to external recruiting, promotions, retirements and the like. New leaders are less effective and, in order to deal with the problems and anxieties of the moment, they may progressively rely on more autocratic methods that alienate followers. Problems are not so readily solved and opportunities are not seized upon with the former effectiveness. Group and organization members gradually retreat from volunteering as much effort and from risk-taking behavior. A general lack of direction and loss of intentionality and control gradually lead to the emergence of chaotic workplace experience.

BUREAUCRATIC VERSUS CHARISMATIC WORK EXPERIENCE

These workplace experiences are, in many ways, opposites in terms of leadership. The bureaucratic approach provides for limited routinized leadership where the leader is closely observed and monitored by followers for indications that he or she is exercising too much unilateral and arbitrary control. In contrast, the charismatic leader is expected to provide considerable unilateral direction that organization members are expected to loyally follow. This leader is also opposed to too much organizational order (policies and procedures) that tends to be limiting in terms of the directions pursued, how fast and in what manner. In general the hope within the organization is that the charismatic leader will tear up the red tape that confines his or her decision-making prerogatives in order to make things happen. In contrast, bureaucratic red tape and rules and regulations serve to confine and restrict the power and authority of leaders, who are not expected to necessarily think great thoughts or achieve great things. There is, then, a substantial contrast between the two types of psychologically and socially defensive workplace experiences.

Change from Bureaucratic to Charismatic Experience

The underlying reasons for this change are similar to those for the other changes from bureaucratic order. There exists an appreciation that the ossified organization is unable to adapt to changes in its task environment and that routinized leadership is not going to provide a way out. In this case some organization members who identify with the idea of order are not willing to give up hope of controlling their anxieties by controlling the organization, and simply plunge into chaotic experience. This expectation is reinforced by the necessity for the organization to continue to function in a predictable manner as might be the case in many organizations such as governmental entities, utility companies and large manufacturers. This appreciation leads to one of two alternatives—charismatic leadership or the balanced group experience. The charismatic leader is intuitively understood to provide a quick way to change (the line of least resistance) while hopefully not abandoning too much of the structure associated with the preexisting order. This choice is further advanced by a deep underlying sentience that the current leaders are the cause of the problems and that what is needed is a much more effective and dynamic leader to, at least temporarily, lead them out of their organizational despair.

Experience of the Transitional Space

This organizational space is filled by a preoccupation of not entirely losing control with what is going on, and perhaps the fantasy that the new charismatic leader can be partially controlled by organization members. Much like a seasoned mountain climber who does not let go of one rope before having another in hand, organization members do not want to lose the control of their anxiety-allaying bureaucratic experience until a new dynamic leader is present who forcefully pries their collective hands off their familiar reliance upon controlling work. Locating the requisite charismatic leader can temporarily make the transitional space distressing as multiple individuals may emerge to challenge for dominance. There may develop an all-or-nothing, win-lose dynamic where only one person is left standing in the end. Often, because of this distressing competitive experience, once a leader does emerge, a vast relief arises within the organization where he or she is now eagerly looked to to provide all the answers and soothe the distressing experience of anxiety. As the leader emerges and gradually acquires more followership and control, there rapidly develops a group of admiring supporters who eagerly submit to his or her control and direction. At the same time there also gradually arises a larger group where the sentience is less accepting and supporting. This dynamic, however, only slowly emerges usually as a response to the ever greater power and control sought by the new leader, who begins to make controversial and unilateral decisions.

Change from Charismatic Leadership to Bureaucratic Experience

The nature of this change lies in trying to bring the charismatic leader under more control by gradually restricting his or her decision-making power and prerogatives. This amounts to routinizing his or her leadership. The leader, as a result of acting too often in a unilateral manner that does not take into account other points of view, begins to make many organization members anxious about the choices being made. The leader further aggravates the situation by identifying a loyal, admiring and unquestioning "kitchen cabinet" that aggressively defends its unique organizational status from others and by so doing alienates a large number of organization members. These group and organizational dynamics lead to a growing appreciation that the leader may have good ideas and offer needed leadership but that his or her baser tendencies (arrogance and narcissism) must be minimized. Therefore, reliance upon internal controls and bureaucratic order will, it is hoped, accomplish this purpose. Initially the leader and his or her closest followers may be resistant. They may in fact be dangerous to take on. However, it is also generally felt change is needed and that it is less dangerous to advocate for more order than to seek to replace the leader. This activity may be made easier due to a growing list of critical incidents where the leader made a mistake and organization performance was compromised. As movement toward a more orderly command and control structure occurs at the request and urging of many organization members, the leader may gradually see the advantage to gracefully yielding to this direction and retaining his or her position rather than facing the alternative. It is also the case that the new order offers him or her protection from the adverse outcomes of his or her unilateral decisions in that many others presumably have to sign off.

Experience of the Transitional Space

This space is filled with a sense of threat and foreboding that arises out of the likely or perhaps certain threat that the leader and his or her close-knit group of supporters will combat any threat to the status quo. Power, it is felt, must be preserved at any cost. There may well arise efforts to dispose of the opposition by labeling them as outcasts and discontents who, naturally, "should leave if they do not like it here." Aggressive actions to isolate, discount, discredit and limit individuals and groups advocating change in the leadership style are expected and feared by many (Allcorn, 2002). Only those who are highly motivated and willing to risk their career provide alternative leadership that makes them a target for the leader and his or her support group. One after another of these leaders may be disabled or disposed of; however, the prevailing sentiment remains that the leader has to be reined in. Efforts may be made to enlist the support of the governing board, stockholders, press and even the public in this effort. The leader may feel that he or she is being "pecked to death by a thousand ducks." This period of a constant press may eventually alienate the leader, who suddenly announces his or her departure thereby creating the potential to appoint a less charismatic, dynamic and autocratic leader. The leader and his or her loyal band of followers may also only gradually and grudgingly yield to more control by organization members. Passive aggression and backstabbing may become the norm. Gradually, however, the group will win out and the change occurs, but only after an occasional "bloodbath" or "coup" attempt. Anxiety remains high for a considerable period after the change process is under way. There also remains a long lasting residue of fear that the leader may regain his or her former power and that he or she and his or her steadfastly loyal supporters will enact countermeasures.

In Sum

Organizational change is seldom tougher to achieve than when a firmly entrenched charismatic leader has created a loyal band of admiring followers. Confronting him or her regarding his or her autocratic, unilateral management style that has created a growing list of problems and failures is an action filled with many perceived risks. Regardless of whether this leader is a ruthless dictator or highly adept at manipulating others (the politician), the individual will invariably see change as a personal threat to him or her. Power, it is felt, must be conserved sometimes at any cost including the potential destruction of self and others. Organizational change in the direction of limiting the leader's decision-making power is, therefore, understood to include a real sense of threat to anyone advocating change who is noticed by the leader. There may exist considerable evidence as well as organizational mythology that those who oppose the leader risk personal annihilation. Change, it may be felt, can only be supported by those who cannot be directly attacked by the leader. Very often external consultants are employed at the urging of upper and middle management in the hope that they can achieve the needed change. Their great cost is balanced by their disposability.

In contrast, change from a predominantly bureaucratic work experience to charismatic leadership is less threatening to organization members. In fact, once a leader is identified, he or she will assume most of the risk in creating change thereby sheltering organization members from assuming personal responsibility. This type of change is often initiated by a new charismatic leader who is hired with the expectation that major change will occur. Preexisting routinized bureaucratic leaders can be safely scapegoated and asked to leave to make way for the new leader or risk being demoted to a subservient role. It is not likely that these leaders will engage in mortal combat with the new leader. It is not their style.

BUREAUCRATIC VERSUS BALANCED WORK EXPERIENCE

These workplace experiences share a desire for organizational structure and organization-based control and coordination of work to permit working effectively on task. Where they differ is how diligently control of organizational experience to minimize anxiety is pursued. Excessive reliance upon routinized leadership and policies and procedures all too often adversely affects the ability of an organization to innovate and adapt to change in its operating environment. Balanced work experience represents an effort to build on the strengths of the bureaucratic approach while avoiding its rigidities. In particular, group and organization leaders are encouraged to provide vision and direction and sufficient administrative structure that are not allowed to become a socially defensive feature of organizational life.

Change from Bureaucratic to Balanced Work Experience

A change from bureaucratic to balanced work experience is generally motivated for the same reasons as discussed above for change from bureaucratic order to charismatic leadership. The order, as represented by policies and procedures, rules and regulations, expectations for impersonal performance of job duties and routinized leadership, may be experienced not only as confining and restricting but also as no longer producing external adaptiveness and internal integration. Organizational rigidities create a context where change is slow if at all, and when it occurs it very often falls short of the change that is needed (too little, too late). Anxiety continues regarding organizational performance. Individual autonomy and personal integrity and responsibility are stifled by the nature of worklife.

Those leading the organization make their contribution by not being willing to self-differentiate to any great extent by offering a new vision and direction to lead the organization away from threats to its survival. Internally organizational fragmentation becomes an ever greater problem as needs for more and more control bring pressures upon managers and supervisors to control everything, including relationships between individuals, groups and divisions of the organization. Protocol and defending one's turf and budget emerge as important elements of daily functioning. These induce vertical and horizontal fragmentation where communication and voluntary cooperation are discouraged in favor of formal controls. Efforts to keep things from falling apart via control paradoxically promote fragmentation and the experience of the organization as falling apart. Anxieties about losses of control, performance and survivability lead to reliance upon the same old solution—more control. This response is, however, eventually understood to be the source of the problem and not the solution.

A change to a more balanced work experience is often seen as the solution when there remains an interest in maintaining some control and there is a deeply ingrained fear of having a leader who is too powerful. Organizational history is often filled with mythology about the hazards of losses of control and leaders who were too powerful, arrogant and indifferent to organization members and organizational success. In these cases, the only viable change seems to be in the direction of the balanced work experience where these tendencies are moderated.

Experience of the Transitional Space

This organizational space is not particularly threatening. There are no overly powerful leaders or groups that may lay waste to those advocating change. At the same time there is a pervasive insistence on doing it by the book. Advocates of change are constantly reminded of historical problems that are thought to have been created by losses of bureaucratic control. Also often heard is the refrain, "We have already tried that," implying trying something like it again is of no use. These familiar responses militate toward retaining the familiar status quo. Those speaking for change must be careful to avoid intimidating or frightening organization members. If this occurs the predictable response is a steadfast retreat to bureaucratic control that makes contemplation of another change effort unlikely. This space is, therefore, filled with patient and persistent efforts to coax change without evoking stressful anxieties about relaxing bureaucratic controls that many feel have worked well thus far even though there is considerable evidence to the contrary. This change process toward a balanced work experience must itself be a model of balance and evenhanded efforts to lead change on the part of others. The emergence of a less socially defensive organizational scheme is gradual. The balanced work experience may come into existence without many organization members appreciating that the change has occurred.

Change from Balanced to Bureaucratic Experience

Pressures to make this change are frequently evoked by one or more critical incidents that are felt to have humiliated the organization and its leaders. A bold but calculated business venture may have gone awry resulting in a temporary loss of profitability and perhaps a public flogging in the press. As a result anxieties increase. There gradually develops a feeling that, in order to avoid problems like this in the future, more controls and layers of review and analysis are needed. Those in leadership roles, it is thought, should have less decision-making autonomy. This shift in thinking toward more control is subtle but once begun, takes on a life of its own as those advocating it are eager to demonstrate that they can do better. Gradually leaders feel less empowered to make decisions and set direction. More organizational energy is directed at developing, maintaining and auditing compliance with controls over decision making and work.

Experience of the Transitional Space

This organizational space, as may be observed from the nature of the change, is less charged with threat and anxiety although change is most definitely occurring. Leaders may be resistant to more layers of review and analysis being added to the decision-making processes. They point out that delays in taking effective and timely action will occur. However, these leaders seldom become threatening when they encounter losses of their decision-making prerogatives. Some may decide to leave without fanfare and are replaced by new leaders who are supportive of being less autonomous regarding decision making. They are, characterologically speaking, the "team players." These new leaders may actually prefer the safety of numbers in that they become less responsible for negative outcomes if a great many people have signed off on the decision. They have plausible deniability and thereby organizational survivability. As the change process continues, group and organization members gradually detect an overall change in the nature of their worklives as the bureaucratic approach emerges. It is only with time that the most negative aspects of bureaucratic work experience emerge.

In Sum

Organizational change from a well-established bureaucratic approach to a more balanced way of managing an organization is fostered by a growing awareness that the leaders and many policies and procedures are not enabling the organization to make needed changes to adapt to the marketplace. Anxiety also exists regarding the personally stifling nature of all of the rules and regulations and expectations of strict compliance with protocol. The omnipresence of poor communications and voluntary cooperation promotes organizational fragmentation and red tape. Change for multiple reasons gradually becomes seen as desirable although not everyone agrees. Organization members are cautious about change and want to avoid the loss of too much control. Similarly, they may want to avoid being subordinated to a powerful charismatic leader. Therefore, as change ensues, a carefully engineered balanced approach emerges where all three types of psychologically and socially defensive group experiences are avoided.

It is also the case that a change from a balanced group and organizational experience occurs with equal care and gradualness. To be avoided are chaos and the emergence of a strong charismatic leader. Change in the direction of bureaucratic work experience is often keyed off by a few critical incidents where problems have developed. It is thought by some that what is needed is better control over decision making and work to avoid making problems in the future. Gradually a persistent press develops to add more layers of review to decision making and more rules about how work should be accomplished. Ever so slowly the bureaucratic work experience emerges where initially little about worklife has changed. It is only with time the negative side of bureaucratic work experience emerges as the desire for control becomes compulsive.

IN CONCLUSION

This chapter has explicated the nature of organizational change based on dynamic workplace theory. In particular, attention was directed to articulating the nature of each type of organizational experience relative to the others. Organizational change is likely relative to the others with the exception of the charismatic versus balanced work experience. This omission provides the reader an opportunity to explore what has been learned in the chapter and ponder how this interaction should be formulated. The chapter provides all of the content necessary for this exercise to be completed. To be kept in mind is that organizational change is likely when a growing dissatisfaction and sense of threat arise. A change process emerges that gradually moves the organization toward another type of workplace experience that promises to regain control of the situation and reduce member anxiety. Also discussed have been some of the psychodynamics of organizational change and the nature of the transitional space and time between the types of workplace experience. It is essential that the nature and experience of this transitional organizational space be appreciated in order to better understand the dynamics of the four workplace experiences. In contrast, in chapter 5 attention is turned to an inspection of the inherent stability of each of the types of workplace experience.

Chapter 5

Finding Stability in the Workplace

The problem is that sick firms run by neurotic managers are often the hardest to change. This is not to say that they cannot be changed; but change will require a long and arduous intervention process. It is not simply a matter of pointing out dysfunctional behavior and prescribing a more appropriate substitute. Instead, much effort must be devoted to providing managers with insight into their dysfunctional behavior and its genesis and to helping them improve by giving them the necessary incentives and support.

(Kets de Vries and Miller, 1984)

Dynamic workplace theory and its many attributes provide insights into how the workplace really works. What seems like a rather simple model of group and organizational dynamics may be observed at this point to contain considerable complexity. The theory contains four types of commonly found workplace experiences. The dynamic nature of the model has been described as having its origins in the deeply embedded and mutually conflicting tensions that lie within and between the four types of experience. There is, however, another element to the dynamic workplace model that merits inspection. This chapter is devoted to a review of the non-dynamic side of the model where points of stability emerge and each of the four types of organizational experience becomes firmly entrenched in the short term and many times for much longer periods. Understanding this stability and how it is created, maintained and lost provides employees, managers, and consultants additional insight into organizational dynamics. The discussion of workplace stability commences with an inspection of the stability of the three psychologically and socially defensive experiences of the workplace. Each type of experience is discussed from three points of view:

the creation of stability, the maintenance of stability and the loss of stability. These perspectives when combined with the transitional space and time discussed in chapter 4 fully articulate dynamic workplace theory.

CHAOTIC WORK EXPERIENCE

Chaotic work experience has been described. It is symbolized by the ascendancy of the struggle for personal survival and autonomy in threatening workplace circumstances. Group and organization members retreat from active participation, voluntary coordination and risk taking to solve readily apparent operating problems. There exists a sense of loss of direction and purpose. Leaders may have been lost to retirement or recruitment elsewhere thereby creating a leadership vacuum. Those rising in their place to offer leadership are rejected or challenged by others who aspire to a role of leadership. Others may feel threatened by the emergence of one or more leaders who have developed a group of followers. The organizational scene is filled with hard to resolve conflict, problems and leadership voids. Consequently employees readily experience considerable personal and organizational threat. It is not uncommon for the best managers and employees to look elsewhere for employment thereby further reducing organizational viability. One may then reasonably wonder what stability may be had within this overarching context.

The Creation of Stability

As unlikely as it may seem, the inherently distressing experience of chaotic organizational space contains within it hard to detect stability that is theoretically characteristic of all types of chaos. In this case, group and organizational fragmentation is promoted by the perceived safety afforded by individual and group autonomy. Psychological defenses that emphasize splitting and projection whereby others not inside the group or division are seen as bad also support this outcome. Individual self-differentiation in the form of providing leadership or achieving outstanding work is understood to be threatening to oneself as a result of being threatening to others who respond by limiting or disabling the individual by any organizational means available (Allcorn, 1991, 2002). It may also be the case from a broader perspective that individuals, groups, sections and divisions may rise to the occasion and distinguish themselves within the scope of what they can control. This outcome not only provokes a sense of threat on the part of other groups and sections but can also create self-defeating outcomes. A marketing division that has outstanding sales when combined with a manufacturing division that has out-of-control costs that create a loss on each unit sold obviously decreases organizational viability. Organizational fragmentation, psychological and social defenses, occasional successes and ongoing compromises to organizational performance, while not desirable, are the familiar and stable elements of chaos. This is further illustrated by the following case example.

A Case of Self-Defeating Behavior

A good example of the tension between the anxiety-allaying predictability of stability and compromises in organizational performance is provided by a department of internal medicine in a large academic health sciences center. This department had a history spanning more than twenty years where the department had weak and ineffective chairmen or none at all. This context fostered the development of strong subspecialty divisions such as cardiology, hematology and infectious diseases. The ten divisions, although all not equally successful, were led by strong division heads who had each developed a small kingdom. The administrative presence of the larger department was weak. Each division pursued its own interests relative to each other, the department and the school of medicine. Despite this level of departmental fragmentation, most divisions were successful.

During the late 1980s it was generally felt among the division heads that they were losing out to departments that had effective chairmen. There had also gradually arisen problems in the survivability of some divisions as well as unresolved conflict between them over the allocation of scarce resources such as space and funding that would normally be resolved by the chairman. The call went out to recruit an outstanding physician executive as a chairman to lead the department and its divisions into the future. The eventual recruitment of a successful interim chairman from one of the top medical schools in the country was initially greeted with enthusiasm. However, shortly thereafter, as the chairman moved to put his house in order, there arose an ever increasing resistance to the chairman's leadership and decisions. He was immediately seen by some division heads as invading what had historically been their purvey. The most powerful division heads were skeptical and some outright resistant. A few frequently and openly challenged the chairman. It became apparent within a year that although the division heads had espoused a desire to be led, thereby presumably indicating a willingness to follow, as soon as their new leader acted, they saw it as a loss of their own power and prerogative. Some articulated a vision that they expected the chairman to lead the department without drawing the divisions into line to develop a coordinated purpose and direction. Overcoming departmental fragmentation was, however, essential if the department was to compare favorably to other departments and effectively compete for additional resources. The chairman was eventually unsuccessful at drawing some of the most powerful division heads into line despite occasional division-based disasters that the chairman had to bail out. The chairman left within three years and the department returned to its formerly underled status by appointing one of its division heads to the role of chairman.

The brief case vignette points toward the enduring stability that lies within chaotic work experience. The hiring of a leader who in this case endeavored to achieve more balance, openness and participative dynamics ultimately failed. The maintaining of individual and divisional autonomy took precedence. Many of these same group and organizational dynamics may be discovered in organizations that seem to somehow survive across time but not because they are effectively managed and coordinated.

The Maintenance of Stability

Chaotic work experience as may be discerned from the above case contains what might be thought of as bounded instability (Stacey, 1992). Even though individuals, groups and divisions are doing their own thing and may actually contribute to serious compromises in organizational performance, there are enough successes by individuals and divisions working autonomously to somehow keep things going. Over time various divisions may contribute to the overall success, and occasionally coalitions and compromises are developed among the autonomous divisions to overcome conflict and imbalances where a win-win solution may be had. The stability is experienced as fundamentally chaotic but at the same time things are happening and successes and progress can be observed to be occurring albeit without any sense of a larger unifying vision. These management styles may be described as reactive and opportunistic.

The pursuit and maintenance of individual autonomy is more desirable than the accompanying distressing experience of anxiety as to how things are going in general. Herein lie the stability and simultaneously the underlying tension for change. So long as there seems to be more to be gained by being autonomous, chaotic workplace experience is supported by the leaders of groups and many of their members. As in the above case, this dynamic may span decades so long as the perception of threat to the larger sense of the organization is not sufficient to create excessive anxiety as to individual and group survival.

The Loss of Stability

The loss of the underlying stability may occur for several reasons. One common generator of instability is the ascendancy of one or two groups to positions of greater power relative to the other autonomous groups and divisions. Much the same can be said of interpersonal relatedness where if one or a few individuals receive more income and promotions, others feel envious and threatened (Allcorn, 1991). These interpersonal and group dynamics can lead to rivalry and destructive interpersonal and group competitiveness that not only threatens the individuals and groups involved but may also threaten the viability of the larger organization. A second common source of stress is the growing perception that the larger organization is failing to compete successfully albeit in a fragmented way with other better organized departments or organizations, as was the case above. There may, of course, be combinations of variables. However, they all share in common attracting sufficient attention to threats to organizational viability that, if realized, threaten to take down all of the autonomous groups and individuals. Everyone is suddenly aware of being in the same leaky boat together. As discussed in chapter 4, this leads to the gradual development of transitional organizational space and time.

In Sum

Chaos often emerges out of events where one or more historically effective leaders are lost and no other effective leader emerges to take his or her or their place. Hard to resolve conflict and operating problems gradually increase, although within large groups and organizations some subgroups or division may still be performing well enough to provide the promise of sustaining the organization despite the lack of direction and the presence of organizational fragmentation. The organization may not rapidly fail but it is clear to many that it is failing to succeed. At the same time the sense of threat and accompanying anxiety encourages individual withdrawal from active participation. Individual and group safety is achieved by not taking chances or offering leadership. This state of affairs, regardless of how unacceptable it may appear, offers participants safety by creating excessive personal and group autonomy and losses of accountability. It is metaphorically playtime in the sandbox. Following direction when it is offered seems to be optional. Many will be comfortable with the autonomy they have and actively oppose leaders who might impose autonomy-limiting direction and order. Herein lies the stability of the chaotic work experience as well as the ever present possibility of change. The existence of many hard to resolve problems and conflict and a growing sense of threat to group and organizational survival can become so distressing that change may seem to be mandatory. However, this is not always the case, especially when chaos is not so threatening and one's survival not explicitly threatened by an enemy without.

BUREAUCRATIC WORK EXPERIENCE

Bureaucratic work experience has been described as a psychological and social defense against anxiety associated with individual survival, the vagaries of interpersonal relatedness and domination and submission issues associated with organizational hierarchy. The optimal outcomes are carefully designed and regulated hierarchical administrative processes and protocols that routinize work and the actions of leaders. Individual autonomy, initiative and creativity are circumscribed. This outcome creates the sense of lackluster leadership, infuriating red tape and many times an inability on the part of an organization to change in order to respond to opportunities in its task environment (the marketplace). Herein arise the seeds of anxiety that may eventually lead to a manifestly felt need to change organizational dynamics and move in the direction of one of the other three workplace experiences. Despite these destabilizing influences many organizations such as federal, state and local governmental bureaucracies are notoriously resistant to change. This stability merits additional inspection.

The Creation of Stability

Bureaucracy, it must be acknowledged, is a familiar response to managing individual, interpersonal and organizational membership anxiety. In particular the attributes of bureaucracy are associated with its counterpart—hierarchical organization structure. This type of structure is compatible with maintaining control via bureaucratic methods when maintaining control is intuitively understood to conserve formal power that resides within a position and not individuals. In this regard these aspects of organizational life reinforce each other. In general, those in roles of power and authority personally benefit from the nature of their hierarchical position by its making them feel important and admired or, failing that, feared. The role and these personal enhancements are conserved by rigid reliance upon policies, procedures, rules, regulations and protocols. Herein lies the seductive and stabilizing nature of bureaucracy and its companion, organizational hierarchy. Those who seek roles of leadership are eventually rewarded with formal power and authority. At the same time those who strive for limited personal responsibility to minimize stress and anxiety pursue roles of followership. Security, it is felt, lies in just doing their job and following orders. Once all of this is worked out (routinized and ritualized) it becomes so pervasive and familiar that calling it into question is experienced as threatening to all concerned. The stability is not open to being challenged, thereby making this defensive solution to organizational life rock solid. Organizational stability, however, is also transformed into organizational rigidity that threatens long-term survival of the organization and creates the threat of eventual and perhaps convulsive change.

The Maintenance of Stability

Based on the above explanation of the compelling nature of bureaucracy and hierarchical organization structure, it is apparent why it has become universally adopted for managing the distressing experience of workplace anxiety. Everyone or nearly so feels that "This is how we do things here." Change is only accommodated in small incremental and carefully planned doses. This desire for metering out organizational change might be thought of as being supported by methods such as continuous improvement and total quality management (TQM), where everything is carefully analyzed and consensus built for controlled change.

The stability of everyone's role and preferably all role-to-role interactions are prescribed and regulated. Anxiety-generating uncertainty is as nearly as possible engineered out of workplace experience. This is such a common element of most work experience that a detailed example need not be provided. Nonetheless it must be appreciated that the stability provided is very important for many of our institutions. Federal and state workers are often thought of as carrying on the work of their departments despite the turmoil created by political appointees with varying levels of management skills and politically driven agendas for change. Inspections of a large federal and state bureaucracy often reveal that what keeps the political turmoil from overwhelming the system is the steady nature of the bureaucracy that is slow to respond to change. This limits the potential damage temporary swings in political points of view have on carrying out the work of government.

The Loss of Stability

It is also not difficult to appreciate that this familiar and stable organization form is frequently threatened by its rigidities. This organization form is slow to take up change even when it is blatantly apparent that change is needed. Departments and divisions of federal and state government may be threatened by such moves as major reforms in programs that do not seem to be working and the outsourcing of much of their work to the private sector. These fundamental threats and the actions of competitors in the private sector may eventually promote considerable distress among organization members, so much so that change becomes seen as the only way out. Losses of stability are assured given a time line of sufficient length. History is replete with examples of once powerful nations, governments and huge business concerns that are no longer with us. The word may go out that the appointment of a new, authoritative and powerful leader is needed. The problem of adaptiveness may also be seen to be one of achieving greater creativity and responsiveness that is translated into organizational flattening and downsizing and placing decision making closer to the customer.

In Sum

Bureaucracy and accompanying organizational hierarchy are known for their stability that contains the possibility of nonadaptive rigidities that make the organization vulnerable to changes in its larger task environment. Like the mighty oak, it may not bend in the wind and thus may find itself uprooted. The search for anxiety-allaying stability through the control of interpersonal and leader/follower interactions is seductive. Control, it is understood within this type of organization experience, is achieved by prescribed impersonal role-to-role interactions that may accordingly be controlled through detailed bureaucratic policies, procedures, rules and regulations that limit how one may act and preferably think and feel. However, as mentioned, this stifling work experience when combined with the need to improve and change becomes the underlying weakness to this psychologically and socially defensive approach to organizational design and administration.

CHARISMATIC WORK EXPERIENCE

Charismatic work experience hinges on the presence of a leader who feels he or she can lead the group or organization out of the wilderness and away from the distressing experience of threat and anxiety. As discussed in chapter 3, this leader often becomes bigger than life and at the same time organization members experience themselves as diminished by comparison via a process of splitting and projection. As a result, the leader's narcissistic qualities are accentuated. He or she is encouraged to see him- or herself as depended upon by organization members to save the situation. So long as the promise of deliverance is fulfilled, most followers will steadfastly and unquestioningly submit to control by this leader. However, inevitably, the leader develops feet of clay as some threatening problems go unaddressed and his or her tightly knit group of devoted followers and sycophants encourage others to feel excluded, threatened and alienated. The gradual increase in operating problems encourages one or more out-groups to become sufficiently mobilized to take on the leader, who is now not only seen to be a problem but also vulnerable. This powerful paternal or maternal figure may be eventually metaphorically killed off. It is, therefore, important to appreciate that the inherent stability of charismatic work experience lies primarily in the arena of wish fulfillment.

The Creation of Stability

The identification of a charismatic leader who is able to martial considerable support while overcoming the resistance of other groups and would-be leaders encourages group and organization members to feel secure. This represents a form of wish fulfillment. There gradually arises a sense of stability as the leader tightens his or her grip on the organization's information systems, resources, processes and methods. The recruitment of a loyal band of insiders who become "lieutenants" who defend and evangelize their leader further adds to the experience of this individual as a great person. One need only think of dictators of the past who seized power and control over governments while ruthlessly extinguishing resisters, who found themselves imprisoned, banished to an organizational gulag or many times simply killed off and outplaced. Organizations with charismatic leaders such as J. Edgar Hoover's leadership of the FBI, the role of the pope in the Catholic Church and the CEOs of some organizations such as Jack Welch at GE may come to mind. These leaders and countless others create a sense of stability and dependence on their leadership.

The Maintenance of Stability

Once the charismatic leader is firmly entrenched, most meaningful opposition is suppressed. The leader, who might be described as a master autocrat, comes to hold almost absolute power over the organization. The individual may aspire to micromanage much of the organization and create information, administrative and other control systems that block access by others who may strive to understand what is or is not going on, while enabling the leader to know in an omniscient manner everything that is going on. This quality of organizational experience is often further supported by a network of loyal "informers" who provide the leader intelligence as to who is naughty and nice. Gradually the leader recasts the organization in his or her likeness by selectively recruiting and promoting employees to create an ever-larger band of loyal followers who occupy all of the major positions. It is, therefore, not hard to imagine that once this level of control is achieved, stability is created. Even though success is highly dependent upon the leader, who may not make the best of decisions all of the time, he or she is much too dangerous to confront. In fact there will usually exist an organizational history and mythology regarding those who used to be a part of the organization and questioned what was going on.

The Loss of Stability

History tells us that the most powerful and tyrannical of leaders must inevitably die or be displaced as a result of growing discontent. Much the same can be said for leaders of contemporary groups and organizations. In many ways the leader's invincibility is only sustained by successes that cannot be continually achieved. The very best athletic team or corporation that has dominated competitors for many years will not succeed indefinitely. Leaders can become out of date, out of touch and preoccupied with their own arrogant greatness that is supported by an organization filled with favored appointees who may not be up to the job. At the same time there are always those who are skeptical and passively and occasionally aggressively resistant. They may exploit the exposure of operating problems that are attributed to the leader in the hope of revealing the leader's feet of clay.

A combination of factors such as these leads to the eventual removal of the leader if the person does not retire or voluntarily leave the organization. The underlying dynamic is the loss of control on the part of the leader as evidenced by attention-getting problems arising out of poor decisions. These outcomes generate considerable anxiety on the part of organization members, who may call his or her leadership into question. The leader may respond by trying to exercise more control, distorting information and redefining the meaning of events (today referred to as "spin") and attacking and eliminating leaders of opposition groups. These actions further polarize the organization where the level of internal ritualized violence is constantly ramped up, thereby creating ever more anxiety on the part of organization members who want a change.

In Sum

Charismatic leaders are supported so long as they succeed in providing adequate direction to allay follower anxieties while not threatening followers by becoming too powerful, controlling and arbitrary. The hope that the leader can get control of the situation and make things happen substantially increases the performance delivery demand that the leader must fulfil while decreasing the personal responsibility that followers feel toward contributing to the solution. This dynamic makes it a real challenge for the leader to be effective. Success, however, creates a stable situation where the leader acquires significant power and modifies the organization to meet his or her control needs. Once stability is achieved the leader may remain in power almost indefinitely. However, the best of leaders may stumble given time or leave the organization for another position. These destabilizing influences are not uncommon in groups and organizations. Followers experience situations like this as stressful and, therefore, undesirable. They may seek to remove their current leader or to obtain a new leader much like the old leader in the case of departure.

BALANCED WORK EXPERIENCE

Balanced work experience arises out of a desire to avoid the negative sides of the three psychologically and socially defensive group experiences. As has been discussed, the optimal experience is creativity without chaotic individual and group autonomy, leadership without excessive dependency on the leader and sufficient organization structure that is at the same time not compulsively relied upon and rigid. The development of balanced work experience may, therefore, be understood to include a willingness to confront individual and group anxieties while retaining personal responsibility for managing the anxiety and the situation that generates it.

The Creation of Stability

The dynamic workplace is inherently unstable because of the constant potential of the three psychologically and socially defensive types of work experience. Achieving the balanced group experience, as may be attested to by the reader's firsthand experience of the workplace, is a challenge. Conceptually a balance must be struck between the tendencies to retreat to the three psychologically and socially defensive groups. The balance arises out of the transitional space discussed in chapter 4. Balance is created when the experience in one type of psychologically defensive group will not be tolerated any longer and retreat to the other two types is also not seen to be a viable alternative. There exists a quality of negation among the three defensive group experiences where their negative sides are avoided. This negation leads to the creation of an organizational setting composed of personal responsibility, interpersonal safety, secure group attachment and creativity without an overriding fear of a loss of control. Individual, group and organizational energy is liberated from the service of maintaining one of the defensive groups that protects against anxiety, unpredictability and the interpersonal world where dominance and submission issues abound. Additionally, optimal levels of leadership and direction become available or nearly so. Group and organization members are supportive of this more open and non-defensive work experience.

The Maintenance of Stability

Once a sense of balance emerges, group and organization members welcome the liberating experience of the balance where things are happening but without being overcontrolled by a leader or organizational structure. Initially there is a growing sense of excitement and a collective energy emerges as the more compulsive and rigidly relied-upon aspects of the three defensive organizational experiences are avoided. Work, thoughts and feelings are open to discussion and group and organization members feel important and respected for what they can contribute to achieving improved organizational performance. Vertical and horizontal communication and coordination is more open and becomes one of the important sources of improved performance along with the assumption of personal responsibility. These changes in work experience are accompanied by an abatement of many of the individual and shared group psychodynamic processes such as splitting and projection. Individual and group experience, regardless of how unpleasant at the moment, are tolerated and inspected for their origins as well as responded to in a meaningful way. Denial, rationalization, scapegoating and many other organizational dynamics are minimized as a result of the ability to openly challenge what is going on without the fear of being personally destroyed in the process. Openly questioning what is going on and why is the fundamental strength of the balanced experience that staves off a retreat to one of the other three defensive group and organizational experiences.

The Loss of Stability

Balanced experience is constantly challenged by the presence of the potential for the emergence of any of the three defensive group and organizational experiences. This tension or threat is accentuated when the organization goes through a stressful period that evokes member anxiety. An economic downturn, a hostile takeover bid or the loss of key leaders can be depended upon to promote employee anxieties. Individuals and groups may well respond by advocating some of the elements of the other three types of defensive groups. The instability created by temporary problems and the occasional failure is challenging for any group or organization to respond to without its members becoming overly anxious and defensive. Firm and effective leadership in the moment can stave off further losses of stability, as may the development of risk taking and creative solutions that are adequately evaluated, planned and implemented. It is also the case that many stresses may be absorbed, at least in the psychological sense, by the presence of an effective organization structure that initially withstands the disorganizing influences of the situation of the moment. These responses, however, cannot be sustained indefinitely if conditions do not improve. This signals to organization members that there are compelling reasons for change in order to assure personal and organizational survival.

In Sum

The balanced group emerges out of a desire to avoid the negative sides of the other three psychologically and socially defensive group experiences while building upon the their strengths—creativity, sufficient structure and optimal leadership. The inherent stability that emerges comes from the growing intentionality that arises out of the assumption of individual and group responsibility. A new openness and ability to question what is going on encourages identifying self-defeating thoughts, feelings, and actions that may make members anxious and compromise functioning. Losses of this stability are most likely to occur when the organization encounters difficult problems, external attacks and the occasional failure that makes everyone anxious about themselves and their and their organization's future. These destabilizing encounters challenge organization members to rise to the occasion by maintaining intentionality and open, thoughtful and reflective processes. They may also encourage desperate voices that advocate for change in the direction of one of the defensive group experiences. These voices combined with ongoing stressful circumstances may eventually degrade the experience of the organization as functioning effectively, thereby leading to entry into transitional organization space and time and to movement toward one of the three defensive workplace experiences.

IN CONCLUSION

This chapter examined dynamic workplace theory from a new perspective. It asked and answered the question, "What makes the four types of group and organizational experience stable over time?" The three psychologically and socially defensive groups, while containing underlying destabilizing tendencies, can achieve stability that can last for long periods of time. Dictators and autocrats may rule for many years or decades. Governmental bureaucracies are, if known for anything, known for their resistance to change. Chaos may also become a long-embraced norm, as is indicated by the seemingly endless revolutions and tribalism in many areas of the world such as Afghanistan, the Middle East and some African and South American nations. The members of these societies suffer interminably from the chaos that destroys infrastructure, food supplies and the rule of law. I now turn to an exploration of the significance of the stability and bounded instability of dynamic workplace theory in terms of how it informs managers and consultants in their work.

Chapter 6

Managing and Consulting Using
Dynamic Workplace Theory

Structures should be designed not only to use the talents of employees but
to increase the potential to tap into and expand on the inhibited potential
of all employees in ways that are respectful of and empathetic to their sense
of self-worth and dignity.

(Czander, 1993, p. 122)

Dynamic workplace theory provides many insights into the workplace—how it
works and how it is experienced. The theory suggests that there are ultimately
only four types of group or organizational experiences and that they are familiar to anyone who has worked in a large or even modest-size organization. The
theory's dynamic nature has thus far been explored in terms of its underlying
stabilities and instabilities. This chapter continues to develop the discussion by
exploring how the theory informs management and consultation. Managers and
consultants who understand how organizations work based on the theory can
locate ways to manage the four types of workplace experience by tapping their
strengths and avoiding their implicit weaknesses. In particular, managers and
consultants can strive toward balanced work experience if they are informed
about the psychologically and socially defensive nature of the other three types
of workplace experience.

MANAGMENT INFORMED BY DYNAMIC
WORKPLACE THEORY

Dynamic workplace theory provides managers and executives a practical perspective for leading and managing individual, interpersonal and group dynamics.

The first step in taking charge is understanding the four kinds of work experience. This appreciation leads to insights into what is going on at the moment as well as the significance of organizational history. Dynamic workplace theory also contains challenges for leaders, who must be prepared to manage themselves (their thoughts, feelings and actions) and their relationships with others and groups. The theory's dynamic nature and complexity also point to the likelihood that there is no one "right" way to manage, or indeed, many times anyway, to directly manage individual, group and organizational dynamics. Rather the theory points toward executives and managers assuming roles of insightful and attentive coaches and facilitators who enhance some dynamics while redirecting or minimizing others. Embracing losses of personal efficacy in the face of monumental workplace complexity leads to the necessity of executives and managers accepting, at least to some extent, the experience of themselves as less instrumental—in charge, in control, in command and calling all of the shots. The humbling nature of this appreciation is the first step toward achieving the balanced group experience where the leader is not all-powerful and the role is not used to fulfil narcissistic needs to feel admired, powerful, in control, loved and failing that, feared. In sum, the complexity of dynamic workplace theory signals the importance of leaders becoming informed and insightful facilitators of organizational change and stability.

Facilitating Group and Organizational Process

Dynamic workplace theory provides leaders a conceptual basis for facilitating group and organizational process. When group and organizational dynamics lead to competition, infighting, undermining, coalitions, delays, confusion, indifference, withdrawal, and ritualistic inactivity, the theory encourages us to look at these organizational outcomes as a system of psychological and social defenses that protect group members from losses of security, individuality, autonomy, personal integrity and self-esteem. Membership in groups that is unrewarding and threatening or associated with the likelihood of a failed effort is most often experienced as aversive. Membership, therefore, creates a dilemma. Being a member is undesirable but nonmembership may be precluded by superiors, peer pressure and economic self-interest. The only resort is to develop defensive coping responses. These responses are focused on changing one's self (denying failure for example) or the group (advocating for more or less control or a change in leadership) (Czander, 1993). When enough members come to share similar defenses the group has developed its own unique and often undiscussable culture and accompanying management challenge (Bion, 1961). The culture may also spontaneously change as discussed in chapter 4. It is at this point of readiness to change that an opportunity exists for a leader to make a process intervention that encourages reflection and thinking that promote change in the direction of the balanced workplace culture.

However, even if change is not being considered, facilitation in the direction of the balanced workplace culture is possible. The elements of balance may be nurtured within the culture of the three psychologically and socially defensive groups. This is no easy task for a leader to accomplish, since many aspects of the culture make balanced behavior and group process interventions threatening to organization members who, by assuming a psychologically defensive posture, are in flight from accurate reality testing and personal responsibility. A successful intervention strategy will share many of the characteristics proposed below. One must, however, keep in mind that endeavoring to facilitate group and organizational process where accepting personal responsibility is encouraged is threatening to some if not many organization members. Anyone endeavoring to make an intervention must have the courage to assume the risks of self-differentiation, thereby becoming a visible target for group anxieties and hostility. This individual, therefore, must have the skills to use organizational resistance to change as a means of understanding organizational culture. In this regard dynamic workplace theory provides a cognitive map that will help him or her to understand and interpret the actions of others in the workplace to accomplish this outcome.

Finally, there are also many instances where the stability of the three psychologically and socially defensive groups is firmly established, as discussed in chapter 5. Anyone advocating change and a more balanced approach to work may be ineffective. Nonetheless leadership can be provided that moderates the negative side of each of the three defensive groups. Success will most likely be achieved when the leader/facilitator understands both the defensive nature of the organizational dynamic and its strengths and weaknesses. In particular it must be appreciated that, as anxiety levels rise as a part of challenging the status quo, the defensive nature of the group and organizational experience is initially reinforced. It is generally felt that the current approach has thus far succeeded in controlling stressful experience and allaying the anxiety of organization members.

A note should be added at this point regarding the efficacy of skilled facilitation and coaching. Familiar authoritative, command and control and possibly autocratic leadership styles seem on the surface to promise executives and managers control and instrumental roles as change agents. However, it has been at least my experience that these more "macho" aspects of leadership are not as effective as hoped for by those who rely upon them. In particular, these methods and personal predispositions tend to create perceptions of top-down and unilateral decision making that alienate organization members and create resistance to change. Facilitating and coaching roles, while less macho and instrumental, are frequently more effective when it comes to enabling organizational change. However, this kind of facilitation in order to be effective requires the development of leadership skills in the areas of individual and group dynamics. The effort to acquire this knowledge and the accompanying skills is worth it in order to improve organizational performance. Effective facilitation and coaching can, in my experience, produce rapid organizational change that is openly embraced by organization members thereby making implementation quicker and more effective.

In Sum

Dynamic workplace theory provides those who aspire to lead a significant challenge due to its underlying complexity that highlights the psychologically and socially defensive nature of the workplace. Leaders who want to promote change in the direction of a more balanced approach or at the minimum away from the more detrimental aspects of the three defensive groups can best facilitate change by using a coaching approach that does not increase stress, anxiety and recourse to defensive coping measures. Leadership in the form of coaching and facilitation is of value in three circumstances. First, when group and organizational dynamics are trending toward change, it is possible to influence the direction of the change toward greater balance. Second, the dysfunctional dynamics of the three defensive groups provide the opportunity to nurture a desire for change in the direction of a more balanced work experience. Last, when one of the three defensive groups is firmly established, change is many times not an option in the near term. In this case leaders can work to improve performance by facilitating work that builds on the strengths of the defensive workplace experience while minimizing the effects of its inherent weaknesses. This improvement work lays the foundation for more change toward greater balance, and organization members begin to see that change is effective.

Making Management Inxterventions

An intervention will be most successful as the group or organization begins to evolve a new culture. Organization members must know that their organization is in trouble before they are receptive to an intervention; otherwise, it may be felt that "If it is not broken, why fix it?" Management interventions should start with an effort to recruit organization members in a brief period of reflection. "How did we get here?" This process should not sound judgmental. Finger-pointing, blaming rituals and scapegoating must be avoided. It is critically important to accurately assess current performance and evaluate unresolved operating problems. This is accomplished by avoiding "the blame game" when painful recollection of interpersonal, intergroup and intra-organizational conflict and dynamics are recovered for inspection. In general, if the leadership group and organization are not able to develop this shared and somewhat negotiated history and do not accept its content, it may not be wise to contemplate an intervention. If no one agrees as to how things are or wants to deal with the reality of the situation, organizational maturity and integration is lacking and the possibility of change may be foreclosed. This sense of foreboding can lead to a felt need by those in charge to forcibly intervene to change the organization, which contains its own threats and dysfunctions and many times less than desirable outcomes. If, however, a historical perspective is patiently developed (and most often it can be), the executive leading the work is seen to be effective and willing to listen and build consensus.

This leadership opportunity should be followed up with an assessment of the current situation. "As we seem to accept we have fallen behind schedule, I am wondering what role our group process has played in this outcome?" In particular, we seem to: (1) "not have established any type of effective leadership" (chaotic), (2) "have developed too much bureaucracy and red tape to get anything done" (bureaucratic) or (3) "have unloaded the entire responsibility for the group's performance on one of our members" (charismatic). "Does this seem to be the case to the rest of you?" It is important to test with group members, and in turn validate their perceptions and understanding. Comments may be offered that support the interpretation. "You know, I agree with you. We have completely bogged ourselves down in red tape." It is also likely dissenting comments will be offered that refute the interpretation. However, all comments, regardless of whether they agree, disagree or are completely off the subject, should be thought of in the light of the manager's self-differentiation as an interventionist. Supportive comments, while certainly welcome, may signal the need of a member to continue in a role of dependency upon the leader. A disagreeing comment may signal the development of a rivalry for the "spotlight of leadership" or be thought of as a useful new way to look at the group's process. Comments completely off task signal flight from an uncomfortable subject that can undermine the intervention. All comments can be potentially incorporated into the intervention if recast as carefully phrased interpretations of all-too-human resistance to change. In particular, others in the group should be asked if they agree or disagree with what others are saying about the group without using the group to attack or otherwise compete with the person offering the comments. Discussion of the group's process leads to another opportunity to summarize. At this point group and organization members may welcome a thoughtful and properly timed summary of the group's perceptions.

The success of the summary will signal that a next step can be taken. This involves suggesting that, since the group generally seems to agree that there is a problem and why, a shift away from the current psychologically defensive group culture is needed. This will entail rethinking the group's structure, its process and the leader's role. This step can be expected to represent a substantial threat to group members. Acknowledging that the group is in trouble because of its process does not necessarily lead to the rational next step—change. Many unconscious individual and group dynamics as underscored by the theory will militate against making a change despite certain knowledge change is needed or else failure may occur.

The person leading the intervention must be sensitive to these irrational trends in group process and be prepared to acknowledge that contemplating change makes everyone anxious and that this shared anxiety can block change efforts. The group's members should be encouraged to discuss change and the problems of implementing change to help diffuse the anxiety. In particular, the process may be facilitated by introducing dynamic workplace theory as an orienting and analytical tool to examine organizational life. The nature of the change may also be hotly debated. Even though there may be many points of view considered (chaos), there also exists effective leadership that provides adequate direction and structure for the change process. The manager's role is clearly important. He or she may be thought of as containing group and organizational anxiety. Effective facilitation and containment of the group's anxiety permits a constant press in the direction of acquiring the attributes of the balanced group. The group should be endeavoring to locate a balance as to how it can function in the future.

There will periodically develop regressive tendencies during the process that threaten to derail the intervention and return the group to one filled with psychological and social defensiveness. The interventionist must be cautious but persistent in challenging these trends. "It seems to me if we decide in favor of this proposal we will be creating some new red tape that I thought we had agreed we wanted to avoid." At any point the group may bolt from balanced group process and become defensive. This tendency should be initially resisted; however, if the pressure seems to be irresistible, it is often wiser to give up for the moment on the intervention or temporarily reduce its speed and intensity to avoid making members overly anxious. An intervention may be tried another day or once again speeded up if the leader has not alienated organization members by being overly resistant to member desires of the moment to not be faced with too much stressful change at one time. However, given the right situation, a leader who is respected by organization members can say that he or she does not accept what is happening and refuse to go along with it. This challenges the members to follow the leader, whom they trust and respect, even though they are anxious and skeptical. The group may be reminded that resorting to a defensive group process will not solve or has not in the past resolved the problem of stress and anxiety.

Toward the end of a successful intervention the leader should make sure it is clear to the group what actions are associated with balance so as to make clear the value system that forms the basis for the maintenance of the balanced group culture. Thereafter, the leader can continue to facilitate the group by pointing out regressive trends that conflict with the group's hard-earned balanced process. The discussion thus far has provided general intervention and leadership guidelines consistent with dynamic workplace theory. The following discussion highlights some of the challenges leaders/interventionists face relative to each of the types of group and organizational experience.

Facilitating Chaotic Work Experience

Executives, managers and anyone in a leadership role are confronted with a maximally challenging organizational context when chaotic work experience is present. An inherent part of the experience is an unwillingness to give up individual autonomy and the personal safety of organizational foxholes to follow anyone willing to lead. At the same time, those who attempt to provide leadership find that their efforts are contested by others who wish to lead but in a different way or direction. Nonetheless the roles of formal leadership that executives and managers do have provide them the means to lead if they have the courage to do so by standing up to be counted. These efforts should be supported by others who also have formal leadership roles and the effort is also backed up by the fact that these leaders are empowered to issue instructions and, if necessary, change personnel assignments. However, the use of brute force may alienate employees and place the individual relying upon it at long-term risk. Therefore, care and *balance* are needed in using formal authority as a part of any effort to facilitate chaotic group and organizational experience.

The exact nature of the facilitated change depends upon the unique qualities of the context in which it is to occur. A number of suggestions can, nonetheless, be offered to anyone endeavoring to lead chaotic organizational experience toward greater balance and improved organizational performance. Facilitation must begin with an appreciation of the organization's history and the events that led to the development of workplace chaos. This information offers insights into how to approach the change effort. The loss of a leader or an unpopular reorganization may, for example, be the cause of the chaos that leads the facilitator in one direction versus another. Given an appreciation of events and organizational dynamics leading up to the chaos, executives and managers working as facilitators can help employees calm down and get focused by showing some leadership that may be thought of as controlling anxiety. Visible efforts to lead provide hope for employees so long as those who are leading are appreciative of what is going on and do not become defensively reliant upon the power and authority of their management role when resistance to change is predictably encountered. In this regard the facilitator must be patient and persistent while providing direction and a constant press for change that promises to overcome the negative effects of chaotic experience. The facilitator will want to revisit policies and procedures and operating protocols for their contribution to the creation and maintenance of the chaotic experience. They may be absent, out of date, irrelevant, not being followed or in such abundance as to be confusing and conflicting and foreclose achieving success. Also to be considered is the contribution leadership styles may have made to creating the chaos, including the facilitator's if he or she was involved in the past. The facilitator is, therefore, modeling reflective behavior aimed at analyzing and appreciating what has been and is with an eye on restoring some sense of order and direction to the situation—the fusion of chaos, bureaucracy and charismatic leadership. The creativity implicit within chaos must be combined with the coordinative and predictable order of bureaucratic process and effective leadership to promote balanced work experience.

Much more could be said about this facilitative process, however, the context-specific nature of any facilitation makes it a self-defeating proposition to be too specific and thereby present the reader with the notion of a "one size fits all" and "do it by the numbers" approach to facilitating change. The above discussion, however, introduces important perspectives that are common and point toward the basic elements of an intervention process that must be adapted to the unique qualities of the leadership and facilitating opportunity. This is under-scored by the discussion of the three remaining leading and facilitating oppor-tunities.

Facilitating Bureaucratic Work Experience

This leading and facilitating opportunity presents the challenge of, figura-tively speaking, prying the fingers of the collective membership off carefully developed and rigidly adhered to organizational controls that allay anxiety. Call-ing the control and accompanying red tape into question is perceived as being critical of organization members and threatening to them by removing their psychologically and socially defensive security blanket. If the intervention is not handled adeptly, feelings of hurt, shame and threat will emerge alongside efforts to more firmly grip the controls (Baum, 1987). The manager endeavoring to lead in this context must be careful to take his or her time to understand the total situation before acting. Doing so demonstrates a willingness to listen and learn and it shows respect for what is. In effect, everyone is watching the manager who calls into question what is going on and presumes to point the way toward what could be.

The facilitator is, therefore, providing leadership that falls outside of being a routinized leadership style, while also trying to relieve or contain anxiety so as to permit organization members to relax their need for control that has stifled individuals, groups, and creativity and has reduced organizational flexibility and adaptiveness. Care must be taken to not move too fast or unilaterally in order to avoid creating more anxiety that will predictably lead to greater reliance upon the controlling nature of the bureaucratic organizational design.

Facilitating Charismatic Work Experience

This leadership opportunity usually arises out of the need to confront a leader who has inadvertently created problems for him- or herself and followers. Con-flict of the leader and his or her closely knit band of loyal followers with the rest of the organization's members may evolve into requests for change from above and may lead to the hiring of a consultant. In this context intervention must once again be approached with care. Attention has to be given to understanding the historical context and the current operating situation. However, anyone who presumes to gather this information will be seen as a potential threat to the leader and his or her loyal followers. It also tacitly signals the threat of being found out and disapproved of and the success of the out-group in attracting at-tention to the situation. These dynamics and others are often present to some extent in interventions of this kind.

The actual intervention may take many forms such as confrontation, coach-ing, leadership training, reassignment and reorganization. It must usually be superiors and in some cases external consultants and coaches who lead this effort. Much depends on the receptiveness of the charismatic leader involved to change. In particular, the intervention may be threatening to his or her self-image, which is at least in part enhanced by his or her leadership role. There are no magic bullets, although the interventionist may rapidly come to wish that he or she had one. This work can be tedious, difficult and threatening to the interventionist, who may be directly challenged by the charismatic leader in an all-or-nothing win/lose dynamic. The charismatic leader may also suddenly resign, leaving turmoil in his or her wake. He or she may recruit employees to follow him or her to a new organization. All of these considerations point once again to being careful, patient and persistent while not being manipulated into relying upon power and authority to defend oneself or enforce one's point of view regarding the need for change. It must also be appreciated that success is problematic and almost entirely dependent upon the charismatic leader's willingness to be reflective. To the extent self-reflection is achieved and coaching accepted, a more balanced leadership style may emerge where everything does not have to necessarily be controlled and micromanaged. The creativity and productivity that lies within organization members can be allowed to emerge even if it is occasionally messy.

Facilitating Balanced Work Experience

Executives and managers are confronted with a different leadership opportunity when work experience is primarily of a balanced nature. It is fundamentally easier to try to maintain balanced experience as compared with changing the nature of the three defensive group and organizational experiences. The goal is to, in a timely and sensitive manner, nip in the bud group and organizational dynamics that may lead to the emergence of one of the defensive groups. Flight toward chaotic experience is countered by taking advantage of its creativity. Clear direction and leadership and paying attention to the need to follow agreed upon policies, procedures and protocols also forestall a retreat to chaos. Flight toward bureaucratic experience is countered by questioning the need for more hierarchical positions, organizational layers, rules and regulations and instances where dysfunction arises relative to too-rigid compliance with them. Trends such as this may be called into question. Their advocacy, however, signals a need to revisit current organizational protocols or lack thereof. Similarly, the emergence of a charismatic leader may be greeted with efforts to coach the individual to avoid the negative side of charismatic leadership. On occasion it may be necessary to find a new leadership opportunity for the individual or encourage him or her to find a new position elsewhere that is more consistent with his or her growing self-expectations. Changes such as these are not uncommon and can be handled in a positive and affirmative manner.

In conclusion, successful interventions by group leaders and members can be more difficult than employing an outside person to facilitate group process. There are two reasons why this is often the case. First, managers and employees are frequently unprepared experientially and educationally to facilitate interpersonal and group dynamics. The above description of the elements of a successful intervention requires considerable skill and insight to carry out. Second, a group member who attempts an intervention will frequently be experienced as threatening and not functioning as part of the group. It is difficult and many times unrewarding to try to lead a group from within as a process interventionist. However, despite these problems, successful interventions by group members and leaders are possible and should be encouraged rather than developing a long-term dependency upon an "external authority." In this regard, if a consultant is employed, he or she should have as an explicit goal enabling organization members to learn the skills and insights necessary to manage themselves.

In Sum

Dynamic workplace theory provides managers and executives many insights into what is going on at work as well as a cautionary note on some of the limitations of managing organizational dynamics. This somewhat humbling perspective encourages executives, managers and other workplace leaders to approach their task from a perspective that acknowledges workplace complexity. In particular, assuming a role such as participant observer and workplace facilitator or coach is consistent with using dynamic workplace theory as a guide to managing and leading change. The challenge is to be able to influence the nature and direction of organizational change toward a more balanced work experience. It is, however, also the case that at least in the short run, groups and organizations may be functioning fairly well by relying upon one of the three psychologically and socially defensive organizational cultures. The challenge in these cases, while not surrendering the goal of promoting change toward more balance, is to avoid the negative side effects of the three defensive organizational cultures. Each defensive mode can accomplish considerable work and these accomplishments can be further enhanced by confronting the negative side effects of the inherently defensive nature of each of these types of groups.

CONSULTING INFORMED BY DYNAMIC WORKPLACE THEORY

Consultants will find many potential uses for the perspectives provided by dynamic workplace theory. The theory informs organizational diagnosis, intervention strategies, client education and change management strategies.

Organizational Diagnosis

To begin, the three defensive group experiences and the balanced experience may be readily observed in the workplace. An entire organization may have adopted one of the defensive cultures or various divisions may have developed different ones. A thorough organizational diagnosis produces large volumes of information about organizational dynamics. The theory permits the sifting of this information for overarching meaning. Perhaps one major division is led by a charismatic executive and a second has come to rely on bureaucratic control such as may be the case of the juxtaposition of an aggressive marketing division with a complex process of producing products. Dynamic workplace theory, therefore, provides an important portal for viewing organizational dynamics in all of its complexity. Information overload is avoided when attention is paid to discovering the fundamental nature of work experience throughout an organization (Diamond, 1993 and Schein, 1985).

Organizational Intervention Strategies

The organizational diagnosis, when framed by dynamic organization theory, very often leads organization members to rapidly self-identify many areas where change will be useful. The types, amounts, and directions of change can be cast in terms of dynamic workplace theory. This permits developing an overarching perspective for thinking about where "we" are and where "we" want to be. The theory may then be used to examine the experience of the psychological and social sides of the change and many of the difficulties that may be encountered while planning and implementing change.

Client Education

There is just about nothing more important for a successful consultation than educating one's client, or more correctly client system, about the nature of the current context, the direction for desirable change and how to manage the change process. Failure can occur at all three stages. Dynamic workplace theory provides consultants a meaningful way to describe organizational experience. Exotic words and phrases need not be relied upon. The nature of the diagnosis can be described in terms of dynamic workplace theory without the threat of making members of the organization feel that the consultant is talking to them in "consultant speak" that, while perhaps making the consultant(s) feel important and superior to the client system, may only serve to frustrate learning on the part of organization members. Dynamic workplace theory permits a thorough analysis of what has been found in the diagnosis that then points to the need for organizational change and direction it needs to take. Organization members can, after reviewing dynamic workplace theory, create their own organizational diagnosis with the help of a consultant as well as locate the amount and direction of the needed change. This approach I describe as "client centered" as compared with "consultant centered" consultation. Client centered consultation grows out of the underlying nature of the balanced work experience in which it is assumed managers know the nature of their organization's problems and the need for change but have not acted. The result is that the client system learns to manage organizational dynamics and not develop dependence upon organizational consultants.

Planning and Implementing Organizational Change

Facilitating organizational change under the best of circumstances is exceptionally difficult. In most instances the best of plans will run into unintended consequences, unanticipated problems and employee resistance to change. Reliance upon dynamic workplace theory does not magically remove these change management problems. However, it informs those planning and implementing change of many of the difficulties that may be encountered along the way. Chapter 4 provides a sobering perspective of just how challenging managing organizational change can become. Dynamic workplace theory directs attention to the nature of the potential and transitional organizational space and the need to carefully plan change as well as work hard to minimize the stresses and strains that employees experience. An appreciation of what is being lost by employees who are invested in one of the defensive group experiences is important. The nature of the plan and the design for implementation should take into account the nature of this loss. An organization or division that has become bogged down in bureaucratic controls must not be made to feel incompetent or ashamed of how they designed their work environment. Bureaucratic process is not all bad, as discussed in chapter 5. Attention can be directed toward some of the red tape, delays, problems in making rapid adjustments and so on without per se confronting the entire context. Many employees will readily understand what is being tactfully pointed out when adequate documentation and concrete examples are provided. They may then be gradually recruited to making small carefully selected changes that gradually but strategically loosen their dependence upon bureaucratic control without their feeling overly distressed about the nature of the change, thereby reinforcing their belief that bureaucratic control is essential.

Although it is not possible to provide a "how-to cookbook" for facilitating organizational change, it is possible to use dynamic workplace theory as an important tool in change management. Consultants, executives and managers endeavoring to lead organizational change can avoid creating excessive anxiety and defensiveness that create resistance to change by using dynamic theory and its notion of transitional organizational space and time as a template for thinking through all aspects of planning and implementing change.

Consulting inside the Context

Consultants inevitably have to start their work at the point where the organization is. The organizational diagnosis usually makes this painfully clear. Dynamic workplace theory provides consultants a way of thinking about the next step—how to help the client system learn and locate the nature and direction of organizational change. The four types of workplace experience provide consultants the starting points and a perspective for thinking through their work.

Consulting to Chaotic Work Experience

Consultants are many times recruited by a segment of senior management to save their organization from the dysfunctional actions of their leader and excessive organizational fragmentation that has pitted divisions and departments against each other. Chaotic experience usually includes an absence of effective leadership combined with excessive individual and group autonomy. Additionally, many employees find their work experience so unsatisfactory that they have retreated into their organizational foxholes to protect themselves and their careers from threatening organizational events.

These are all challenging parts of a complex context that the consultant rapidly diagnoses. Dynamic workplace theory provides consultants with a frame of reference for making this assessment and locating the variables that may be influenced to achieve balanced work experience. A consultant may want to work with and coach formal leaders to become more effective. This may translate into overcoming divisive, competitive and autocratic leadership styles and very often a larger dysfunctional subculture among senior executives. Dynamic workplace theory encourages consultants to use it to point to the problem "out there" where the executives can inspect what is going on in a less threatening and defensive manner. It is frequently safer to talk about a theory and encourage "silent learning" on the part of executives, who may come to more fully appreciate their contribution to the leadership vacuum, and the dysfunctions of their marginal leadership styles.

Chaotic work experience may also be approached depending on the severity of the context by providing clear direction that organization members must pursue in order to stabilize their organization's functioning. Often lost in the chaos are the vision, mission and strategic and business plans. This loss can be profound where autonomy, losses of accountability and hiding out abound. The leadership group and mid-level managers can be enlisted to locate the most serious problems and how to remediate them in a tactical sense. At the same time the consultant may point out the absence of a larger and longer-term strategy that must be approached via a strategic planning process that ideally should include a variety of employees—a diagonal slice through the organization.

Consulting to chaotic work experience, therefore, includes improving the quality of leadership, stabilizing organizational performance by repairing operating problems and engaging management and employees in a collaborative process of revisiting vision, mission, values and planning. Gradually the consultant coaxes and prods organization members toward a less threatening and more balanced work experience where leadership and some appropriate institutional controls are available without stifling individuality and creativity.

Consulting to Bureaucratic Work Experience

Consulting to bureaucratic work experience presents consultants with a substantially different organizational context from that of chaos. The challenge here is to enable leaders and organization members to gradually relax their dependence upon meticulously designed and rigidly enforced organizational protocols that suppress individuality, creativity and organizational flexibility and adaptiveness. Once again dynamic workplace theory permits both locating the organizational diagnosis and encouraging an inspection of the diagnosis in a non-defensive manner that encourages learning. Very often facilitated meetings with senior management will gradually permit not only an inspection of what is but also how bureaucracy and organizational hierarchy have tended to limit what they can think of or consider doing to improve organizational performance. This realization may then be gradually nurtured to a more complete assessment of the organization's context and what may be done to moderate the agreed-upon excessive dependence on defensively employed policies and procedures, rules and regulations. In most instances senior management must be coached into locating, planning and implementing change since most employees are firmly locked down and in many instances have been recruited, retained and trained to not question what is going on.

This raises a second aspect to the design of an intervention strategy. If management is moving to plan and implement change, this must be done with maximum care relative to the employees who will feel threatened by the change and anxious to maintain control via familiar bureaucratic mechanisms. It is often the case that it seems that there cannot be enough communication. Inevitably employees will generate their own understanding of the reasons for and the nature of the change process. This resistance to change is threatening to the leaders, who may well feel guilty about what they are doing and threatened by losses of employee loyalty. Inevitably there will arise confusion, conflicting and different points of view and hard to address feelings of guilt, shame and anger (chaos). Therefore, planning and implementing change is a major challenge for the consultant to manage.

Consulting to Charismatic Work Experience

This organizational context presents the consultant with a difficult situation where the CEO and his or her loyal senior management team control the engagement. Many times the consultant, as in the case of chaos, is recruited into the situation by a subgroup of out-group senior managers who are influential enough to get a consultant involved. In this regard these individuals may see the consultant as the only hope of countervailing the dysfunctional nature of their charismatic leader's leadership style. Dynamic workplace theory, in this case, not only permits the consultant to locate the organizational context but also the difficult nature of the consultation. The consultant must appreciate several things. He or she cannot please everyone all of the time. The subgroup that initially sponsored the engagement will inevitably seldom have their expectations for change met, expectations that may tacitly include removing their leader. At the same time the leader and his or her close circle of supporters can be expected to work to limit the scope and influence of the consultant's work and perhaps occasionally threaten to stop funding the work. The consultant, therefore, often finds him- or herself between a rock and a hard place. Dynamic workplace theory underscores the problematic nature of the work and of achieving meaningful change.

Nonetheless, work must begin on carefully developing an organizational diagnosis that includes capturing subjective as well as quantitative data such as survey results. The quantitative analysis permits presenting unwelcome but nevertheless concrete data that is hard to dismiss by the leader and his or her management team. The central issue here is coaching the leader to accept the data so that he or she will permit work on it which is felt to be threatening to the leader in terms of both change and being identified as part of the problem. In the event the leader is willing to proceed with the engagement he or she can be expected to be less than fully supportive and occasionally to resort to language that implies his or her power may come into play. It is also the case that many times upper and middle managers become enlisted in the change work with their leader becoming a reluctant participant who assumes a role of judge and jury of the ideas being generated. This appreciation once again reminds the consultant of the problematic nature of the work. Most often some progress is made at the risk of creating a more empowered out-group of executives and managers that is at least temporarily mobilized by the consultant's presence to countervail the negative effects of their leader's style. The consultant may, therefore, be seen as leading a revolution that, while seductively flattering, must be strictly avoided.

Consulting to Balanced Work Experience

The nature of this engagement should be considered to be a relief as compared with the above three defensive group experiences. Management and employees are working hard, usually in a coordinated and collaborative manner, to improve organizational performance and confront the risks associated with growing their organization. Within this context organizational consultants are often employed to look into specific areas that have been resistant to improvement. The scope of the engagement is therefore limited, which is not always a good thing for the organization or the consultant for the obvious reason few localized problems are merely that. The diagnostic work may reveal a systemic set of operating problems that collectively act to create the situation under inspection. Therefore, consultants who believe the organization is balanced are encouraged to confront management over narrowly defining the scope of the work. In most instances management will be open to the notion that systemic thinking is appropriate if indicated by the diagnosis, although also worried about the greater cost associated with an expanded scope of work.

The remaining work of the consultant usually involves carefully diagnosing the situation and locating possible solutions to improve performance that are fed back to management for their consideration. The consultant may assume a less directive role in helping management locate, plan and implement change. The consultant should find management receptive to drawing organization members into the work of planning and implementing organizational change. Employees should be consulted as appropriate, and information flows regarding operating problems and change must be thoughtful, timely and complete. Employees, as a result of receiving adequate communication and being allowed to participate, will most often feel included and supportive of the direction of the change and how it is being implemented. The consultant may, therefore, focus his or her attention upon smoothing out rough spots along the way since no amount of change planning addresses all the possible unintended consequences.

In Sum

When it comes to the most negative outcomes of the three psychologically and socially defensive group and organizational experiences, consultants are often looked to by at least some organization members to save them, their group and their organization from creating self-destructive outcomes. These explicit and implicit expectations tend to encourage consultants to see themselves in roles that are not necessarily the most conducive to being effective consultants. Feelings that they must save individuals and an organization essentially amount to rescue fantasies that are seductive and make the consultant feel important, powerful and needed. Therefore, an important aspect of dynamic workplace theory as it pertains to organizational consulting is the interaction of the cultures of the defensive group and organizational experiences with the consultant's inner needs, desires and fantasies. Remaining objective and in touch with the psychologically and socially defensive nature of the work experience is important.

Dynamic workplace theory also provides consultants many insights into how to work with leaders, leadership groups and employees in an effective manner. In particular, the theoretical perspective improves the process of organizational diagnosis and its communication to organization members. It is also important to appreciate that the cultures of each of the three defensive organizational experiences as well as that of the balanced work experience individual provide consultants many challenges in terms of facilitating organizational learning and change.

REALITY TESTING—THE THEORY IN THE REAL WORLD

Executives, managers and consultants must take a mental time-out to examine their work, their leadership style, and the types of groups that are found in their workplace. Is there a lack of effective leadership and commonly accepted direction? Is there too much red tape that bogs down decision making and work? Is there a powerful unapproachable leader who has collected around him or her a small group of loyal supporters? Is there an effective mix of leadership, creativity, risk taking and organizational structure? Questions such as these point the way to a reflective process. Does your workplace fit within dynamic workplace theory?

In final analysis, only you the reader can decide if dynamic workplace theory makes a contribution to understanding the workplace based on your experience and insights. Based on my experience as an executive, manager and organizational consultant, this theoretical perspective possesses considerable explanatory power in terms of understanding and talking about what goes on in most organizations.

IN CONCLUSION

Dynamic workplace theory provides executives, managers, supervisors, employees, organizational researchers and consultants a perspective for understanding organizational dynamics grounded in the workplace. The four types of group and organizational experience may be seen to exist in organizations simultaneously in different places and sometimes sequentially when analyzed from a historical perspective. The theory not only makes intuitive sense, it makes sense of workplace experience that is many times hard to locate, identify, think about and discuss. The theory provides many insights and clues as to how to be more effective designers, leaders and agents of change within our organizations, which are invariably hierarchies that create overarching organizational cultures that contain the theory's four types of workplace experience. However, one might ask, "Do organizations always have to be hierarchical and so often bureaucratic?" It is indeed difficult to imagine an organization that does not inherently possess hierarchical features. The next chapter begins the process of presenting a thought experiment about how to create a nonhierarchical organization. This envisionment will confront readers with a challenging new perspective for organizational design. This new organizational design is described in chapter 8 and analyzed in chapter 9 by using dynamic workplace theory to test its veracity.

Chapter 7

The Search for the Organizational Solution to the Industrial Revolution

There is, in the growth of modern organization, an ending of all that has gone before. The newcomer entering bureaucracy from society steps into what, in the social evolution of humankind, is an entirely new world. . . . Is there no escape from this future incorporated in our present, in which humankind is dehumanized and its survival put in question? If we have the courage to draw the logical conclusions from what our investigation of the underlying rationalizing movement of bureaucracy forces on us, we must deny ourselves all false hopes. Bureaucracy has been, is now, and will be the carrying institution of an irresistible rationalization process riding roughshod over any opposition. To the extent that a civilization actualizes its underlying values to the bitter end, bureaucracy is our fate for the foreseeable future.

(Hummel, 1982, p. 218)

This chapter is the first of three chapters that inspect the nature and pervasiveness of the bureaucratic hierarchical organization design and how difficult it is to envision any other way to design our organizations for the twenty-first century. Bureaucratic hierarchies are so common today as to be merely accepted as the only way to design our organizations. However, what must be appreciated is that bureaucratic hierarchies are a relatively new organization form growing out of how goods are produced and the accompanying societal changes associated with the industrial revolution. It is also important to appreciate that dynamic workplace theory has thus far been discussed within the context of the bureaucratic hierarchical organization design. Indeed, it is at this time the only organizational design context to which it may be applied. Therefore, the question may be asked whether dynamic workplace theory will apply to an organization that is neither bureaucratic nor hierarchical. In order to make this assessment chapter 8 presents an organization design that avoids as nearly as possible the controlling nature of bureaucracy and organizational hierarchy where issues of power and control, dominance and submission and superior/subordinate relations predominate. Chapter 9 continues the analysis of ring organization design and dynamic workplace theory by inspecting ring design through the lens of dynamic workplace theory. Does the theory apply to an entirely new and essentially foreign organization design? Does ring organization design offer a realistic possibility of creating a bureaucracy- and hierarchy-free organization design for the twenty-first century? This challenging bidirectional analysis offers additional insights into the complexities of understanding the workplace and possible redesigns that may be considered in the future.

Returning to the task of this chapter, I commence the process of understanding the nature of organizational design by providing reflections on a literature review that delved into the development of bureaucratic hierarchies as a response to the industrial revolution and the development of allied management theory to improve their operation. This review is streamlined to compare the past (pre-1950) with the near present (last fifteen years). The literature reviewed focused on the better-known authors of each period who have provided insights into how to make bureaucratic hierarchies more efficient and effective.

THE LITERATURE REVIEW AND ANALYSIS

The literature selected for overview dated back to Taylor's conception of scientific management and testimony before Congress in 1911. Also included are Mary Parker Follett's work in the 1920s and Chester Barnard's theorizing in the 1930s. These and other early works were then compared to the contemporary writing of popular business and management authors who have sought to improve organizational performance. Creating public, private and voluntary organizations that optimize their performance has been a challenge. The amount that has been published toward this end is impressive, ranging from many popular "quick fix," management guru and self-efficacy testimonials to, at times, impenetrable research and abstract conceptual works that atomize the subject matter to the point that it is questionable that the content may be applied in practice or generalized to any other context.

The content of these two periods is rich and abundant and it is regrettable that space limitations limit the many comparisons that can be made. To begin, it is not difficult to discern from the literature that the problems managers and employees face today are much the same as in the past and that many of the approaches to solving the problems are likewise similar although different buzzwords and concepts are mentioned. In particular it become clear from the review that the bureaucratic-hierarchical approach to managing large-scale organizations has become so omnipresent as to create a pervasive context for problem generation and resolution. No matter how much one studies old or modern-day organizations, they are invariably hierarchical organizations that are most often bureaucratic at their foundation (Waring, 1991). This paradox is highlighted by Bergquist (1993), who asserts that the postmodern organization (postindustrial revolution) will contain elements of both a nostalgia filled pre-industrial (pre-modern) period when life was simpler, such as was the case with cottage indus-try, and the complex and alienating capital-intensive industrial period (modern) organizations. Postmodern organizations may, therefore, according to Bergquist, be understood to have their design bounded by not one but two past organiza-tional paradigms.

The review revealed that early authors were working hard to discover what worked and what did not in the new organizational and production frontier of the industrial revolution. These understandings were, in most instances, created by individuals with firsthand experience of managing in the new context, as was the case for Frederick W. Taylor, who as a manager came to question how work was designed and how employees were organized and led. As a result of this in-timate familiarity of early writers with the workplace, it is logical to assume that what was learned from experience fifty or one hundred years ago may also apply to today's similarly designed and operated organizations. Certainly many of the seminal works of these authors continue to be issued as reprinted editions as well as being frequently cited by contemporary authors. At the same time, ob-jective reviewers of contemporary literature cannot avoid being impressed with the fact that not only are these authors not saying much that is new, but they have managed to so fragment the literature that entire books are often devoted to elaborate but one idea offered by an author of the past.

Indeed, one gets the impression that there is of late a churning of manage-ment and organization theory and literature to create yet another of the 2,000 or so books published every year. For example, Argyris (1982) addressed the problems organization members have in learning from experience. This think-ing is most recently further elaborated by Senge (1990) in *The Fifth Discipline*, where the notion of organizational learning is popularized. This somewhat reified notion is then further elaborated by McMaster (1996), who takes the po-sition that, if organizations can learn, then organizations must have intelligence (another reified notion). A more cynical view of much of the popular and influ-ential management books leads to the appreciation that self-marketing for fame and profit is frequently an underlying motivation. Certainly the "biggest sell-ers" provide simplistic fodder for the would-be manager or executive by pro-viding yet another reiteration of principles and lessons from the past. These manuscripts appeal to busy executives because of their seemingly easy to im-plement multi-step management cookbook style of presentation. Many of these books appear to pander to the "quick-fix" "no pain" "feel-good" side of human nature (Covey, 1989; Peters, 1982, 1985; Senge, 1990; Vaill, 1989). This rather critical analysis of popular contemporary management writing is underscored by John Micklethwait and Adrian Woolridge in their 1996 book titled *The Witch*

Doctors. They note: "Humble businessmen trying to keep up with the latest fashion often find that by the time they have implemented the new craze, it looks outdated. The only people who win out are the theorists, who just go on getting richer and richer" (p. 15).

In general, if one steps back from recent publishing, what is basically being said is not particularly new although many contemporary buzzwords, phrases and images are employed for product differentiation for marketing purposes. In fact this lack of self-insight combined with ruthless self-promotion seems to often escape awareness on the part of some popular writers as illustrated by the following quote.

At bottom, my conviction is that in a world of permanent white water, all bodies of knowledge and speculation are themselves in a race to stay just one jump ahead of obsolescence and irrelevance. To the extent that the subject of *excellence and peak performance* [emphasis added] becomes the property of a cultish in-group of cognoscenti, the subject risks being overtaken and passed by the actual issues real managers and leaders are facing, and then we may begin to hear the managers say ruefully, as they have had to say so many times before about once-promising approaches, "Excellence? Oh yea, right, we've already tried that." (Vaill, 1989, p. 66)

It is ironic that Tom Peters, the advocate of excellence in the early 1980s had, by the end of the 1980s, abandoned this notion. Buzzwords like peak performance are also dated in the later part of the 1990s and headed for the management buzzword junk heap. The lament, "We have already tried that" that I have heard articulated by managers and supervisors while I interviewed organization members as a consultant may well apply to most contemporary writing aimed at telling executives, managers, supervisors and employees how to better operate their business.

I conclude with some degree of comfort based on my inspection of the literature that there really is not much that is fundamentally new in the management literature in the last 100 years, although the constant pursuit of something unique to justify yet another book has led to exploring a vast number of "nooks and crannies" in the historical literature on management. Interestingly, when this assertion was presented to a room full of business and public administration professors none disagreed, nor did an editor of a scholarly administration journal. I, therefore, do not feel that I am alone in reaching this conclusion.

This trend toward nothing new is also contributed to by the seeming inability of modern-day managers to adopt the most fundamental aspects of solutions to the problems the bureaucratic-hierarchical form of organization creates. This is such a persistent problem that one might wonder if the paradigm, itself, serves in some way to block the location and implementation of the solutions to the problems it creates. Myriad authors working in the area of organizational psychodynamics provide compelling insights and arguments that bureaucratic-hierarchy, when combined with psychological distortions in personal development, provide a ready mechanism for attempting to fill narcissistic deficits and act out paranoid, arrogant and sadistic tendencies (Allcorn et al., 1996; Allcorn, 1997; Allcorn and Diamond, 1997; Baum, 1987, 1990; Diamond, 1993; Hummel, 1982; Kets de Vries, 1984, 1991; Schwartz, 1990; Stein, 1994). To the extent this is true bureaucratic-hierarchy may be understood to contain contextual elements that are readily bonded with elements of the psychology of their leaders and organization members that serve to create a self-sealing, self-fulfilling and self-perpetuating approach to organizational design and management. It may then be appreciated that, not only are the production and social changes arising out of the industrial revolution the primary underlying driving force behind the selection of the bureaucratic hierarchy as an organization design, many of those who grew up with the design like it that way. Change and innovation, therefore, seem unlikely. This appreciation leads to the need to understand to a greater extent the compelling historical context for the development of the omnipresent bureaucratic-hierarchy and what it portends for the future.

In Sum

The most influential writers of the first half of the twentieth century were writing about the rise and perfection of the rational bureaucratic-hierarchy that evolved to accommodate the production and social changes generated by the industrial revolution. A review of some of the most recent authors of management literature reveals that they are fundamentally laboring in the shadow of their predecessors. They, in fact, may be observed to be dealing with many of the same problems and using many of the same approaches to resolve the problems created by the bureaucratic-hierarchical organization form. With but a few exceptions, such as the psychodynamic inspection of the workplace, there is little that is very different when the two periods are compared even though the language and buzzwords and phrases are different. This is the result of, I believe, the fact that the bureaucratic-hierarchy has become the only organizational context in which ideas are being generated. In effect the bureaucratic hierarchy is an organizational paradigm that bounds thinking and limits the development of new organizational designs.

OUTCOMES OF THE INDUSTRIAL REVOLUTION: LOOKING BACK, LOOKING FORWARD

As we begin the twenty-first century the astounding abundance of an organizational form that has its origins in the eighteenth century seems to point to the hard to deny fact that little to no progress has been made in creating new organizational designs that transcend the bureaucratic hierarchy. There is, therefore, something to be gained by briefly inspecting what history has to offer regarding the success of this organization form. Daniel Wren (1979) writes:

Early management thought was dominated by cultural values which were antibusiness, antiachievement, and largely anti-human. Industrialization could not emerge when people were bound to their stations in life, when monarchs ruled by central dictates, and when people were urged to take no thought of individual fulfillment in this world but to wait for a better one. Before the Industrial Revolution, economies and societies were essentially static, and political values involved unilateral decision making by some central authority. While some early ideas of management appeared, they were largely localized. Organizations could be run on the divine right of the king, on the appeal of dogma to the faithful, and on the rigorous discipline of the military. There was little or no need to develop a formal body of management thought under these nonindustriaized circumstances. (p. 40)

Wren (1979), as quoted in chapter 3, contends that a cultural rebirth created the preconditions for industrialization and the need for a rational, formalized, systematic body of management knowledge as to how best to utilize resources. Modern management, therefore, came to be based on rational ways of making decisions and not on the whims of a few. Perhaps no truer words could be spoken at the beginning of the twenty-first century. It is apparent from the above review of management and organizational literature that we, today, continue to perfect these same old ideas despite ever-improving technology, and to creatively recast management writing.

If much of what is being published today is intellectually bounded by the bureaucratic-hierarchical paradigm, the question may legitimately be posed as to what can be done to break out of the paradigm. This is, of course, easier said than done. There is, however, today a new workplace looming before us, one that did not exist before, as was the case with the development of large factories and mass production during the Industrial Revolution. The *virtual workplace* potentially networked to every node in the world is something that is new (Allcorn, 1997). However, this virtual workplace, while providing a setting for information sharing and knowledge generation, does not in any way solve the problem of how to organize the physical world to avoid the bureaucratic-hierarchical organizational paradigm. In this regard new non-bureaucratic, nonhierarchical thinking must occur. But how might one conceive of a non-bureaucratic and nonhierarchical postmodern organization?

In Sum

The Industrial Revolution with its underpinning in the eighteenth century led to production and social changes that nurtured into existence the need for rationality in organizing what were becoming capital-intensive manufacturing organizations. Their greater complexity generated a new class of nonowner managers who were responsible for their operation. The creation of the bureaucratic-hierarchy is the product of these efforts to design a rational organization that controls processes and people to achieve a predictable return on investment. It is certainly the case today that these same elements are a critically important feature of our management and administrative landscape. As a result, little has in fact changed in several centuries. The problems of managing huge organizations are the same and invariably addressed in much the same ways as management writers of the first half of the twentieth century discovered were essential for success. Nonetheless, our modern-day organizations include many dysfunctions that are contributed to by their organization design and its interaction with human nature. They are not perfect and perhaps not an essential feature of the twenty-first century management landscape where the virtual workplace may be nurtured into existence, thus creating the potential for a new organization form. In sum, the organization form for the twenty-first century has yet to be discovered, or indeed envisioned.

ENVISIONING A POST-INDUSTRIAL
ORGANIZATION DESIGN

The development of a vision for a new form of organization necessarily raises fundamental questions about the need to do so to avoid the trap of meaningless paradigm proliferation and contributing to the proliferation of management literature that contributes little that is new. This is a major challenge when one takes into account that thus far it is apparent that progress in developing management and organization theory is bound by the context of the extraordinary predominance of bureaucratic-hierarchical organizations. Waring (1991) writes:

Such compromises [referring to dehumanizing quantitative methods] with bureaucracy [symbolizing rational structure and methods] almost always occurred, and each ultimately corrupted corporatism. Corporatists wanted management without bureaucracy, believing that worker participation in management would decentralize power, unify tasks, and bring harmony between individual and firm. But they did not want management to wither away; they sought management based on hegemony rather than tyranny. They never understood that management was bureaucracy. They never considered that transcending Taylorism required more than installing a few participative mechanisms; it required a revolution in American society as a whole, in its values, economic structures, educational institutions, and macrogovernment. So however much they talked about democracy and industrial clans, they still presumed the rightness of the management theory of value and the rationality of managers. They could scarcely do otherwise if they wanted to sell ideas in the manager market.

   The management theory of value, whatever its form, amounted to a bureaucratic ethic. Empowering managers inevitably limited participation and autonomy, foreclosing real harmony; if cooperation came from centralized power, their corporatism was self-contradicting and chimerical. Centralizing power established a managerial will more important than any combination of individual wills. It allowed managers to establish collective goals transcending individual interests. In doing so, it imposed the rationality Weber had defined as central to bureaucracy. When swept out, bureaucratic ideas always crept back into microcorporatism. (pp. 197–98)

Waring (1991) concludes: "But the theory of good business government remained essentially the same as in Taylor's day. Management experts were still shoveling the same stuff, although with at least ten new kinds of shovels." (p. 203) Micklethwait and Woolridge (1996) also arrive at the same conclusion, that contemporary management theory is a hodgepodge served up by many for personal commercial success. Donaldson (1995) further underscores the hodgepodge notion by asserting that there is excessive paradigm proliferation in the service of self-promotion and presumably personal financial success, success that can only be acquired by providing managers tools to perpetuate their existence.

It therefore seems appropriate and perhaps necessary to develop new concepts for management theory and organization that challenge the status quo even though they profoundly and unprofitably question hierarchical bureaucratic organization and the accompanying legitimization of management roles. In this regard, ring organization design described in chapter 8 challenges bureaucratic rationality and hierarchical control. Also to be considered is that, while challenging the legitimacy of patriarchy and matriarchy as the psychological stuff of bureaucratic hierarchies, ring organization design does not advocate the elimination of constructs such as power, authority and specialization within organizations, but rather the transformation of the utility of these constructs by placing them into a new, less pathological context.

In Sum

The historical nature of the bureaucratic-hierarchy and its superabundance as the predominant organization form at the start of the twenty-first century present organization theorists an outstanding challenge to think beyond its thought-limiting paradigmatic nature. At the same time, anyone endeavoring to do so will encounter stiff resistance from those trying to continually perfect the bureaucratic-hierarchy as well as those who fill management positions created by and maintained by it. Nonetheless, the challenge remains to locate other forms of organization design that may be nurtured into existence by new management thinking that appreciates the psychodynamic and virtual workplaces.

IN CONCLUSION

This chapter provided a historical, theoretical and conceptual basis for understanding the development and proliferation of the bureaucratic-hierarchical organization design. This design is so common as to constitute a paradigm that heretofore has limited our ability to think outside of the box that it creates. Most contemporary literature directly or indirectly supports this contention. There is indeed little that is truly new in the literature that one cannot find in the literature prior to 1950. The exceptions are a growing understanding of the psychodynamic nature of the workplace albeit arising out of the development of psychoanalytic theory developed prior to 1950, and the potential represented by the virtual workplace that may reasonably be understood to have been created post-1950, although the theoretical basis for its creation may also be located prior to 1950.

The chapter concluded with an inspection of the bureaucratic-hierarchy for the challenge it poses anyone trying to envision non-bureaucratic and non-hierarchical organization design. Also to be appreciated is that whatever is offered must not be seen to be an extension of earlier thinking that amounts to just so much more repetition. In this regard I do not believe many will believe that ring organization design presented in the next chapter merely represents an extension of earlier thinking arising out of the Industrial Revolution's organization design, the bureaucratic-hierarchy.

Chapter 8

Ring Organization Design

Although one must gaze in wonderment at the accomplishments of these hierarchical modern organizations and the improvements they have made in the world, one hopes perhaps there could be a "better way." Theorists and teachers of business are constantly responding to this hope, and they do so by continuously proposing new and exciting organizational structures, procedures, technologies, programs, and processes to make the organization more effective and efficient and at the same time to increase commitment and esprit. Invariably they come up short.

(Czander, 1993, p. 1)

More specifically, new insights fail to get put into practice because they conflict with deeply held internal images of how the world works, images that limit us to familiar ways of thinking and acting.

(Senge, 1990, p. 174)

This chapter is devoted to the notion that coming up short in redesigning our organizations is not going to be good enough for the twenty-first century. Our modern-day reliance on hierarchical and invariably bureaucratic organizations challenges anyone trying to think of a new form of organization structure to have to think outside of the box. In this case the box amounts to an organizational design paradigm—the bureaucratic-hierarchy—that bounds thinking.

Postindustrial organization theory building has as one of its challenges conceiving of organizational forms for large-scale organization that are not based on the principles of bureaucracy and hierarchical structure while also avoiding simplistic thinking associated with a return to small preindustrial forms of organization (Bergquist, 1993). Notions of positions containing power and authority, people reporting to others of higher organizational status and reliance upon professional managers have to be avoided according to these prerequisites. Also to be avoided are rule-bound decision making that follows predetermined policies and procedures aimed at controlling human behavior in the workplace. If we, in fact, remove these familiar attributes of contemporary organizational life from the theory building process, we are confronted with a blank organizational design slate and no repertoire of ideas to write upon it. This is the challenge posed by postindustrial organizational and management thinking.

How indeed can an organization structure be conceived that does not contain hierarchy at its core? This has proven to be a challenge for management and organization theorists and consultants. It is only with the advent of cyberspace and information systems technology in the form of networks that a new form of organization structure can be conceived that does not implicitly or explicitly depend on some form of hierarchy and its accompanying routinizing, controlling, power and position conserving bureaucratic nature. Ring organization design described here represents but *one* possible way of getting unstuck from the bureaucratic-hierarchical paradigm.

The following discussion highlights a number of the attributes of a postindustrial ring-based organizational design that postulates the existence of three distinct workplaces within one organization—physical, potential and virtual. These workplaces are first described to orient the reader to the elements of ring organization design. This discussion is followed by a description of how a ring organization will operate in practice. Next a few thoughts are provided as to how ring organizations might be created. The chapter concludes with a consideration

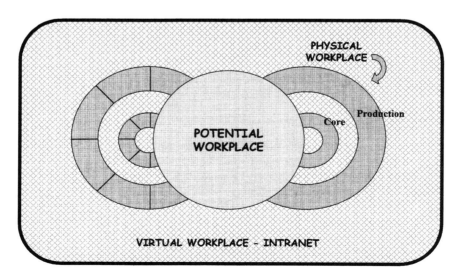

Figure 2. Ring Organization Design

of what it would be like to work within a ring organization. What might be the culture and values of a ring organization?

A proviso must also be mentioned. Ring organization design will confront the reader with many new thoughts that will appropriately promote skepticism and questions that have not been addressed by the description and discussion of ring organization design. Chapter 9 is devoted to an inspection of the efficacy of ring organization design using dynamic workplace theory. As far as the unanswered questions that will inevitably arise about ring organization design—my apologies.

RING ORGANIZATION IN THE WORKPLACE

Ring organization design embraces the true complexity of the twenty-first century workplace by acknowledging the presence of the physical, potential and virtual workplaces (see Figure 2). These workplaces coexist and interact to create what can become an anxiety-ridden experience of the workplace if not understood from a unified perspective.

The Physical Workplace—The Rings

The physical workplace of a ring organization provides a setting that supports the work of the core and production functions. Core functions are shared by all parts of the organization. These have historically been referred to as staff functions. Production functions are directly involved in the production of a product or service. Each function occupies its own physical space (offices or manufacturing site) and shares meeting/creative spaces with all of the functions.

Core Functions

Typical examples of core functions are: personnel, finance, accounting, payroll and information systems. Depending on the purpose and size of the organization, others may be added or some excluded. Ring organization design involves organizing employees and process into rings, one for each core function. Each ring represents a core function with its own specialized purpose (such as the personnel function) as well as specialization within the ring among members (such as compensation or benefits administration) as represented by the ring sections (see left side of Figure 2). These rings symbolize the *physical workplace*. They each have their own geographic location and they share the *potential workplace* as represented by a sphere through which the rings pass (Figure 2). The potential workplace exists for the purposes of sharing information and coordinating work. This shared conceptual organizational space and accompanying physical space provides much of the connectivity that "glues" organization members together. It creates a work setting where members of the core functions interact with each other and with members from the production rings to support global organizational activities such as organizational planning, decision making and implementation.

Physical space is designed to support the potential workplace by providing shared workspaces. Conference and meeting facilities and many other types of potentially creative spaces such as exercise facilities, gardens and eating places compose the physical setting of the shared potential work space. The creative and coordinative activities of this shared physical space are extended to the *virtual workplace* as represented by the intranet. Core organizational functions are, therefore, linked to each other and to the production functions not only by the potential of shared physical spaces but also by an intranet—the virtual workplace that provides a seamless sharing of information and ideas among organization members. It, like the shared physical spaces, provides a *virtual potential space* for organizational dialogue that continually creates and recreates the organization and its work (Bergquist, 1993). In sum, the shared physical and virtual potential workplaces provide flexibility, connectivity and organizational fluidity advocated by many organization theorists. Together they represent the creative chaos of the balanced workplace experience described by dynamic workplace theory. The potential and virtual workplaces are discussed further below.

Production Functions

The core functions and potential physical and virtual workplaces are joined to another set of rings (the production areas) that are created based on an in-depth understanding of the nature of the organization's work. Production functions usually possess their own physical locations as well as many more abstract qualities such as processes that must be managed. An important proviso of ring organization design must be mentioned. All rings are considered to possess organizational equality just as all members are organizationally equal. This proviso removes hierarchical values by creating an absence of organizationally based power, status and subordinancy.

Many possible production ring based design envisionments might be discussed. Two examples are considered here. They are the development of specialized and interdisciplinary production rings. A ring may be composed of specialists all of whom do the same work as part of a larger production process, such as work groups specialized in assembling different parts of a car or providing an element of a larger service for a specified group of customers (a ring without sections, see Figure 2). Rings may also be composed of interdisciplinary skill sets, such as a work group that assembles a complete car or provides a comprehensive service to customers or clients (a ring with sections, see Figure 2).

These and other types of production rings not mentioned pass through the same shared sphere of the potential workplace. The reader is reminded that the potential workplace serves to coordinate work and share information among the production and core rings. The production rings are, like the core functions, also surrounded by the intranet—the virtual workplace, which links them together through universally shared information. The virtual workplace creates a forum where operating problems, decisions, threats and opportunities are discussed and addressed by organization members.

In Sum

The physical workplace is composed of discrete work locations and shared creative spaces where core staff and production functions collaborate to develop and produce products and services. Each of the core and production functions represents a coequal ring in the organization that passes through the sphere of shared physical and virtual organizational space where information sharing and mutual coordination of work are achieved.

The Potential Workplace

The potential workplace is a conceptual setting where organization members meet to discuss work, problems, decisions and opportunities (Figure 2). It is a place where work is planned, implemented, coordinated and monitored. The potential workplace contains what has historically been management's areas of responsibility—planning, organizing, leading, managing human resources and coordinating and controlling work. These are all important functions for large organizations to accomplish that have historically been handled by a management hierarchy and policies and procedures that tell workers what work to perform and how and when to perform it. An important quality that is the key to the potential workplace's success is that this workspace must be a psychologically safe and open holding environment where all sides of a discussion are explored (the balanced workplace described by dynamic workplace theory). The absence of formal positions of power and authority and the avoidance of an overdependence upon rules and regulations contribute to the ability to create and sustain this attribute of the potential workplace.

Another important aspect of the potential workplace is its ambiguous nature. It symbolizes how an organization's work might be accomplished if no one were formally in charge (a characteristic of hierarchical organization design). It becomes a bossless creative skunk works (discussed further below) where traditional bureaucratic hierarchical protocols are absent. Anyone who has experienced in-groups in the hierarchical workplace has very likely experienced an outcome where a group came to have a life of its own. It functioned in ways unanticipated at the start. Surprising creativity and innovation may have emerged. Groups left to their own devices possess many potential leaders who volunteer their leadership to support the group's work. Leaderless groups or groups that do not follow the direction of their hierarchically appointed leader are not leaderless for long. Most often the roles of leadership have a temporary and intermittent quality to them as work progresses from one point to another. The initial leadership provided by one individual is eventually supplanted by the leadership of others who have something to contribute to a given phase of the work.

It is, therefore, a fundamental premise of ring organization design that members of rings will spontaneously find the means to work together on self-identified tasks in support of a jointly derived, shared and continually revised organizational vision and operating plan. Similarly, inter-ring collaboration spontaneously arises in the interactive space of the potential workplace. The potentiality of the space is, therefore, put to good use as a result of the natural desire on the part of organization members to accomplish work. Ring organization design is, it should be noted, based on the proposition that people can develop a balanced work experience as well as maintain it over the long run. Creativity is accessed without chaos. Structure is created without compulsive needs to control everything via rules and regulations. Leadership is provided without an overdependence developing upon the leader, who does not seek excessive authority, power and control.

In Sum

Potential workspace is a conceptual space for shared creation and innovation for all organization members in all rings. It is referred to as potential in that it provides resources and conceptual space for accomplishing coordination and leadership of an organization. However, it does more than this. Potential space creates a vacuum that pulls organization members together to create, maintain and operate their organization. In this regard it is a potential that acts directly on organization members so as to fulfil its potential. This notion underlies the assertion or perhaps assumption that if people are simply left alone by managers in hierarchies they will get the work of the organization done (Hall, 1994). It is the nature of human behavior in an organizational context to volunteer information, leadership, direction, ideas, risk taking, coordination of effort and hard work. Leaderless groups are not leaderless for long. Groups created without direction are not directionless for long. Potential space is, therefore, filled with the many qualities of the people who create an organization every day that they come to work.

The Virtual Workplace

The technology to support organization-wide networking in the form of intranets is available and continually improving as we commence the twenty-first century. It is not my purpose here to discuss the nature of this technology, but rather to focus on the organizational implications of its use. The proposed post-industrial revolution organization, the ring organization, will place all aspects of its operation onto the intranet for inspection and discussion by all employees (Allcorn, 1997). Exceptions to this approach may be made for highly confidential individual information such as payroll and benefits. Organization members will be trained to use the intranet and encouraged to use it. They will be provided access to computers either at their desks or in shared spaces such as libraries and multimedia learning centers. User-friendly software will be provided to further enable employees to inquire into the organization's virtual space. In particular, employees are encouraged to think critically about what they see and hear as well as use online analytical tools to evaluate database information to test out their own ideas. In order to fully tap the creative potential of all employees, they are provided protected time to explore and contribute to their virtual workplace and rewarded for its use in successfully locating problems and solutions to problems. Additionally, the intranet capability will provide Internet access to the global community where operating problems may be discussed and answers and information obtained. All organization members will know any exclusions such as a secret formula and confidential information.

It is fair to say not all employees will be motivated to explore the potential of virtual workspace, but many will. Opinion leaders and individuals with inquiring minds can be expected to make use of this potential. Others may participate in ways better suited to their interests, such as in online chat groups. At the very least, organization members will not readily feel that secret information and decisions are being made in a top-down and unilateral fashion as occurs in hierarchical organizations. Those that do not choose to use the virtual space will at the very least hear from others who may carry forward their ideas and messages from the physical workplace into the virtual workplace. The virtual workplace is, therefore, consistent with the balanced work experience described by dynamic organization theory.

In Sum

The organizational equality of the social and physical workplaces is mirrored in the organizational equality of the virtual workplace. Nearly all available information about the past, present and future operation of the organization is available on the intranet in a user-friendly manner. This information is accompanied by many easily understood analytical tools that facilitate employees in performing their own analyses of the data. The virtual workplace is, therefore, filled with exceptional potential for communication, sharing of ideas, testing ideas and creativity that enhances organizational performance.

The virtual workplace will also contain home pages for the organization as a whole, rings and ring sections and individual organization members, social groups and so on. Any aspect of the potential and physical workplaces may appear on the intranet. The virtual workplace will also support open discussions and exploration of the workings of the organization. These discussions may range from highly detailed discussion of operating problems to the actions of competitors and the discovery of new threats and opportunities. These discussions will include the stakeholders involved with the topic to insure all sides of the problem, threat or opportunity are explored. The virtual workplace will, therefore, also provide the potential for the creation of a community of employees and their interests and by doing so will transcend its virtual nature.

The nature of ring organization structure has been described as containing three distinctly different workplaces (physical, potential, virtual) that together, I suggest, create a context for a functional postindustrial revolution nonhierarchical and non-bureaucratic form of organization. The discussion of these workplaces no doubt raises many additional questions in the hearts and minds of anyone reading about them. In particular, one might wonder how a ring organization will operate and how it might be created given the nature of current organizational design and operation.

RING ORGANIZATION DESIGN IN OPERATION

Organizations have implicit and explicit prerequisites for their functioning. Ring organization design is not an exception. Ring organizations must accomplish the traditional management functions such as planning, directing, staffing and monitoring of organization performance. These and all other related management functions are accomplished within the potential workplace discussed above. Leadership in the management of the organization is expected to spontaneously arise within the potential workplace as well as within the rings (the physical workplace) with the virtual workplace also making many contributions. It becomes the task of those working within the potential workplace to synthesize and balance the knowledge, ideas, interests and concerns articulated in the physical and virtual workplaces. Consensus-building interpersonal skills will be valued within the potential workplace. Other aspects of organizational functioning such as the management of human resources will occur primarily within each ring, supported by a core human resources management function. Similarly, other activities such as budget management and individual ring task assignments will be managed in much the same way. Decision making within rings is, however, open to inspection by other rings and by all activities carried out within the potential and virtual workplaces. In this regard a healthy sense of inquiry and critical and systemic thinking occurs to optimize organizational performance. To be avoided are competitive and self-serving interactions that often seem to create interminable group process, as is the case in hierarchical organizations. The openness, sharing and reflectivity of the potential and virtual workplaces as well as the physical workplace are a strength rather than a weakness when viewed from the unilateral, take-charge, command-and-control culture of bureaucratic hierarchies.

The importance of organizational planning, implementation, performance monitoring and coordination cannot be understated for twenty-first century organizations. These aspects of ring organization design merit further elaboration. To be noted in the discussion is the availability of information, and the presence of organizational dialogue and consensus building. I also suggest that these organizational prerequisites may be set as ring organization tasks from the start or discovered to be essential by ring organization members as they press forward to accomplish work.

Organizational Planning

This critically important activity, informed by performance information and the ongoing dialogue within the physical and virtual workplaces, is best performed by a work group assembled by including one or more members from each ring. The result is an interdisciplinary group drawn from all aspects of the organization. The work group decides upon its own leadership and process and will receive support from planning expertise within the core functions. Group process expertise is also available from the core human resources management function. Plans are shared with organization members in the virtual workplace for discussion and feedback before being adopted and acted upon. Decision making to arrive at a final plan is by consensus where everyone's point of view in the organization is heard if offered, but not necessarily incorporated into the final plan. Planning is viewed to be a process and, therefore, subject to constant scrutiny by all organization members and the subject of an ongoing dialogue in the physical and virtual workplaces, leading to continual renewal of the plans. This work group as well as those to be discussed is expected to include members from the other two work groups to further promote coordination and information sharing. Additionally, a free flow of meeting minutes and other information is shared in the virtual workplace.

Planning Implementation and Decision Making

Many daily operating decisions are made by those closest to the decision arena. The rings are responsible for developing decision-making groups as needed to address intra-ring processes (discussed further below). However, inevitably, there are many decisions that must be made for the organization as a whole (inter-ring decisions). The decision-making work group is assembled from members of all rings. Its work is informed by the work of the planning group and information contained within the physical and virtual workplaces. Its tasks are planning implementation and the making of organizational decisions. Tentative decisions sometimes referred to as trial balloons are shared with organization members in the physical and virtual workplace for feedback and discussion. The emergence of consensus is expected to build toward a final decision. A second decision-making process, when time is short, is to ask each ring to recommend a decision and locate the commonalities among these decisions to create a final decision (not unlike parallel computing). Decisions, once made, are allocated to the appropriate rings for implementation based on a plan of action that is also discussed in the physical and virtual workplaces.

Monitoring Organizational Performance

Ring organizations possess information- and knowledge-rich physical and virtual workplaces where organization members, individual rings and the performance-monitoring work group (also assembled from ring members) share information and insights about organizational performance. Rings are individually responsible for monitoring their own performance. Organization-wide performance issues that may include performance issues relative to one or more rings are addressed by the work group, which will, once again, work in the open and share its thoughts and ideas for remediating performance problems before they are implemented by the decision-making work group. Solutions to operating problems may include changes to one or more rings, including the possibility of dissolution of a ring when its work is at an end. Ring members will preferably be distributed to new rings or among rings short of members. The planning and decision-making work group will be constantly kept informed of this group's work.

Intra-Ring Management

Each ring is responsible for its own operation, such as hiring members as well as rewarding and disciplining members. Each ring is assigned tasks and resources by the above planning and decision-making work groups, and is monitored for performance. Instances where resources allotted to tasks need to be adjusted will be carried back to the performance-monitoring work group by the ring members participating within the work group, as well as posted to the virtual workplace (Allcorn, 1997). Each ring is expected to create its own planning, decision-making, and performance-monitoring work groups as well as assume full responsibility for human resources management and intra-ring leadership. In this regard intra-ring work groups are in parallel with those of the larger organization. Rings may organize themselves in any way their members see fit, with the results posted to the intranet for understanding, inspection and discussion. For example, each ring must address the issue of compensation and rewards for good performance. Some rings may choose to reward individual performance while others may focus on the ring as a whole. Compensation will be governed by ring resources, the marketplace and compliance to externally imposed laws. Additional compensation is not permitted for participation in ring or organizational work groups, which implies an organizationally based status differentiation. Rings are also expected to locate a balance between numbers of members and compensation. Last, the notions of career advancement and personal development are managed both within rings and by the core human resources and organizational development functions. Given that a hierarchy of roles is absent, organization members can, nonetheless, gain experience and new skills that permit them to take on new and different work that is more highly valued by the rings and organization.

The Absence of an Excessively Controlling Bureaucracy

A final operating consideration is how the absence of detailed rules and regulations will affect work. Rules and regulations are of value to respond to the legal environment, such as the proper legal steps to pursue progressive discipline or standardized aspects of work such as the use of electronic forms. The presence of some policy, rules and regulations in and of themselves does not translate into a rule-bound and red tape-filled bureaucracy. The entire ring organization must be committed to avoiding this negative side to operating procedures. At the same time, many user-friendly approaches can be developed to both guide and educate organization members on the routine side of organizational life. The virtual workplace may be filled with guidelines and decisions-support software, question and answer material and case examples, all of which serve to inform and educate rather than limit and control.

Incorporating the External World

Ring organizations, like bureaucratic-hierarchical organizations, operate within a larger socioeconomic sphere. In particular, interest groups such as customers or clients as well as vendors and the local community all have a stake in an organization's operation. Ring organization accommodates these interests by enlisting participation in interest group–specific rings. Vendors, for example, may be organized into a ring devoted to understanding and improving organizational performance. Their voluntary participation in their respective ring creates the potential of a win-win working relationship with the ring organization.

I now turn to a discussion of the attractiveness of ring organizations to their members and how the organization is created and experienced. The question must be asked, "What's it like to work here?" This question introduces the perspective of organizational culture and values. However, before proceeding to this discussion a brief note must be added on the relationship of this discussion to contemporary management literature.

In Sum

Ring organization creates a non-bureaucratic, nonhierarchical workplace where everyone within the organization and each ring possesses equal organization status. The language used to describe the new organization is simple and should avoid the use of buzzwords and metaphors such as teams that conceal hierarchical organizational attributes. The actual operation of a ring organization promotes information sharing and consensus building to manage the organization as a whole and each ring individually. The collegial nature of the balanced workplace experience encourages creativity and productivity in the service of organizational success.

A NOTE ON RING-RELATED THINKING IN THE MANAGEMENT LITERATURE

There are, as has been alluded to, substantial dysfunctions that are a part of the traditional bureaucratic hierarchy. This appreciation has led to many innovations within the paradigm that may be seen to be precursors to the proposed ring organization model. Kanter (1983), for example, discusses the parallel participative organization. She writes:

An innovating organization needs at least two organizations, two ways of arraying and using its people. It needs a hierarchy with specified tasks and functional groupings for carrying out what it already knows how to do, that it can anticipate will be the same in the future. But it also needs a set of flexible vehicles for figuring out how to do what it does not yet know—for encouraging entrepreneurs and engaging the grass roots as well as the elite in the mastery of innovation and change. (p. 205)

This parallel organization advocated by Kanter provides a creative space where employees are free to work together regardless of their field or level. This need for a parallel organization unencumbered by the limitations of the bureaucratic hierarchy is also implicit in Peters and Waterman's discussion of a skunk works in their book, *In Search of Excellence* (1982).

A more contemporary view of how to change bureaucratic hierarchies that contains aspects of the proposed ring model may be drawn from Hammer and Champy's 1993 book, *Reengineering the Corporation*. They write:

In companies that have reengineered, however, organizational structure isn't such a weighty issue. Work is organized around processes and the teams that perform them. Lines of communication? People communicate with whomever they need. Control is vested in the people performing the process. Consequently, whatever organization structure remains after reengineering tends to be flat, as work is performed by teams of essentially coequal people operating with great autonomy and supported by a few managers—few, because while a manager can typically supervise only about seven people, he or she can coach close to thirty. (p. 78)

Many others have provided useful content that supports ring design. Lawler (1988) asserts that everyone in the hierarchy above the production level produces nothing of value. He speaks of self-managing work groups and emergent leadership. Howell and his coauthors (1990) discuss substitutes for leadership. Barry (1991) discusses distributed leadership and managing the bossless team. Hall (1994) asserts employees know how to be productive if managers will simply let them assume responsibility. Taylor, Friedman and Couture (1987) report on an organization experiment that successfully turned most management responsibilities over to employees.

All of these authors are speaking to the problem of trying to "wire around" the limitations of the bureaucratic hierarchy. Some suggest forming separate entities that are for the most part free of the dysfunctions. Others suggest that hierarchy can be minimized, suspended or in some way eliminated. All of these considerations offer support to any effort to envision a new nonhierarchical and non-bureaucratic organization design such as ring design.

In Sum

Ring organization design may on the surface seem to be a radical departure from the past. However, many of its elements have been proposed by consultants and scholars in the past as well as used by organizations to improve their performance. What has been missing is the envisionment of a larger context into which to place these many different perspectives. Ring organization design, therefore, represents one effort to provide this larger context.

THE ORIGINS OF RING ORGANIZATIONS

Ring organization design, I conjecture, may arise in a number of ways. Much like in the discussion of the industrial revolution, consideration must be given to the changing ways in which work is performed and products created along with a gradual shift in our society. It is always hazardous to speculate on what is happening at the moment and where events are taking us. Having duly noted this, one possible understanding of where we are now is at the leading edge in a fundamental shift in the nature of how work is performed and how products are created. Some have said we are beginning the information age or are in the midst of an information revolution supported by ever more sophisticated information technologies that speed data collection and knowledge generation and sharing. Ring organization design represents one possible response to these interpretations of where we are. And, to the extent that these changes are a reality, the direction of change is also fairly clear as we look toward the notion of the generation of intellectual products of all forms—hardware, software, biological, mathematical, chemical. When one takes these considerations into account the context in which ring design may arise emerges.

The Interpersonal and Social Context of Creation

The prerequisites of avoiding position-based power, status and subordinancy lead one to think of organizational structures that by their nature serve to promote organizational equality and the absence of superior/subordinate relations that implicitly include interpersonal issues pertaining to dominance and submission. These new organization structures that maintain personal integrity and individual diversity must also avoid homogenization where individual differences and self-differentiation are stifled. Homogenization tends to eliminate important organizational contributions such as spontaneous leadership and location of valued skill-sets for problem solving and work accomplishment (Allcorn, 1991 and Allcorn and Diamond, 1997). The problem is, of course, to envision an organization form that achieves both of these outcomes. One possible organizational form that meets these criteria is the circle.

When people enter a room full of scattered chairs to work on a task they most often and without discussing it arrange them into a circle. It seems safe to say that virtually everyone in our society has had occasion to experience this dynamic that implicitly provides an organizational structure for task accomplishment while simultaneously promising interpersonal equality. Conceptually, a circle contains an infinite number of points that are all the same distance from the center, which symbolically represents the locus of power. The circle is, I believe, perceived by its members as creating a social context of organizational equality that promotes interpersonal safety, self-differentiation and personal integrity. The circle or ring, therefore, represents a basis for the design of a non-hierarchical organization where, by its nature, members tend to experience themselves as socially equal but also self-differentiated.

Ring equality seems to be intuitively sensed as secure by its members. Attachment to the group comprising the circle, it is suggested here, is not inherently conflicted by issues such as dominance and submission. In its purest sense it is a round table without a king. Everyone is coequal. However, ring organization design provides for more than implicit equality. The purpose of ring organization design is to create an organization culture (discussed below) that explicitly provides for interpersonal equality and integrity where members of a ring or members of many rings have as their starting point coequality. In a sense, everyone is hired into a ring organization as equals.

One might reasonably wonder at this point if this dynamic of interpersonal equality within and among rings is true if created. My experience as an executive and consultant tends to support this assumption. I have created this organizational context in a number of large organizations for the purposes of improving organizational performance as an executive and as a strategic planning consultant. It is my observation that if people are left alone to work together, coequality not only emerges but they also accomplish a lot of good work (Hall, 1994). In the case of strategic planning this dynamic is achieved by selecting participants by making a diagonal slice through a hierarchical organization. The planning group that results contains the CEO, many senior level executives as well as secretarial and clerical staff and other workers. Everyone's voice is treated as coequal by the facilitating consultants. The outcome of this approach is that ideas and leadership are just as likely to arise from staff as from the executives. Everyone joins together for the planning work after the initial testing of the new work context by many who are suspicious that the hierarchy of power and authority has not been left out of the process.

In Sum

Firsthand experience combined with observations of group dynamics provides anecdotal evidence to support the notion that the inherent equality that lies within the nature of rings can create the basis for a new organization design that can get things done. The absence of organizational hierarchy and accompanying rules and regulations must, however, raise more questions than thus far answered. We are still left with the problem of taking the observation that rings can work in specific instances and transforming it into a workable organization design.

CREATING RING ORGANIZATIONS

Ring organizations may arise from three likely sources. Each of these origins, it must be noted, contains difficult and problematic aspects that have to be overcome to establish a successful ring organization design or redesign. It is perhaps the easiest to start a new organization using the ring design although changing a traditional organization to a ring organization is equally possible if effective leadership is provided. The three likely sources and some of the challenges are briefly discussed. It is not possible to provide greater detail about the complexities of this organizational design/redesign work due to the peculiarities that reside within every organizational setting. The challenges mentioned do, however, provide an indicator of how demanding the change to a ring design may be. It should also be noted that the three sources are not intended to exhaust the possibilities for creating a ring organization. They merely represent three of the most common starting points of any type of organization design or redesign.

Entrepreneurial Redesign

Ring organizations may arise from the efforts of entrepreneurs and business owners who have created or inherited a traditional hierarchical organization. The founder and/or owner is presumably empowered to change the organization as he or she sees fit. This amount of power and control, however, does not mean that change can be unilaterally imposed. If a ring redesign is undertaken, the nature of the change process must be consistent with ring organization culture and values (discussed below). It is also important to appreciate that the first and greatest problem to be faced is that the entrepreneur must accept that a successful ring organization redesign eliminates his or her unique status of president or CEO, but not that of owner who expects a return on investment. The entrepreneur must simultaneously provide the needed leadership in the service of change while gradually nurturing the functioning of the ring organization into existence.

As ring organization redesign unfolds and the accompanying culture and values are embraced by organization members, the role of the entrepreneur will gradually atrophy. During this process the entrepreneur must be careful not to reassert his or her formal role as the ring redesign emerges. To be avoided is sending the wrong signals to organization members, who will be alert to the possibility that the redesign is just another screen to conceal traditional organizational hierarchy.

It is not my purpose here to provide a detailed explanation of exactly how this migration to ring organization design can occur. It is, however, easy to image the many challenges that will have to be met to address peculiarities that reside within the entrepreneur, the leadership group and employees as well as the technical features of the organization. Some turnover will no doubt occur as the nature of the roles within a ring organization design is embraced. In particular, many in management will have to adjust to what is essentially their losing their hierarchically based jobs and status. They may choose to locate new positions in other hierarchical organizations. Last, ring organization design requires the creation of a rich and robust information system to support the virtual workplace. This will invariably require considerable investment of time and money to create. It is, therefore, essential to appreciate that a successful ring redesign must be coordinated with the development of this enabling information generation and sharing feature of ring organization design.

Bureaucratic–Hierarchical Redesign

Ring organizations may also arise from traditional bureaucratic-hierarchical organizations where the governing board, leadership and members agree to try a ring organization redesign. The migration to ring organization will be more challenging than that led by an owner/entrepreneur. More specifically, it will be maximally challenging in terms of unlearning traditional organizational concepts and values and learning the new ones for the ring design. Once again transitional leadership is essential and it must be accompanied by a constant focus on educating employees about the nature of the change, how ring organization works and the accompanying culture and values.

The leaders in this case are not the owners of the organization and will not feel as threatened in a monetary sense. They should also not feel as personally invested in their organization as it is not "their baby." The major challenge in converting a large bureaucratic-hierarchy to a ring design is overcoming the deeply entrenched nature of the bureaucratic-hierarchical culture and values that can be expected to generate considerable resistance on the part of organization members to the change. Also to be considered is the essential redesign of the information system into one that supports the ring organization's virtual workplace. In this case many large organizations will have to carefully design their information system migration path in order to avoid excessive costs. Once again, coordination of the change in design, operations, culture and values with the evolution of the information system is essential.

Startup Ring Design

An individual (an entrepreneur) who recruits others to form a ring organization may create a ring organization from the start. Recruitment into this new organization, while confronting prospective members with a radical new organization design, should not be difficult because of the very nature of the design. This recruitment assumption is supported by the alienation many workers feel toward their bureaucratic-hierarchical organizations. These organizations have a long and well-documented history of stifling the most creative and dynamic employees, who invariably seek opportunities to work within organizations where their talents and skills are valued (Downs, 1967). Many may find this new risky endeavor to their liking, which will further invigorate organization members by creating a sense of participation in something new and exciting.

Despite the fresh start, anyone who is attempting the start-up of a ring organization has several challenges that must be met. First, the individual must keep the focus on nurturing the development of the ring design and accept that his or her influential role of initially leading the development must atrophy. Second, organization members must be constantly worked with in order to reinforce the ring organization design, culture and values. There is always the tendency to ask the hierarchically based question, "Who is in charge here?" Last, a new information system design must be created and implemented to support the ring organization's virtual workplace. In this case it will evolve with the growth of the organization and this, while creating many challenges, will permit the timely and sensitive adaptation of the system to the realities of a growing and changing ring organization design. Creating a ring organization presents a major challenge for anyone with the wherewithal to lead the change. The nature of this challenge is further underscored by the unique nature of organizational culture and values that must be simultaneously nurtured into existence.

In Sum

Ring organizations contain familiar aspects associated with professional organizations where coequality exists to a large extent and with democratic organizations where everyone gets to participate in decision making. Ring organization is essentially a blend of these two approaches to designing an organizational culture. In this regard ring organization design is not per se so foreign after all. There are elements that are familiar to everyone. The actual creation of a ring organization is, however, a challenging undertaking for anyone endeavoring to lead organizational change. This may be fairly easy to do for an entrepreneur/owner who initially has the power to initiate the change. However, he or she must also accept that his or her control over the organization must be eventually lost. A more challenging context is changing a large preexisting bureaucratic-hierarchy to a ring organization. In this case the leaders should be less personally invested in the organization as it is not "their baby." At the same time, they still stand to lose their hierarchically based position of power and authority. Also to be overcome will be the deeply entrenched culture, values and operating protocols of the bureaucratic-hierarchy as well as the need to redesign information systems to support the ring design. Last, and perhaps the easiest to do is to start a new organization based on ring design. In this case the person leading the development of the new organization (the entrepreneur) must start with the appreciation that his or her hard work as leader will eventually be taken over by the very nature of the ring design. Recruitment into this new organization design is expected to be relatively easy and very likely to attract many who will be excited to try something new. Information systems in this case will grow with the organization.

RING ORGANIZATIONAL CULTURE AND VALUES

The ring organization is a culture of interpersonal trust, respect, openness, collaboration and inquiry where the pursuit of the best ideas to make the organization more effective is the primary task. Information sharing is a norm that encourages the generation of new insights, ideas and knowledge that are shared and tested in all three workplaces—physical, potential and virtual. All aspects of the organization and its operation are open to inquiry. This dynamic helps to sustain balanced work experience by calling into question psychological and socially defensive trends of in-group and organizational process.

Decision making, as noted, becomes a product of the entire membership of the organization. Organization members openly discuss and work through problem identification and resolution as well as strategic and tactical direction within the three workplaces. The directions and problem resolution emerge as an outcome of a system-wide or systemic search for improved performance. Leadership as mentioned arises spontaneously. Individual members of rings and participants in potential and virtual workplaces are expected to provide leadership as the need arises. Individuals who are enthusiastic about the work or who tolerate less ambiguity than others can be depended upon to assert their leadership when it is needed.

This presumption regarding human nature represents the "energy" that fulfills the need for leadership in the ring design, and it merits reemphasis. In my experience as an executive and consultant who has intentionally created many leaderless groups to accomplish clear and important workplace tasks, I have seldom been disappointed with the ability of these groups to locate leadership as needed and to achieve their assigned task. Groups invariably include individuals who are looked to by others to provide leadership. These individuals may have provided leadership in the past or have been depended upon to provide key information and their opinions. They are simply perceived to have the "right stuff." It is also the case that groups often contain one or more individuals who are enthusiastic about the group and the assigned task. They respond to the stress of accomplishing the task and working within the group by seeking to work on the task. They are often so personally energetic and eager to get on with the work that they facilitate those providing leadership (carry out work on key tasks) or willingly assume personal risk by providing direction to accomplish work. This eagerness is an integrated and mature response to the situation as compared with the next observation. Leadership and the taking of action in an initially ambiguous situation may also arise from individuals who are personally distressed about the stressful ambiguity that resides in the leaderless group context where the group is being depended upon to accomplish an assigned task. Their aversive experience of anxiety motivates them to act to provide leadership or direction or to take some action to change the situation. In this regard, all psychologically defensive coping is not per se bad. It may well lead to good work by the individual and group. To be avoided, however, is the compulsive pursuit of power and glory by an individual who, out of immediate awareness, is seeking to prop up shaky self-esteem and compensate for a narcissistic deficit. This outcome is not consistent with the values of ring organizations. These considerations of the origins of leadership in an ambiguous context are also mirrored in the larger organization where organizational boundaries may also serve to alleviate workplace anxiety.

The notion of organizational boundaries, while existing between rings in the physical workplace and between ring members and those participating in work groups such as in the potential workplace, does not exist in the virtual workplace where organizational "us/them" splits are overcome as discussed below. The lack of a rigidly adhered to organizational hierarchy avoids the development of anxieties that may arise out of dominance and submission issues. The absence of hierarchy in ring organizations avoids many of the perverse organizational dynamics associated with the psychologically and socially defensive group dynamics described by dynamic workplace theory. The culture and values of ring organization design lead to a consideration of how exactly the organization will be experienced.

In Sum

The much more open and interpersonally safe operating context of ring organizations creates a shared context where the assumption of personal responsibility is encouraged. Greater trust and respect and the avoidance of the dominance and submission issues associated with hierarchical organizations that alienate organization members from themselves, their work, their skills, each other and the organization are avoided. Organization members are, therefore, much less focused on personal survival and defending against threatening interpersonal and group membership experience. The avoidance of the defensive group and organizational experiences explained by dynamic workplace theory releases considerable creative and productive energy back into the service of making the organization a better place to work and more successful.

THE EXPERIENTIAL CONTEXT OF RING ORGANIZATION

There exists a bidirectional interaction between the form an organization takes and the unconscious proclivities of its members (Czander, 1993). Bureaucratic-hierarchical organizations, while providing rational prerequisites for coordination of a specialized workforce, also create a context for individual functioning and interpersonal relations that is invariably influenced by unconscious and frequently dysfunctional intrapsychic, interpersonal and group dynamics (Allcorn and Diamond, 1997). Organizational structure itself may, therefore, as dynamic workplace theory indicates, be an outcome of psychological and socially defensive systems aimed at mastering member anxiety. This interplay appears to be especially vulnerable to acts of psychic compensation by individuals who possess narcissistic deficits as well as by those who have paranoid and sadistic tendencies.

It is not my purpose to further elaborate these bureaucratic-hierarchical attributes and their accompanying dysfunctions. They have been described and analyzed by many authors (Allcorn, 1994; Allcorn and Diamond, 1997; Baum, 1987, 1990; Czander, 1993; Diamond, 1993; Downs, 1967; Gabriel, 1999; Hummel, 1982 and Schwartz, 1990). However, it is important to note that all organizations, including post-industrial organizations, possess this interaction between structure and the personalities of members. The following discussion explores some of these dynamics within the larger context of a ring organization design. In particular, it is important to appreciate how a ring organization may be experienced in a manner that will promote anxiety and concomitant psychological defensiveness that adversely affects performance.

Ring Organization May Promote Member Anxiety

Ring organizations can be expected to promote anxiety in at least four ways. First, the lack of power and authority associated with management positions and status differentials associated with hierarchical positions can be expected to evoke anxiety on the part of some members. Employees who perhaps out of awareness seek to develop idealizing attachments with powerful leaders or their superiors will not be able to accomplish their unconsciously motivated interpersonal agenda. Psychologically, the desire to make these attachments is often profoundly influenced by infant, child and adult experience associated with poor quality interpersonal attachments to other powerful parental figures and significant others (Diamond, 1993; Horney, 1950 and Kohut, 1984). These strongly held and unconsciously motivated desires to form idealizing and frequently self-effacing attachments will, in large part, be frustrated by the lack of incumbents of traditional roles of power and authority. Worse, these individuals may be asked to assume roles of leadership when they prefer to follow and be taken care of by a leader.

A second anxiety-promoting aspect of a ring organization work setting is that it eliminates the ability of those who unconsciously wish to rival and replace powerful authoritative figures from acting out these tendencies as is readily possible in hierarchical organizations. Attacking and competing against others is inconsistent with ring organization values and is discouraged by organization members. In contrast, deeply felt needs to assume roles of leadership to acquire admiration and narcissistic supplies, rather than being frustrated by organizational design are supported by ring design, although the arrogant and vindictive use of these roles is inconsistent with ring organization values.

A third aspect of ring organization that promotes anxiety is the ambiguity as to who is in charge. Members who have unconscious and often compulsive needs to control their anxiety by making sure others and situations are under someone's control will feel anxious about the ambiguity and the lack of any one individual who is permanently in charge. The lack of a rigid organizational structure with designated hierarchical leaders may be thought of as moving organization members closer to a sense of organizational chaos where they must trust in the nature of bounded chaos and emergent and self-organizing organizational experience (Diamond, 1999 and Stacey, 1992). The outcome, as Diamond (1999) notes, may be a good enough holding environment and transitional space between order and chaos if member anxiety does not become excessive, thereby introducing psychological regression. Additionally, the use of task groups and consensus building will not provide a setting for acquiring control and dominating others. These anxious individuals may constantly point out how ineffective and slow groups are in providing organizational direction and leadership even if it is present (Allcorn and Diamond, 1997).

The fourth area of consideration is that the ability to work hidden interpersonal agendas in the hope of personally benefiting is stifled by the open and inquisitive nature of a ring organization. This aspect of contemporary organizations is often threatening and demoralizing to those who do not choose to "play the game," which often entails ingratiating oneself to powerful authority figures. This method of managing one's anxiety by attempting to control others is inconsistent with ring organization values and process and the inability to pursue it can be expected to frustrate individuals who prefer to cope with their anxieties in this manner.

These four aspects of ring organization do not exhaust the possible list of anxiety-promoting elements that this new organization structure contains. However, also to be appreciated is that the ring structure may also allay many anxieties surrounding the quality of the attachment of the individual to the organization. The more open, trusting and participative nature of a ring organization may well allay anxieties about being engulfed and dominated by the organization and powerful others or unexpectedly abandoned. In this regard, the four origins of anxiety discussed, while often unique to individuals who bring unconscious motivations into the workplace, may be ameliorated at the individual, interpersonal, group and organizational levels by the reflective, inclusive and participative values and structure of ring organizations. The management of member anxiety and concomitant psychological and interpersonal defensiveness becomes an important consideration as is underscored by dynamic workplace theory. Anxiety will inevitably be present in every type of organization. It is, therefore, essential to explore not only how ring organizations promote anxiety but how their culture facilitates its management and, better yet, avoidance. This anxiety management process is discussed in terms of intrapersonal, interpersonal and group membership anxiety. However, discussed first is the presence of organizational boundaries as an anxiety-allaying organizational attribute.

In Sum

The bidirectional influence that exists between organizations and the unconscious nature of their members contains both positive and negative outcomes. Organization members who have essentially grown up with the bureaucratic-hierarchical organization model will find that many of their approaches to managing themselves, their anxieties and others are no longer effective in ring organizations. Ring organization members will not be facilitated by organization dynamics that encourage interpersonal competitiveness and clawing one's way to the top. At the same time, the lack of powerful authority figures in high positions may make many ring organization members anxious about who is in charge and who will make the decisions. The much greater collegiality and consensus-building aspects of the ring organization, it must be appreciated, will inevitably make some organization members feel anxious. At the same time many of the more perverse psychological and socially defensive tendencies of the hierarchical workplace are avoided. Organization members will feel more trusting and accepting of themselves and each other and, therefore, less defensive.

Organizational Boundary Management as a Means of Managing Member Anxiety

Hierarchical organizations are filled with many vertical and horizontal boundaries (layers and silos or smokestacks). Ring organizations also possess internal boundaries. Each ring is a work group that is differentiated from other rings. The potential organization is a conceptual organizational space with a boundary. The presence of work groups that plan, make decisions and manage performance also imply boundaries between organization members and membership in these groups within the potential workplace. Boundaries such as these within ring organizations can be expected to introduce some anxiety-allaying structure as well as anxiety-promoting difficulties in communication and coordination and provide the context for an "us versus them" experience. In this regard, hierarchical and ring organizations are understood to contain internal boundaries that share in common anxiety allaying and promoting aspects.

The challenge for ring organizations is to build upon the positive contributions of boundaries while minimizing their negative outcomes. Boundaries within ring organizations must be recognized as potential problem areas that can be avoided by continually promoting communications, maintaining open participation and developing working relationships throughout the organization.

The goal is to recognize that the boundaries do exist and that their negative outcomes can be avoided. In particular, the negative effects of these organizational boundaries may be overcome by the boundary-collapsing nature of the virtual workplace. The virtual workplace presents organization members with as near as possible a boundaryless context that may, it must be noted, promote anxiety about its operation and what will happen to oneself when participating within the virtual workplace (Allcorn, 1997). At the same time, the virtual workplace creates an exceptionally open (boundaryless), interactive and creative setting for organization members. The full realization of its potential, it may be readily appreciated, depends on the presence of the anxiety-busting ring organization values of trust, respect, openness, collaboration and inquiry. The anxiety-provoking aspects of ring organization and its three workplaces may, therefore, be envisioned to be a problem of managing intrapersonal, interpersonal, group and organizational anxieties. These anxieties must be effectively addressed by organization members to avoid the creation of yet another workplace—the psychologically defensive workplace (Allcorn and Diamond, 1997).

In Sum

Organizational boundaries offer their members a context that is at once abstract but also reassuring. Organization members know that "I am here and you are there," and "We are here and others are there." It is likely no organization form can be conceived of that will not implicitly or explicitly contain internal and external boundaries and if one could do so their members would very likely create their own, so reassuring and anxiety-allaying are boundaries. It is, therefore, essential within ring organizations that the existence of boundaries and their anxiety-allaying function be appreciated along with the many rigidities and communication and collaboration barriers that they may also create. The challenge for ring organization members is to avoid the negatives and build upon the positives of ring organizational boundaries.

Managing Intrapersonal Anxiety

The above mentioned anxiety-evoking aspects of ring organization (and many possible others) will have special meaning for each organization member. The ambiguity of the physical organization coupled with the mysterious nature of the potential workplace and the boundarylessness of the virtual workplace will have as many meanings as members of the organization. These conceptual contexts can be discussed from many psychodynamic perspectives. I limit my discussion here to an object relations approach to understanding psychological defensiveness (Ashback and Schermer, 1987; Greenberg and Mitchell, 1983 and Ogden, 1989, 1990).

Splitting and projection is an outcome of life experience that includes both what the individual brings to the situation as well as what lies within the situation or others to draw projections—projective hooks (Shapiro and Carr, 1991). An individual who possesses unresolved conflict regarding a parent with whom a secure attachment was not achieved will, very likely, bring this unresolved conflict into the workplace for continual reenactment (compulsive repetition) in the false hope of eventually resolving the conflict. This intrapsychic context creates a potential for splitting and projection that is realized when objects that possess attributes of the frustrating parent and his or her behavior are located in the workplace. A supervisor or executive may be instantly adored or hated. In the case of the hated other, this outcome is explained by unconsciously splitting off good aspects of the supervisor or executive and leaving only the bad and threatening personal attributes. It may also be the case that the executive's good aspects are taken into oneself (introjection) while simultaneously denied and split-off bad aspects of one's own self-experience are projected into this individual. Both the person (the object) and self become split (fragmented), with bad attributes amassed in the executive and good attributes amassed for oneself. The result is an all good self and all bad other. The reverse may also occur, where bad parts of the other are introjected and good self parts projected, thereby creating an all good other worthy of idealization and all bad and despised self unworthy of respect from others. This certain or pathological knowledge of the other is highly familiar, as it arises out of prior life experience with a frustrating parent(s), which fuels transference of historical feelings attached to this bad life experience upon the similarly offensive or threatening supervisor or executive. The response is disproportionate. A "hot button" is created and then pressed.

This brief description of object relations–based psychologically defensive process represents but one way to understand the psychodynamics and psychologically defensive workplace. However, even this brief description serves to illustrate the powerful and often destructive intrapersonal and interpersonal nature of intrapsychic process. Given this limited review, one might wonder how intrapsychic defensiveness will be acted out in a workplace devoid of individuals who, by the nature of their position, possess power, authority and status.

Two of many possibilities are discussed here. First, ring organization may diminish the anxiety the individual experiences by encouraging appropriate and adequate organizational attachment while, at the same time, presenting many fewer "targets" for splitting and projection. Problems with authority figures and organizational boundaries are minimized by the absence of these figures and by the minimization and permeability of organization boundaries. One might speculate that this absence will result in the individual having to work harder to better integrate good and bad self-experience that is facilitated by the organizational context. A second, less desirable outcome that may arise in the absence of this personal effort is that the need to split and project is increased as these unconscious processes become frustrated within the ring organization experiential context.

Second, the ring organization, since it is composed of people, will contain individuals who, while not possessing formal organizational power, authority and status, will present projective hooks. Members who possess parental attributes or special skills for which they are recognized or who participate in the task group governance process or perhaps overtly seek organizational-based power, authority and status will attract the attention of others who are especially attentive to these dynamics.

The fact that people are not perfect is a truism. Every organization, regardless of its design, culture and values, contains individuals who seek positions of power and authority to control their anxieties. Even though organization members may value avoiding these tendencies, they will, nonetheless, exist. Their presence may result in these individuals drawing the projections that would normally be associated with individuals in formal roles of power and authority. Adoration or hostility may result. In either case, the group dynamic will be affected, which can be expected to result in interventions by organization members who seek to support ring organization values. This elaboration of intrapsychic management of anxiety permits a briefer discussion of interpersonal, group and organizational anxiety.

In Sum

Unconscious processes abound in the workplace. An example borrowed from object relations theorizing is psychologically defensive splitting and projecting. An all bad (or all good) external object is created by first locating behavior and personal attributes in another that resemble those of a frustrating parent. All bad self-experience is then placed within the person (the object), followed by the transferring of one's deeply held and in many cases painful and hostile feelings onto this object. The individual is then subsequently not only known to be like the frustrating parent, he or she is treated in much the same way. This appreciation makes it clear that ring organization will not eliminate these psychologically defensive outcomes. However, its culture, values and operation will promote better self and self-other integration, which, if successful, will minimize the presence of the psychologically defensive workplace (Allcorn and Diamond, 1997). A second likely outcome is that those individuals who are unable to resolve their conflicts and who consistently and compulsively introduce their psychologically defensive processes into the workplace may well find themselves the subject of remedial action and eventually choose to leave this "frustrating" organizational design, or perhaps be terminated.

Managing Interpersonal Anxiety

The values of trust, respect, openness, collaboration and inquiry are values of an interpersonal nature. Achieving these values within a ring organization will become an unending struggle against psychological defenses that are acted out in intrapsychic and interpersonal space. Dynamic workplace theory also supports the notion that this struggle exists. Interpersonal rivalry, competition, envy, acceptance and rejection are open to inspection within the three workplaces—physical, potential and virtual (Allcorn, 1991). All organization members are faced with the same challenge, that of self-reflection that leads to learning and changes in thoughts, feelings and behavior (Senge, 1990). Skills such as conflict resolution will become imperatives in this new interpersonal context. However, to be avoided is the development of a retreat to cult-like rituals and language that may be readily associated with the new more open and accepting interpersonal context. Members do not magically become undifferentiated brothers and sisters or associates. A higher level of interpersonal authenticity is being sought in this new organization form.

Managing Group Anxiety

Groups that exist in the three workplaces will contain the many familiar group dynamics that exist in all groups. Disagreements, conflicting points of view, strong debate and the creation of many new and possibly distressing ideas will be encountered. However, ring organization structure and values promote a constant inspection of group dialogue, dynamics and process with a watchful eye on avoiding devolving into basic assumption groups or group relations training formats (Allcorn and Diamond, 1997; Bion, 1961; De Board, 1978). Members must feel free to question group dynamics without becoming obsessed by their interpretation. Organizational values are used as a baseline for evaluating and intervening in group processes that appear to be becoming dominated by individuals or subgroups, a process that may be facilitated by group process consultants located within the core human relations function. The virtual workplace raises these considerations to a higher level of abstraction by introducing virtual groups. However, ring organizational values and culture permeate the virtual workplace, which may also contain virtual group process consultants.

Managing Organizational Anxiety

The presence of three distinct workplaces within one organization can be expected to be confusing and very likely distressing to some organization members. Organization members will have to be informed about their nature and purpose as well as ring organization values and culture in order to allay these anxieties. Some members, it is expected, will feel more comfortable working within one or two of the workplaces. An organization member who prefers to avoid the virtual workplace, while being encouraged to participate, will not be disciplined or ostracized for nonparticipation so long as performance is adequate within the remaining workplaces.

Also to be considered are the coordinative and communicative relationships between the three workplaces. Members of rings and participants in the potential and virtual workplaces will have members who are active in two or more of the three workplaces, which will insure information and knowledge generation is shared among the three workplaces. Rings and the potential workplace will also maintain intranet Web sites to further advance communication and knowledge sharing.

In Sum

Appreciating the complexities and challenges of individuals and groups managing anxiety within the workplace is a critically important first step in avoiding the psychologically and socially defensive workplace. Ring organization design, as mentioned, avoids interjecting many of the anxiety-inducing elements of the bureaucratic-hierarchy while, at the same time, introducing other forms of anxiety-promoting work experience. Managing anxiety-evoking intrapersonal, interpersonal, group and organizational experience can become, it is suggested here, an explicit task of working within a ring organization design. In particular, a constant press of organization values is needed to keep the workplace before organization members as they go about their work in order to develop and sustain ring organization culture.

IN CONCLUSION

This chapter has presented what amounts to a "thought experiment" as to how one might envision a postindustrial, nonhierarchical and non-bureaucratic organization form. Ring organization design has been explored for how it might be created and operated as well as how it might be experienced. This experiment may be understood to be one possible start at describing a new organization form that promises improved organizational performance. This experiment also directs attention to the difficulty of envisioning a non-bureaucratic, nonhierarchical organization form as well as challenges the reader to ponder whether there might be other equally valid criteria that a postindustrial or postmodern organization might meet. This is the challenge left to management thinkers to ponder as a result of the apparent dead end in management thinking to date.

Ring organization design will have no doubt raised more questions than it has answered. These questions and reservations may be further addressed using dynamic workplace theory to gain more insight into ring organization design. Chapter 9 provides this comparative analysis. However, before proceeding to this comparative analysis a final reflection in the form of a "reality check" is in order.

Ring organization design has thus far been discussed in a relatively purist manner in order to illuminate its attributes, problems and possibilities. Admittedly, achieving a ring organization design as discussed is without a doubt problematic as we start the twenty-first century. However, ring organization design does provide organization leaders and entrepreneurs an important frame of reference for assessing current organization designs and their functioning. It also provides concrete ways of thinking about organization design and improvement. In its purest form everyone is coequal. However, I suggest that many of the attributes of a ring design may be achieved by an enlightened leader and management team that, while retaining their hierarchical positions, advocate a ring design. In this case they remain as authority figures that hold the ring organization accountable for its performance and address hard to resolve issues that the ring design is having difficulty overcoming.

In sum, ring organization design does provide organizational leaders, executives, managers and employees a way of thinking about the workplace with an eye on improving member experience and organizational productivity. Partial implementation of a ring design may well be better than no implementation at all. And finally, ring design considerations may be somewhat recast as issues of maintaining organizational vitality, resilience, adaptability—issues related to dynamic adaptiveness and organizational plasticity discussed in the concluding chapter.

Chapter 9

An Analysis of Dynamic Workplace Theory and Ring Organization Design

By definition, innovative strategic directions take an organization into un-charted waters. It follows that no one can know the future destination of an innovative organization. Rather, the organization's managers must create, invent, and discover their destination as they go. If no one can know where the organization is going, then no one can be "in control." Instead managers have to create conditions in which behavior within the organization is con-trolled even though no one controls it. If managers cannot know where the organization is going or what the right business philosophy for the future is, they should not all believe in the same things, as the "cohesive team" and "common culture" myths hold. Instead, they should question everything and generate new perspectives through contention and conflict.

(Stacey, 1992, p. 4)

This chapter provides a critical evaluation of dynamic workplace theory and ring organization design. Each perspective offers the reader a somewhat if not sub-stantially different perspective of how the workplace works than might have been thus far discovered in the literature. It is also a truism that new perspec-tives and ideas always have their strengths and weaknesses. They may seem to intuitively make sense or they may not. Most of all they may be envisioned to be of practical use in the workplace, or only represent interesting insights with little utility. It is, therefore, appropriate to step back from the content of this book and assume the perspective of the critic and the role of the devil's advo-cate. Do dynamic workplace theory and the concept of ring organization design make sense? Are they of any potential value to executives, managers, supervi-sors, employees and organizational researchers?

To begin, it must be noted that dynamic workplace theory has been articulated and explored to a much greater extent than ring organization design. It is also very likely the case that ring organization design represents a much greater departure from traditional management thinking than dynamic workplace theory, which draws upon readily observable aspects of the workplace. Ring organization design also admittedly represents a first effort to envision a nonbureaucratic and nonhierarchical organization form that will no doubt merit more articulation. We then start with the premise that dynamic workplace theory is a more fully thought-through idea as compared with ring organization design, which represents a first effort to conceive of a new organization form. This leaves ring organization design more vulnerable to criticism.

It is also the case that each of the perspectives may be used relative to each other to further illuminate the strengths and weaknesses of each. Dynamic workplace theory arose out of experience within bureaucratic-hierarchies, and exploring its efficacy relative to ring organization design permits acquiring new insights into its merits and deficiencies. At the same time ring organization design may be evaluated from the perspective of dynamic workplace theory. This juxtaposition of the two perspectives, therefore, offers yet additional ways to understand each.

In sum, this chapter provides three discrete analyses. First, dynamic workplace theory is inspected for its strengths and weaknesses. Second, ring organization design is evaluated. Last, the two are joined to locate what may be learned from understanding ring organization design through the lens of dynamic workplace theory. The discussion of each point made is limited in favor of discussing more points. It is, of course, also important to note that this chapter represents an effort at self-evaluation, with all of its attendant biases and losses of insight. In this regard it has been challenging to create, in the sense of my not being able think of more potential problems and questions that may be raised about this work. The reader is, therefore, encouraged to reflect on the content of this book to locate additional insights that may only be gained by others not personally invested in developing the content.

A CRITICAL REVIEW OF DYNAMIC WORKPLACE THEORY

Dynamic workplace theory and its many facets have been discussed in considerable depth. The fundamental premise of the theory is that its elements are readily recognizable as existing within the workplace. In this regard, the theory represents an effort to acquire greater appreciation and awareness of common aspects of the workplace by providing a "cognitive map" for thinking about it in terms of understanding and interpreting workplace experience. It also draws one's attention to the complex dynamics that exist within organizational change and stability when they are placed within a vast arena of difficult to understand and contend with change in the marketplace. Several questions may have come to mind relative to the theory and the fundamental nature of its assertions.

Is the Typology Exhaustive?

Dynamic workplace theory suggests that all workplace experience is accounted for by the four types of workplace experience—chaotic, bureaucratic, charismatic and balanced, as well as the nature of the transitional space between the four types of experience. Several aspects of this assertion can be examined.

First, these four kinds of workplace experience may be referred to by other terms that are perhaps nuanced to explore one particular aspect of one of the four experiences. It is certainly the case that much has been written about powerful and authoritative leadership and the experience of large organizations as monolithic, unadaptive and unyielding structures. It is not my purpose here to review these many possible additional terms and points of view. Rather, I suggest that, regardless of the exact terminology used or the specific facet of organizational life explored, all of this work is circumscribed by the bureaucratic-hierarchical organizational paradigm. This thought-limiting context seems invariably to lead back to the four kinds of group experience. In this regard a careful examination of one's firsthand experience and the language and the ideas of others may, without being overly diligent about fitting this experience and language into one shoe, seem to, in most instances, comfortably lead back to one of the four kinds of workplace experience. This outcome occurs regardless of whether one thinks of the workplace in terms such as a team activity or one big family where both metaphors contain implicit hierarchies and layers of participation.

Second, discussed below is the likelihood that a nonhierarchical organization design may well introduce new types of workplace experience. This once again points to an appreciation of how limiting one's thinking and experience may become when that thinking and experience occur within the pervasive presence of bureaucratic hierarchies.

Does the Nature of Organizational Change and Balance Really Permit Better Management?

The discussion of organizational balance and change in chapters 4 and 5 may have reminded readers who have experienced organizational change of the many complexities and unintended consequences that arise during periods of major change as well as during the constant presence of lesser change. Many familiar aspects of organizational life and long-established working relationships may be obliterated by organizational events such as mergers, downsizing and reengineering. At the minimum, creeping organizational change to adapt, adjust and improve performance and products as represented by a concept such as total quality management very often requires constant adjustment on the part of organization members. It is, therefore, important to appreciate that organizational dynamics create a context where stability may be preferred over change. This leads to the familiar problems of organizational rigidity and maladaptiveness.

At the same time, there are many instances where a high-performing organization loses its balance, so to speak, and tumbles into operating and performance problems. In this regard the notion of organizational balance cuts both ways. This book makes clear that overcoming rigidities to create change often only occurs when the collective sense of the organization and its performance draw into question survivability (Levinson, 1972). In these instances sudden and many times extreme change may occur (Allcorn et al., 1996 and Hammer and Champy, 1993). At the same time, in those instances where organization members experience their organization as functioning well, it is logical not to want to lose this dynamic. Nonetheless, almost irresistibly this loss occurs as a result of external pressures and internal forces that break down the balanced group experience. In this regard those who aspire to be effective leaders are provided considerable insight into what it is they must accomplish in order to lead their organization in a process of change, or conversely sustain it when organizational dynamics are highly productive.

Dynamic workplace theory, while perhaps discovering little that is entirely new about organizational change, does organize, integrate and articulate the complexity that is always involved with change. Keeping organizations productive and leading organizational change have historically been elusive even for the best executives and managers. The theoretical perspective provided here illuminates the problematic nature of organizational life created by this psychosocial complexity and by doing so hopefully provides leaders insight into how to better manage performance and change. A close inspection of the nature of organizational change as represented in chapter 4 provides those aspiring to lead change a way to think about the nature of the transitional space between the way things are and the way they should ideally be. In this regard an appreciation of these complex organizational dynamics is sobering and challenging.

In Sum

Dynamic workplace theory even when viewed with a critical eye seems to have merit in terms of understanding organizational life as well as providing insights that may be used by executives, managers and supervisors in their daily work. Admittedly the theory contains a reductionist tone by asserting that the four types of group experience account for all workplace experience. It is certainly the case that a great many other insightful perspectives and nuanced insights into the workplace have not been explicitly accounted for. However, the assertion that a large percentage of these are directly linked to bureaucratic-hierarchical work experience seems to still hold water. Many authors and consultants have developed ideas about how to make bureaucratic-hierarchies run better and, at least in some cases, suggested ways of improving organizational performance that might be thought of as paradigm busting or shifting. In conclusion, it is the case that few theoretical perspectives end up accounting for all aspects of experience of the many innovative and divergent thoughts of others.

Nonetheless, dynamic workplace theory is firmly grounded in everyday work experience and provides an integrated approach to understanding work experience and organizational dynamics.

A CRITICAL REVIEW OF RING ORGANIZATION DESIGN

The conception of ring organization design, it is acknowledged, must promote considerable skepticism as a result of its substantial departure from conventional management thinking. Admittedly there is much more that might be thought through and said about ring organization design that has been left undiscovered, unexplored and unsaid here. Nonetheless, the notion of ring organization design is sufficiently articulated to promote critical thinking about what might be involved in conceiving of a new non-bureaucratic and nonhierarchical organization form. Once again a number of questions about ring organization design may have come to mind. Hopefully some of the more pertinent ones are covered here.

Is Ring Organization Design a Radical New Idea?

Mention was made in chapter 8 of linkages that ring organization design shares with a considerable amount of traditional management literature. In particular, academics and consultants have suggested on many occasions and in many different ways that something is awry with the actual performance of bureaucratic hierarchies. In particular, it has been argued that organizational rigidities and barriers to creativity, communication and voluntary coordination must be overcome. This seems to be even more essential for modern-day organizations in order for them to become more flexible, adaptive and innovative to survive in the ever more competitive, dynamic and rapidly changing world marketplace. Chapter 10 further explores this need to be flexible and adaptive.

Many of these advocates for changing bureaucratic hierarchies and how they function point to the necessity of conceiving of an organizational design that is, at the minimum, less dependent upon the basic underlying command and control aspects of the bureaucratic-hierarchy. At the same time one can also be assured that there will arise maximum concern about the losses of the command and control that form the basis of the bureaucratic-hierarchical organization paradigm. The question will be asked, "Who is in charge here?"

Is Ring Organization Design Galloping Egalitarianism?

There is without a doubt a wish harbored by most individuals in the workplace of being treated fairly, equally and respectfully or conversely not like a number or a human resource. These expectations translate into specific aspects of organizational life such as being kept informed of organizational happenings, being provided opportunities to offer input into what is going on, and more importantly being listened to and respected as an individual. Additionally, the notion of fair play also applies to the interpersonal realm where some individuals are not favored over others. If, in fact, employees are treated equally, one has to a large extent created an egalitarian organizational culture. Based on this description of the hoped-for attributes of workplace experience, it must be appreciated that there also exists a negative connotation to the notion of egalitarianism (galloping or otherwise). This reservation is most often thought of as being operationalized in the form of a group or organization becoming preoccupied with taking care of everyone's feelings and balancing out the politics of influence. The feared outcome is that taking care of people and avoiding perceptions of unfairness and disrespect become more important than taking care of business. Ring organization design does create an organizational structure that encourages a culture of equality, fair play and interpersonal respect. It does not, however, turn the workplace into a focal point for social work. It must also be appreciated that our traditional command and control organizations are often filled with individual and group experience filled with personal authority issues relating to dominance and submission. This reality, I suggest, tends to create bruising experience that adversely affects self-esteem. In this regard, the negative connotation of egalitarianism in the workplace seems to be linked to bureaucratic hierarchies where distortions and preoccupations about losses of the positive contributions of a more balanced, fair, respectful and trusting workplace arise.

Does Ring Organization Design Represent a Collectivist Approach to the Workplace?

Collectivism refers to a political or economic system where the people as a group control production and distribution. It is a term most often used to refer to state-sponsored activities that are implicitly understood to be opposed to capitalism and free enterprise. The means of production is owned by individuals and distribution is determined by free trade and the profit motive. Collectivism holds that the interests and welfare of the collective group are more important than the interests and welfare of any individual. It is, therefore, a political-economic theory that differs little from theoretical socialism but also revolutionary communism where not only capitalistic enterprise but also most private property is abolished. This brief description of collectivism shares some things in common with ring organization design; however, there are also substantial differences. Ring organization design encourages organization members to work in groups to manage their organization and, once again, respectfully view each other as equally important contributors to the organization's well-being. However, in contrast to the above definition, ring organizations remain capitalist enterprises that must contend with the marketplace. Also to be taken into account is that individual performance will yield differential organizational rewards such as increases in compensation and career advancement.

Is Ring Organization Design Management by Committee?

Ring organization design presents the reader steeped in work experience acquired in bureaucratic hierarchies a serious problem as to who is in charge. How are decisions to be made? Who is running the show? And who is responsible in the event a blameworthy scapegoat is needed? Certainly an aspect of contemporary organizational life is the notion that groups and committees are not as effective as a single individual who calls all of the shots. Does ring organization amount to management by committee that very often takes on pejorative overtones in bureaucratic-hierarchical organizations?

Ring organization design and members of this postindustrial organization design will have to be effective at working in groups where leadership emerges as needed and dissipates when the leadership opportunity ends. This is, in fact, frequently the case in our contemporary organizations despite the command and control nature of the bureaucratic-hierarchy. Notions such as collaboration, participation, organizational flattening and bottom-up management share in common a limiting of the command and control nature of our organizations. This is not to say these approaches always work well or that they are not employed to conceal the command and control structure by providing the illusion of open participation and respect for all organization members. In fact, accessing the potential of these management techniques usually requires training and a shift in organizational culture.

Training in group and organizational dynamics as well as within-group coaching must be provided to make these management techniques effective in bureaucratic-hierarchies. It is similarly the case that this training is the foundation for the successfully functioning ring organization. Individuals who possess autocratic and authoritarian tendencies will either have to master them or perhaps look for employment with bureaucratic-hierarchical organizations that tacitly if not explicitly support these tendencies.

A second area of concern is that the process of building consensus is too slow to be effective. Building consensus does take time; however, the time taken will be reduced by the use of effective group process and the virtual workplace where discussion of ideas may be exhausted in hours or a few days. Participation on the front end usually results in less resistance to change and improved implementation on the back end. If one examines the entire cycle of decision making, implementation and the degree of success achieved, participative processes are very often superior to the traditional top-down, unilateral command and control approach of the bureaucratic hierarchy. Also to be considered is that this form of organization is more dynamic and flexible than bureaucratic hierarchies and may well avoid many crises and the accompanying need for crisis management.

A third area of interest involves the traditional notions of power and authority, which have been defined and discussed in many different ways. Hierarchical management positions answer the question, "Who is in charge?" In this regard hierarchically based power and authority minimize ambiguity for organization members while providing rewarding roles for those who seek power and authority not always for the most rational of reasons. The proposed ring organization recasts these aspects of organizational life into a group context independent of position. This change can be expected to increase ambiguity, which may be distressing to some organization members who do not readily tolerate ambiguity. Nonetheless, the ring organization work groups are "in charge" of planning, decision making and control that are the critically important elements of work that need to be accomplished. Psychological issues related to power and authority in the proposed ring organization design suggest the possibility of a post-oedipal or parental (patriarchal/matriarchal) relationship where separation and individuation are achieved as well as a higher level of self-integration and self/other acceptance.

Is Ring Organization Really Implementable?

This is a critically important question to ponder. Many management ideas that have been articulated during the past 25–50 years have sounded good on paper. They have made consultants a lot of money. They have made CEOs and managements look good to stockholders and governing boards. Alas, they have also had little effect on organizational dynamics or performance (Micklethwait and Woolridge, 1996). I recall chatting with an executive from a large corporation who said that his company was implementing Japanese-like principles where employees were to meet regularly to discuss performance improvements. When I subsequently asked how it was going he grinned broadly and basically said no one thought it was going to work. Nothing was going to really change regarding how top management ran the show. I also recall a more recent example where a former consultant was hired to manage a large outpatient facility for a university hospital. He made a big show out of the notion of developing self-managed teams. The physicians who used the facility on a daily basis waited expectantly for improvements that never arrived. After several years I questioned staff about their progress in managing the self-managed teams. Many reported that the idea did not work at all because the executive in charge sat in on most meetings, had to approve all changes and essentially micromanaged the entire facility which, in hindsight, exceeded his skill sets and contradicted the philosophy of the self-managed teams. The bottom line of these two examples of change that implicitly or explicitly contain some of the cultural attributes of a ring organization is that these changes and many others often become "management speak" and the fad of the quarter. Little is really changed about how the executives in charge command and control their organization and its employees. Employees all too often inwardly grin when they hear of a new effort such as lean and total quality management or the like.

This problem of whether management actually embraces the espoused change of their theory in practice is the "soft underbelly" of any type of change of this nature and in particular any change to embrace a ring organization design (Argyris, 1982). In many ways, while ring organization elements are not as great a departure from the present as might be thought, when taken together and placed into the larger context of a ring design, one can only imagine the undiscussable resistance senior level executives will have toward any real effort to implement a ring design that they understand will ultimately eliminate their hierarchical role and importance. Governing boards, stockholders and other stakeholders in the organization's performance may also be skeptical and in particular be concerned about their interaction with a form of organization lacking a formal management hierarchy.

In this regard, implementation of ring organization design must be thought of as a major undertaking that may well benefit from long-term external consultation that facilitates the change as well as informs and educates others such as board members and stockholders. This seems advisable in that an independent point of view may become essential for accurate reality testing as well as providing a caretaking guiding hand to nurture the change process along.

It is also worth mentioning that in order to avoid the above mentioned problems of management by fad and management speak, efforts to adopt a ring design must be carefully thought through and embraced by management in order to stand any hope of successful implementation. It is much better to decide not to attempt to embrace ring organization design than to casually enter into a change process to implement it in a month. It may, therefore, be concluded that the implementability of a ring organization design or redesign is challenging and will require the utmost of courage, persistence and sacrifice on the part of those who lead the change effort. Nonetheless, it is an implementable design that may be more appropriately considered for organizations that have reached or are near failure and it is generally thought some new "genetic" material must be infused to survive. In this regard a ring redesign might be welcomed by most employees in the hope that its promise can be realized. It is also the case that ring organization design may be most implementable at the front end of the growth and development of an organization where constant change, adaptability, flexibility and creativity are valued.

In Sum

Ring organization design presents the reader with a new concept for organizing the workplace. It is also, however, inclusive of many previously suggested changes in how our traditional bureaucratic hierarchies should operate. Ring organization design is, therefore, not entirely new. Rather, it builds upon a long tradition of trying to find ways to make contemporary organizations more efficient and effective. Ring organization design's very nature, however, must be considered to be a challenging new organization structure for those contemplating implementing it. In particular, many of those in powerful hierarchical positions can be expected to be resistant to losing their hierarchical-based status. They may ask, "Who will be in charge?" and assert ring organization design is an attempt to run their organization by a misplaced egalitarian or collectivist philosophy that amounts to management by committee that will compromise organizational performance and profitability. Ring organization design is not, however, intended to be management by committee with all of its attendant hierarchical organization-based negative nuances, even though a premium is placed upon group process and consensus-building skills. Neither is it entirely egalitarian, although there exists a basic assumption on a peer-to-peer basis of interpersonal equality. This advocacy of equality is not, however, extended to all aspects of the workplace. Individual employees will receive different salaries for their skills and different rewards for their contributions. Last, ring organization is not a collectivist philosophy where collectivism is considered to be opposed to capitalism. Ring organization design is not implicitly for or against any particular social or production philosophy. In final analysis ring organization design places a premium on personal flexibility and the assumption of individual responsibility to achieve improved organizational performance.

DYNAMIC WORKPLACE THEORY AND RING ORGANIZATION DESIGN INSIGHTS INTO THE OTHER

The application of dynamic workplace theory to understanding the organizational dynamics implicit within a ring organization design introduces a challenging opportunity to study each in theory and speculate about their efficacy in practice. Perhaps there is no better place to start than to examine the ring organization design for the presence of the four types of group experiences described by dynamic workplace theory.

Will Ring Organizations Contain the Four Types of Dynamic Workplace Experience?

Ring organization experience presents organization members with, as near as possible, a non-bureaucratic and nonhierarchical organization structure where members do not assume roles arrayed on a vertical scale of importance, although there may certainly exist differences in, for example, salaries. Everyone within this organization culture is coequal. This aspect of ring organization design may most immediately bring to mind a potentially chaotic situation where leadership and direction are lacking.

Chaotic Experience

This is, I believe, the most likely experience of a ring organization and it will most certainly be accentuated by prior experience within hierarchical organizations where the chain of command provides control. However, ring organization design is not implicitly chaotic and not intended to be chaotic. The assumption that organization members will provide leadership and direction as needed and that organization members can successfully collaborate within potential and virtual organizational space is, I believe, a reasonable assumption to make. Organization theorists have advocated many of the attributes of the open, participative and collaborative nature of the ring design. My experience within groups within a hierarchical setting also tends to support the notion that leadership and direction may arise from just about anyone at any time. If chaotic tendencies exist, it is likely that they will most often arise during the transition to a ring design and during its early functioning where some organization members are anxious about the new workplace context and speak to the need to have someone in charge. This appreciation also echoes with dynamic workplace theory in that these same voices are always present within our traditional organizations.

Bureaucratic Experience

The distinction was made in dynamic workplace theory between bureaucratic features that contain utility and contribute to organizational performance and the routinization and red tape that come with excessive reliance upon these same features to control as near as possible most aspects of organizational life. Ring design represents an effort to create a flexible administrative structure where leadership and organizational protocols, policies, procedures, rules and regulations may be questioned for their utility at any time by anyone. Ring organization design recognizes the utility of providing a regulated work setting that avoids becoming experienced as underled and filled with red tape and other compulsively and rigidly relied upon control elements that inhibit member and organizational flexibility and adaptability.

Charismatic Experience

Everywhere that there are groups of people, some individuals will invariably be felt by others to be good leaders whom they are willing to follow. Ring organizations will not be an exception. There reside within the design many opportunities for individuals to provide leadership for their task group, ring and the organization and it is likely some of these individuals will be looked to for leadership more often than others. The culture of ring organizations, however, discourages individuals from presuming that they can become formal leaders who occupy a permanent position where they are empowered to take charge on an ongoing basis. As described in dynamic workplace theory, the negative side of charismatic leadership lies in the overdependence of organization members upon a designated leader and the often out of awareness desire on the part of the leader to feel powerful and admired. The ring design discourages this outcome in favor of providing an open setting where the desires of an individual to assume such a role or a group of individuals to have such a leader may be called into question.

Balanced Experience

The above discussion of the three psychologically and socially defensive group experiences has focused on the culture of ring organization where it provides for creativity, sufficient administrative structure and adequate leadership without becoming overly chaotic, bureaucratic or dependent upon a charismatic leader. This amounts to balanced work experience.

Will Organizational Stability and Change Resemble that Described in Dynamic Workplace Theory?

Ring organization design represents an effort to develop and maintain the balanced workplace experience and avoid the three psychologically and socially defensive workplace experiences. In this regard the design of the organization and its accompanying culture offer the promise of stability in the form of organizational balance. This may be compared to hierarchical organizations where the hierarchical nature of the organization contains deeply embedded qualities that encourage a retreat to the defensive workplace experiences of chaos, bureaucracy and charismatic leadership. Each of these tendencies can be understood to be tacitly if not substantially supported by hierarchy and is perhaps a by-product of it.

The issue of organizational stability and change will, therefore, remain much the same as proposed in dynamic workplace theory. Recourse to hierarchical and psychologically and socially defensive workplace experience will remain a constant threat to ring organization worklife. This threat will achieve its greatest potential when operating and performance problems are encountered. In particular, the lack of a clear hierarchy of command and control limits the ability of organization members, board members and stockholders to locate the source of the problems in others (formal leaders) who may then be blamed and scapegoated. The ability to achieve this comforting psychologically and socially defensive outcome may, therefore, be understood to be frustrated by ring organization design where the notion that "the enemy is us" serves to locate responsibility with all organization members. Herein, however, lies the organizational dynamic that may foster a retreat to the seductive organizational context where others are thought to be blameworthy. In order to achieve this outcome the attributes of organizational hierarchy must be reasserted. This leads to a further retreat from ring organization design in the direction of chaos, increasing dependence upon bureaucratic controls or the location of a charismatic leader to take charge, assume full responsibility and lead everyone out of harm's way.

Does a Ring Organization Design Introduce a Type of Group Experience Not Accounted for by Dynamic Workplace Theory?

The description of ring organization design contains the four types of work experience described by dynamic workplace theory. In particular it has been noted that ring organizational design can be understood to be a form of organizational design intended to support balanced work experience. However, one might, after reflecting upon the proposed nature of ring organization design, come to the conclusion that other types of workplace experience might be created. The reader is encouraged also to ponder this aspect of ring organization design. The following discussion highlights some of the possible alternative group experiences that may well be different enough to be considered as falling outside of dynamic workplace theory. However, a few notes are added to relate each discussion back to dynamic workplace theory to demonstrate an underlying compatibility.

Coequal Workplace Experience

The presumption of coequality is an explicit aspect of ring organization design. Hierarchical roles and organizationally dictated status and power differentials are absent. Given this context, it is reasonable to assume that a new kind of workplace experience exists. The open, participative, collaborative and trusting nature of ring organization culture promotes a cooperative and noncompetitive interpersonal experience accompanied by the underlying value of the importance of reflective individual, group or ring and organizational process. Everything about organizational life is open to being questioned, at the minimum in the virtual workplace and preferably within the physical and potential workplaces as well. It is this quality of ring organization design that serves to hold at bay the psychologically and socially defensive aspects of the dynamic workplace model while simultaneously supporting a balanced experience of the workplace. However, coequality also seems to reasonably extend balanced workplace experience into a new kind of organizational space. Therefore, coequal workplace experience may well constitute a new type of workplace experience not a part of dynamic workplace theory. At the same time a counterpoint may also be argued. Coequality and interpersonal respect are implicit qualities that support the balanced workplace experience. In this regard coequality is understood to provide the interpersonal basis for being sufficiently open, collaborative and trusting to develop and sustain the all-important reflectivity that staves off defensive retreats to chaos, bureaucracy and charismatic leadership.

Democratic Workplace Experience

Western democratic ideals start with the notion that everyone is born equal and in this case the notion of equality is extended into the workplace. Democratic process suggests everyone has a vote and everyone may contribute to decision making and the taking of action. Democratic ideals, therefore, operationalize the notion of equality. Ring organization design, in addition to fostering a culture of equality and interpersonal trust and respect, implicitly includes a philosophy of supporting the contribution every organizational member may make to organizational decision making, the implementation of decisions, the accomplishment of work and performance evaluation. Everyone may have a say in the virtual workplace and participate in the potential workplace that lies within the rings and the organization. Also to be included is the physical workplace where ring culture promotes openness, participation in daily activities and collaboration. In a sense the development of consensus that is an important attribute of ring organization design creates a context where everyone may be heard, although every point of view may not be integrated into the decision-making process. Democratic workplace experience may also then be appreciated to be a new kind of workplace experience not explicitly a part of dynamic workplace theory. However, as a counterpoint, democratic values are an important element of the balanced workplace experience where consensus building is important. The openness, trust and respect that are essential for maintaining reflectivity that fosters the maintenance of the balanced experience implicitly contain democratic ideals. Everyone may be heard. Additionally, it is worth noting that there are some types of workplace experience that are not intended to be a part of ring organization design.

Preindustrial Workplace Experience

Bergquist (1993) has suggested that the preindustrial or premodern workplace based on agriculture and cottage-like industry (small units of production) represents a nostalgic counterpoint to the monolithic organizations that arose during the industrial revolution. In a sense the small and individualized production units provided individuals maximum freedom from the control and oppression of having to submit to the domination of others. Ring organization design, however, is not described as containing this kind of workplace experience. A larger organization does exist where rampant individualism and autonomy associated with chaotic workplace experience is avoided.

Quasi-democratic Workplace Experience

A fundamental problem with traditional organization experience is the appearance of the presence of openness (open door policy is an example), collaboration and cooperation where many aspects of the workplace may be called into question. However, employees most often intuitively understand that what is being said by management (management speak or espoused theory) does not accurately reflect what they are doing (theory in practice) (Argyris, 1982). They may say that they are willing to listen to everyone when employees understand that the decision has already been made or will be made as planned even after listening to employee input. At a more devious level, management may have defined the problem to be addressed in such a way as to guide the selection of the decision-making process. The power to define the problem is often the power to choose the solution. Management, therefore, may be seen to be seizing upon the management fad of the moment and espousing participation and inclusion when in fact little is really being offered. This amounts to a quasi-democratic leadership style where the iron fist of management control is gloved in velvet. Things are not as they appear. Ring organization design and balanced workplace experience discourage these kinds of manipulations on the part of those taking leadership roles by permitting organization members to openly question discrepancies between espoused theory and the theory in practice.

In Sum

An inspection of each theoretical perspective relative to the other introduces new insights. Dynamic workplace theory points to the presence of four types of workplace experience. Ring organization design is not immune to the psychologically and socially defensive experiences (chaos, bureaucracy and charismatic leadership) degrading its performance. At the same time, ring organization culture and balanced group experience share much in common and ring design may be understood to explicitly support balanced workplace experience. In this regard, ring design promotes the stability of balanced workplace experience. Ring organization also introduces at least two new kinds of workplace experience—coequality and democracy. The explicit equality of organization members and the ability of organization members to contribute in the virtual, potential and physical workplaces within a ring organization promote coequality and democracy. These are, however, also principles and qualities of the balanced workplace experience and are, therefore, subsumed by the balanced workplace experience. Last, ring organization design does not create other less effective types of workplace experience. It is not a return to a preindustrial workplace experience based on small units of production. Neither is it intended to become a quasi-democratic workplace where participation, respect and equality are espoused by hierarchical executives who are actually using the notions to conceal their hierarchically based command and control structure.

IN CONCLUSION

It is always humbling to attempt to critique one's own work, not so much from the point of view in my case of being personally resistant to inspecting it for deficiencies, but rather from the point of view of not being able to locate new ideas and insights as a result of being bound up with the work. Hopefully I have raised at least some of the issues that may come to mind about the content of this book. It is also most certainly the case that many other pertinent ideas, criticisms and perspectives have been overlooked along a range from differing with a single aspect of the book to global reservations about much of the content. In this regard the book may, however, still have fulfilled an important role by stimulating critical "yes, but" thinking. I now turn to the concluding chapter and a discussion of how this work and the future may collide to create, using a particle physics metaphor, every smaller particles of understanding as well as a grander theory of what the universe of organizational dynamics may hold.

Chapter 10

In Conclusion

This book has been directly or indirectly devoted to better understanding the bureaucratic-hierarchy. It is the most successful organization form of the nineteenth and twentieth centuries and may well be for the twenty-first century. Understanding it for what it is and is not is essential to understanding what it portends for our worklives spent within its confines and our private lives dominated by its influences. Bureaucratic control has become an ideal partner to hierarchies of power and authority. Our contemporary organizations, public and private, are ultimately dominated by deeply embedded and seldom acknowledged or inspected issues related to power and control on the part of those who manage them. Gabriel (1999) underscores this observation. He writes:

Since their earliest beginnings, theories of organizations and management have been preoccupied with control. Standing for order, predictability and reliability, control is an integral part of what most people understand by 'organization.' Control is what distinguishes organization from its opposite, chaos. Management itself has come ever closer to mean being in control—control over resources, information and people. Much of the theory of organizations is aimed at putting the manager ever more firmly in control (p. 280).

We therefore return to the dynamic elements of the workplace—chaos, bureaucracy and charismatic leadership that are played out within the context of hierarchical organizations. However, as underscored by the dynamic nature of the theoretical perspective discussed here, the only thing that is truly predictable is change, the direction of which is ultimately hard to predict. Anyone who has endeavored to design and implement organizational change is familiar with Murphy's Law and the notion of unintended consequences. Leaders and organization members often appear to be furiously paddling their raft down the perpetual white water of the future (Vaill, 1989). At times things are calm and going as planned. Occasionally midcourse corrections need to be made and unavoidably there are occasions where, despite the best efforts to control events, the organization is swept along and control and predictability are for the most part lost. This unpredictability is underscored by the Enron/Andersen and Ford/Firestone commercial disasters that ultimately led to the replacement of their leaders. Theories of complexity and chaos account at least to some extent for this experience.

We are, therefore, left the harsh realities of this moment in time. The bureaucratic-hierarchy promises control and predictability and the conservation of management power. Management, however, is unavoidably faced with a larger context where there is never enough power and control to assure predictability. The world marketplace, our evolving culture and a landscape of ever changing laws and technology assure change is inevitable and many times unpredictable. Dynamic workplace theory further underscores the limits of management power and authority. Organizational dynamics fueled by conscious and unconscious intrapersonal, interpersonal and group dynamics create a context that, when closely inspected, has always been beyond the control of management.

Dynamic workplace theory directs our attention to the unavoidable and uncontrollable nature of these variables that lie in dynamic tension with each other. It is also the case that envisioning an organizational design that does not implicitly include management and status hierarchies that support individual needs to feel powerful, in control and admired presents theorists a paradigm that is hard to bust. Ring organization design represents one attempt to think outside of this box. However, ring organization or any other nonhierarchical and nonbureaucratic form of organization is not likely to rapidly emerge at the start of the twenty-first century. We are, therefore, left with the problem of envisioning how we can better manage our current organizations to accommodate the realities of dynamic workplace theory and the irrational embrace of the illusion of control and predictability. We are also cautioned by Czander (1993), who believes that thus far finding a better way to improve our organizations has come up short. The following discussion recasts dynamic workplace theory in the hope that by using it as a basis for rethinking the operation of bureaucratic hierarchies I can avoid, at least to some extent, coming up short. This recasting suggests an approach to re-envisioning our organizations so that their members focus on creating greater fluidity that can arise out of the balanced workplace experience. A sense of organizational life is created by focusing on organizational fluidity that serves to ground the experience of organization members in the realities of the workplace and marketplace. Change, I suggest, can be embraced as a primary task thereby making individual flexibility a goal and a supportive organizational context a necessity.

DYNAMIC ADAPTIVENESS: ENVISIONING
ORGANIZATIONAL PLASTICITY

The dawn of the twenty-first century finds organizational survival is all too often at stake in the Darwinian worldwide marketplace. Big organizations are making themselves into small ones and small ones into big ones in order to find the right mix of organizational attributes that permit self-perpetuation into the distant future as well as to take advantage of near-term opportunities. Change is omnipresent and its pace is becoming faster, as illustrated by the rapid collapse of the dot coms. These are the facts of life in corporate America as we commence the twenty-first century and they are not without their implications for the public sector.

Much has been written about organizational change. The problems of managing and creating organizational change are well documented.

- Change is frequently driven top-down, which minimizes employee participation and results in poorly informed interventions at the operating level. Employee alienation and distrust is often further encouraged by marginal or no communication, communication coached in "management speak," and manipulative uses of information to support management decisions.

- Change is frequently driven by reliance upon expert authority either on the part of internal specialists, or these days, consultants. Expert authority isolates and alienates employees who do not or minimally understand the information base from which the authority is drawn. To this must be added the use of technical or jargonized language that further impresses upon employees their inability to know and understand and, therefore, their dependence upon the experts driving the change.

- Executives who function as internal change agents frequently seek to fulfil a vision placed upon them by a governing board in a rapid, no-nonsense way that disregards organizational history and culture. Also disregarded are employee interests, fantasies and feelings, thereby assuring anger-filled resistance to change that, in turn, encourages greater uses of unilateral power by the change agent to overcome the resistance. The notion "lead, follow or get out of the way" generates terminations or organizational downsizing and reorganizing that ejects resistant employees out of the workplace (see the Corporate Killers cover of *Newsweek*, February, 26, 1996).

- Organizations that must change are often poorly prepared to plan and implement change. They are already operating under extreme pressure to improve performance, often with the same or reduced staffing as a result of the lack of previous well-timed adaptive changes to organizational structure and work design.

- Those responsible for implementing change at the operating level and end users of technological innovations are all too frequently not properly trained to accomplish change and use the new systems.

- Employees are frequently resistant to change because they must work harder to plan and implement it as a result of having to continue to perform their regular duties. The lack of organizational slack in hard-pressed organizations tends to create a self-fulfilling prophecy of employee distress and alienation.

- Employees are frequently resistant to change for psychological reasons associated with losses of familiar patterns of workplace relationships and work. This results in disorienting anxieties about future performances and, in the case of major change such as mergers, a very real sense of loss of one's sense of the organization, its history and culture.

These are not new findings. Nor are they unique to any one type of organization. They are, in fact, commonplace not only in a historical sense but also in a contemporary sense. It is this latter case that is noteworthy. If these problems are so well documented, researched and published, one must ask the obvious rhetorical question, Why do they continue to be a problem? The equally obvious answer is that organizations and change do not create problems, people do, and herein lies both the problem and possible solution. Implicit in the above well-documented problems related to change is the fact that executives who lead change and employees who must implement it create a chaotic psychologically defensive stew of missed opportunities to be more effective (Allcorn and Diamond, 1997). My purpose here is not to further document and explore these many organizational, leadership and employee-driven resistances to successful organizational adaptation. Rather, it is important to look elsewhere for potential solutions that will not merely facilitate organizational change but provide a vision that embraces the dynamic nature of worklife by creating an organization that possesses a culture, values and relational patterns that enable timely change driven by all the employees.

THE CREATIVE CONTEXT

Developing a new and better vision for accomplishing work and change in organizations is informed by acknowledging attributes that limit creativity by routing critical thinking and reflection down familiar and comfortable paths. These include organizational structure, a variety of formal workplace protocols that are encapsulated under the heading of policies and procedures, the design of work and processes and, of course, people who contribute leadership and followership. All of these are familiar aspects of the workplace that can, according to dynamic workplace theory, contribute varying degrees of dysfunction. At best they contribute to the near-term performance and at the worst they form the basis for poor organizational performance that in the long term threatens organizational survival. These considerations present anyone envisioning a new form of dynamic organization that readily adapts and adjusts to its operating environment a challenge not unlike that presented in ring organization design precepts.

Paradigm-Bounded Thinking

Each of the above contexts for knowing and thinking about organizations, as outlined in chapters 8 and 9, limits thinking and creative vision. Organization structure contains both rational and irrational elements that account for its form and function. The exponents of the rational point of view argue that the requisite organization avoids organizational dysfunction by scientifically aligning roles relative to each other and placing the right person in the right position. These notions are not new by any means. The presence of familiar organizational protocols and policies and procedures that inform routine decision making are experienced as gospel and beyond question. Their de facto existence becomes reality. It is hard to envision an organization without them. Similarly, the design of work usually involves systematic, sequential and scientific elements in the form of systems analysis. Work is work and how it is arranged is usually taken for granted by many employees or at the minimum it is difficult and potentially threatening to call it into question. Of equal concern is that employees often perpetuate these familiar attributes of the workplace to sustain the predictable and avoid the chaotic aspects of change. Change often implies more work at a time when stressful change takes place in the form of the loss of familiar and secure working relationships and performance predictability, that, it must be noted, does not always contribute to organizational performance. In sum, thinking about organizations is necessarily limited by our ability to envision something substantially new. Like colors on a painter's palette, it seems natural to use them to paint a new picture of organizational life, one that is limited by the medium at hand.

Utopia in a Teacup

When it comes to locating a bold new vision for the future, one is reminded of unrealistic, idealistic, implausible utopian thinking of the past. It is easy to commence a process of re-envisioning with a romanticized and quasi-religious or spiritual quality of a vision quest. My purpose here, while advocating new vision, is not to abandon the grimy realities of the workplace and the need to organize and produce work, products and services. The following discussion is grounded in accepted aspects of management and organizational dynamics that promise to provide a platform for re-envisionment grounded in workplace realities. To this end the notion of organizational plasticity is overlaid upon the reality of our contemporary organization design and operation.

ORGANIZATIONAL PLASTICITY—A PATH TO DYNAMIC ADAPTIVENESS

Organizational plasticity and dynamic adaptiveness are theoretical constructs that must be defined and elaborated before commencing a discussion of how to implement them in the workplace. Dynamic adaptiveness represents the goal for organization change. Dynamic workplace theory has, if anything, demonstrated that managing our organizations by trying to control their members' thoughts, feelings and actions is a lost cause. However, it is not a cause that is easily let go of. The problematic nature of trying to control or manage our organizations has been a large part of the discussion in this book. The starting point of dynamic adaptiveness is, therefore, embracing the true nature of the hard to control and manage workplace that invariably produces outcomes that cannot be anticipated and certainly not consistently planned to any great extent. The acceptance of this single premise leads to the conclusion, if control and predictability are not ultimately achievable, then one must design an organization and manage it in such a way as to be able to constantly adjust and adapt to the dynamic nature of the organization and its larger task environment (Stacey, 1992). Dynamic adaptiveness is, therefore, the response to the grudging acceptance of the ultimate failure to achieve sufficient control to create predictability. It represents a conscious and intentional strategy for managing our organizations that accepts that control is not ultimately possible and that adaptive responsiveness is not only possible but essential to organizational survival.

Operationalizing Organizational Plasticity

Organizational plasticity is one way of operationalizing dynamic adaptiveness. I do not suggest that it is the only way to create the needed organizational flexibility that responds to accurate and timely reality testing. Like ring organization design, it offers but one way to think about redesigning and recasting organizational life. Organizational plasticity represents an effort to achieve dynamic adaptiveness by promoting awareness of the organizational dynamics and an organizational culture and values that embrace personal flexibility and organizational fluidity in the service of constantly changing the who, what, where, when and how of organizational life. In an engineering sense it manages down the dynamic mass. The lighter the moving parts of a machine are, the less energy is required to keep them in motion. Organizational plasticity represents an effort to keep the organization in motion in the service of adaptiveness while lightening the load represented by employee resistance to change. In this regard, organizational plasticity is not ultimately a notion that is renderable in engineering terms but rather one that embraces the indeterminacy of human nature.

In Sum

Creating organizational plasticity is much less a challenge than that represented by ring organization design. Organizational plasticity and its accompanying fluidity is an overlay upon the bureaucratic-hierarchy that, while embracing it, also strives to fundamentally change its operation to avoid many of its dysfunctions. In this regard, it is one way of conceiving of an organization that achieves organization balance. It is also important to appreciate that any effort to change an organization in the direction of plasticity must start with an evaluation of where an organization is at the moment. In this case the assessment takes the form of locating organizational identity.

ORGANIZATIONAL IDENTITY

Locating a starting point irresistibly leads to stepping back and rediscovering the identity of one's organization (Diamond, 1993). The questions are: "Who are we?" and "What do we do?" They must be answered to create a starting point for achieving organizational plasticity. This discovery process leads to the development of insights into how the people and parts of one's current organization are connected together and how well they are functioning, thereby creating the basis for recasting organizational identity in new and possibly unfamiliar organizational terms. This organizational diagnosis explores the organization as a product of management and employee conscious and unconscious dynamics. Organizational culture is viewed to be a by-product of the subjective and intersubjective aspects of organizational life. Who we are is a question that yields an answer that is more than simply an "industry leading organization developing the finest product or services." Who we are in this context describes the organization as it is known and experienced from within by the executives and employees who create it every day when they come to work. In sum, organizational identity represents the substance of workplace experience that includes functional and dysfunctional aspects of leadership and followership that enhance and inhibit organizational performance and adaptiveness. Exploring these elements of organizational identity permits inspection and reflection upon the fundamental nature of the organization. Called into question are human motivations and behaviors, some of which may be distressing to discuss if not foreboding and threatening when the thoughts, feelings and actions of powerful executives become the focus (Argyris, 1982). However, it is from just this level of analysis that the potential for achieving dynamic adaptiveness and organizational plasticity emerges. The discovery of organizational identity folds back upon dynamic workplace theory. The subjective and intersubjective nature of organizational life is the "stuff" of the theory. The psychodynamic nature of the theory resides in intrapersonal and interpersonal space where many usually unseen and uninspected conscious and unconscious dynamics cast many shadows upon the outward appearance of the organization and its performance. The theory, therefore, informs this discovery of organizational identity by providing a cognitive map. What it is like to work here is the nature of the experience of the moment, whether it is chaotic, bureaucratic, charismatic or balanced. It is in this space between the theoretical construct of organizational identity and dynamic workplace theory that discovery and creativity takes place to understand where we are and where we want to be. These perspectives also point to the direction and means of change to achieve organizational plasticity necessitated by the need to accept the limits of control imposed by human nature.

ORGANIZATIONAL VISION

The development of a vision statement flows naturally from the above work on organizational identity. Given the starting of point of where we are (organizational identity), the question is who or what do we wish to become. Vision statements typically set a new direction that inspires fulfillment. However, the development of a vision statement based on the later part of the above discussion of organizational identity creates the possibility of creating a new organization that includes dynamic adaptiveness and recognition of the psycho-social-technical elements of organizational life that must support it. Restating, the organizational vision must foremost become one of dynamic adaptiveness.

ORGANIZATIONAL VALUES

The values that govern organizational culture and work must be aligned with this challenging new vision if the principal precept of this new organizational vision is organizational plasticity in the service of dynamic adaptiveness. The values to achieve this will ultimately contain many unique properties specific to the business and industry of the organizations developing them. It suffices here to note some of the more important values that must be incorporated in a values statement that supports organizational plasticity.

Perhaps of foremost value is carefully monitoring the organizational task environment for change that points to the need for organizational adaptation. Also to be considered is organizational change or drift that is inevitably present as a part of the chaotic nature of the workplace. A new manager may introduce incompatible values or work methods and processes that change to some extent what is going on. There are, of course, always those unintended consequences of change that must be constantly addressed at a systemic level.

Information sharing, openness and inclusiveness are values that support organizational plasticity. Employees, supervisors, managers and executives must feel included in the process of locating change and planning and implementing it. Top-down decision making is antithetical to achieving organizational plasticity and avoiding resistance to change. I have always been impressed with how flexible and even enthusiastic employees can be at implementing change if they feel that they have been a part of the change process.

A Word of Caution

It is also important to appreciate that organizational downsizing and restructuring is a commonplace feature of the workplace as we begin the new century. It is not uncommon to hear of major manufacturers suddenly laying off tens of thousands of employees and closing plants, an outcome that I conjecture can often be avoided by improving organizational plasticity where adaptiveness is timely. Achieving dynamic adaptiveness must inevitably embrace the necessity of adjusting, from time to time, the size and nature of an organization's workforce and facilities. These adjustments, however, can be effectively and compassionately addressed by organizational plasticity. First, as discussed, by carefully monitoring change within and without, organizational change may be achieved on a timelier basis. Timely change may avoid the announcement of a major layoff or bankruptcy that every employee feels is a threat to him or her thereby draining away valuable creative and productive energy into personal survival. It may also be conjectured that by becoming more effective at organizational change, major external threats can be effectively met thereby creating a more vital and resilient organization. It will also be the case that the adjustments that must be made will involve smaller numbers of employees and may be accomplished by more compassionate means that may include retraining and relocation in place of being escorted to the front door by a security guard. In those cases where organizational plasticity must include flexing a workforce up and down, the supporting values must support employees in making these changes. For example, employees may be hired into positions that may be flexed. They may be compensated for their willingness to accept the flexing.

This consideration introduces a last factor to consider. Organizational values in support of organizational plasticity include such notions as respect and compassion for employees. Organizational plasticity is achieved by a workforce that does not feel that it has a target painted on its collective back or that it is greatly overextended thereby encouraging a sense of exhaustion from trying to carry on with fewer and fewer resources.

In Sum

Organizational plasticity represents a conceptual means of achieving dynamic adaptiveness where control ultimately fails to achieve predictability. An organization that is metaphorically fast on its collective feet translates into being able to locate what is going on and to changing in response to the many times chaotic nature of work and the marketplace. Achieving organizational plasticity in the service of dynamic adaptiveness, however, presents those in charge and employees a maximally challenging organizational vision that can be ultimately achieved only by embracing organizational values that support timely, effective and compassionate organizational change. Values such as inclusion, participation, openness, the availability of information and consensus building promote timely recognition of the need for change and its implementation with minimal resistance.

In sum, dynamic workplace theory informs our understanding of organizational life and design and the need for organizational plasticity to achieve dynamic adaptiveness. It is also the case that dynamic workplace theory informs living our lives outside of the workplace.

THE BIGGER PICTURE

The significance of the content of this book transcends the workplace. Dynamic workplace theory contains more than insights into the workplace, it provides insights into life in general. It provides insights into how we understand our families and the social groupings and organizations that contain many of the stresses and strains of organizational life. In fact, one of the central elements of dynamic workplace theory is the presence of the bidirectional porous boundary between worklife and the balance of one's life. Many of the psychologically defensive tendencies that energize dynamic workplace theory are directly imported into the workplace from our lives outside of work. It is also the case that many of the trials and tribulations as well as joys of workplace experience affect our experience outside of the workplace. It is, therefore, appropriate to inspect the contribution that dynamic workplace theory makes to understanding life outside of work.

The starting point for this discussion is an appreciation that our lives are filled with intrapsychic, interpersonal and group dynamics not unlike the workplace. Our thoughts and feelings affect how we relate to others and they to us. We may experience others and ourselves as trustworthy, trusting, respectful and open. Conversely we may find our thoughts and feelings and those of others disturbing, distrustful, not respectful and interpersonally defensive. These are the omnipresent potentials that dominate our lives with others and within groups. Dynamic workplace theory may then be thought of as a dynamic theory of life that informs how we understand our experience of ourselves, others and social groups.

Individual Dynamics

Discussion of dynamic workplace theory has focused attention upon the inevitability that we all, from time to time, rely upon psychological defenses to mediate distressing and anxiety-ridden self-experience. If we are not the keepers of others, becoming keepers of ourselves is in many ways equally problematic. Our thoughts and feelings may race out of control and lead to utterances and actions that we may regret. No one is metaphorically without sin and may cast the first stone within this context. Dynamic workplace theory underscores the significance of these kinds of dynamics that lead us to prefer autonomy over participating in a team, order and routine to fend off the experience of the unpredictable and control and mastery over others who it may be felt are inferior and must be led or threatening and must be controlled. Our psychological selves are indeed the baggage that we bring to every occasion. To the extent that we are more vulnerable to feeling anxious about others and events, the more likely we are to retreat to psychological defense mechanisms to manipulate, fend off or control the pain-filled experience. These intrapsychic dynamics are many times expressed within our relationships with others.

Interpersonal Dynamics

Interpersonal relationships can be filled with chaotic elements as well as instances where relations are overly controlled or dominated by one of the participants. It is an understatement to say that people can be unpredictable. However, just as in the workplace, these chaotic elements within relationships can become the wellspring for creativity and innovation to renew and refresh the relationship. It is also not hard to find instances within relationships where interaction has come to have many gradually developed, routinized and familiar aspects that are not easy to change. They provide stability and predictability while simultaneously restricting what may be thought, felt and done. In this regard the relationship may have gradually lost its adaptiveness. It is also the case that many relationships are dominated by one individual who presumes to call all of the shots. Others must essentially submit to his or her leadership and control. And last, there are those sought for relational outcomes where the participants create a true balance between themselves that serves to create respect, trust and open communication that maintains the relationship in a dynamic and adaptive state. Life with the other person is exciting and fulfilling.

These brief mentions of how the components of dynamic workplace theory fit within the larger context of our private lives need not be further elaborated. The applicability, upon reflection, is self-evident. It is the case that much of what was learned about dynamic workplace theory (the origins of chaos, bureaucracy, charismatic leadership and relational balance) informs our lives outside of work. Exploring all of these potential connections cannot be accomplished here as they would constitute the basis of yet another book. However, a few noteworthy aspects of the crossover of the theory into our lives outside of work should be mentioned.

The elements of the theory provide us a cognitive map that informs our thinking about what we and others are thinking, feeling and doing. In particular, the psychologically and socially defensive nature of the interpersonal world produces many of the harder to understand and appreciate nuances that we all have encountered in our relationships. Others and we continually introduce defensiveness into the anxiety-ridden side of our relationships. Why am I mad all of the time? What in the world was the reason he or she did that to me? Underlying many of these outcomes is defensiveness that is hard to locate and most often even harder to discuss. Controlling anxiety within the relationship just as is the case in the workplace can lead to outcomes not unlike those discussed in dynamic workplace theory. Things can become chaotic and unpredictable where efforts to achieve interpersonal intimacy and some type of dependable relatedness are constantly sabotaged by unanticipated thoughts, feelings and actions. Anxieties about commitment and giving up one's personal autonomy are at stake here. There may also be many efforts made by one participant to lay out the rules of engagement. You can do this but not that. We will do it this way, not that way. Always take off your shoes after you take out the garbage. Relationships are very often filled with constant tensions as to who may impose the rules to create predictability to allay anxiety. Similarly the anxiety that resides within relationships about who may do what to whom may in part be allayed by one person seizing control of the relationship and the other submitting. Once again anxiety-allaying predictability emerges. It may, therefore, be appreciated that many aspects of dynamic workplace theory can be observed to be present within relationships outside of the workplace.

It may also be understood that the discussion of stability and change described by dynamic workplace theory also applies to our relationships outside of work. There will inevitably develop many tensions when one member in the relationship seeks to change its dynamics. Greater intimacy may be desired that threatens to engulf and limit the autonomy of the other person. Perhaps all of the rules need to be revisited as they have become confining and not realistic. They may in fact be draining the life out of the relationship. It may also be the case that the heretofore submissive partner no longer accepts the continued dominance of one of the partners in the relationship. In each of these cases, as discussed in chapters 4 and 5, there are some aspects of the relationship that serve to promote continuing stability, including avoidance of the distressing experience of change. It is also the case that if change is to be undertaken, the process will be filled with many tensions and difficulties that must be overcome in order to migrate to another type of relationship, perhaps one filled with more exciting and chaotic elements as compared with the routinized condition of the moment. It is, therefore, not the case that yesterday we were that way and today we are this way. There is, as described in dynamic workplace theory, a long and sometimes arduous migration path that must be traveled to achieve the desired change that might create a more balanced and less interpersonally defensive relationship. What is true of our dyadic relationships is also true for our experience in social groupings.

Group Dynamics

If our relationships are filled with the same complexity articulated by dynamic workplace theory, it is also the case that our participation in many formal and informal groups outside of work is also filled with the same complexity as for those groups that reside within the workplace. Our social groups include chaotic, bureaucratic, charismatic and balanced types of experiences no matter where the group exists and regardless of its purpose of composition. We have all had occasion to be involved in groups that were chaotic and seemed to lack effective leadership and direction. Infuriatingly, nothing got accomplished. Everyone wanted to do it his or her way. A small social gathering may have maximal difficulty choosing an evening's entertainment. We have also all had occasion to participate in groups that seemed to be rule bound or highly political where one person seemed to have all of the power with perhaps others in hot pursuit. Our most fulfilling experiences have been those that contained a more balanced effort to be creative but under control and adequately led. A successful outing to take a long hike or participation in a well-coached sporting activity might be among our fondest and most fulfilling memories.

Once again, dynamic workplace theory offers insights into how our groups outside of work function. In fact the crossover is so readily apparent that further discussion is not really needed. It suffices to note that all of the dynamics of the theory are at work in our groups outside of work, including those aspects of group experience that make them stable over time and the tension-filled aspects of changing group dynamics.

In Sum

Our private lives are, upon closer inspection, much like our worklives. We are all individuals who possess psychologically defensive tendencies that are seamlessly interwoven into the workplace as well as our lives outside of work. It is also the case that our many relationships outside of work contain the same elements of those within the workplace, as is also the case for our experience in groups. Dynamic workplace theory, therefore, informs the lives we live outside of the workplace, providing some of the same clarity that it provides for our lives within the workplace. Dynamic workplace theory is a perspective for living our lives in general.

IN FINAL ANALYSIS

In final analysis we all hold within our minds a tacit theory of how the workplace works. These theories are often revealed when groups are asked to draw organization charts. In a large group no two are the same and some will be massively divergent. Dynamic workplace theory represents an effort to make the tacit and implicit explicit and, therefore, discussible by organizational participants. In this regard, it provides a cognitive map that enables discussion and exploration in the service of promoting dynamic organizational adaptiveness as well as adaptiveness in our lives outside of work.

Dynamic workplace theory represents an effort to more fully understand and appreciate the workplace and our lives outside of the workplace. The dynamic nature of the theory ultimately points to the limits of controlling the workplace, our lives, others and our experience. It represents an effort to more fully and comfortably embrace theoretical perspectives such as chaos theory where the notion of management power and control ultimately confronts the reality of the limitations of these notions. Ring organization design has been described as one possible way of busting the bureaucratic hierarchical organizational design paradigm that aims to control our thoughts, feelings and actions in the workplace. Ring organization design, therefore, underscores the difficulty and problematic nature of any endeavor to move beyond this organization design that has its roots in the eighteenth century. And finally, even if ring organization design is not embraced as a viable new organization form, it is possible to try to capture the benefits of balanced workplace experience in the form of dynamic adaptiveness.

References

Allcorn, Seth. 2002. *Death of the Spirit in the American Workplace*. Westport, CT: Quorum Books.

———. 1997. "Parallel Virtual Organizations." *Administration & Society* 29 (4): 412–439.

———. 1994. *Anger in the Workplace*. Westport, CT: Quorum Books.

———. 1996. *Workplace Superstars in Resistant Organizations*. Westport, CT: Quorum Books.

———. 1989. "Understanding Groups at Work." *Personnel*, 66 (8):28–36.

Allcorn, Seth, and Michael Diamond. 1997. *Managing People During Stressful Times: The Psychologically Defensive Workplace*. Westport, CT: Quorum Books.

Allcorn, Seth, Howell Baum, Michael Diamond, and Howard Stein. 1996. *The Human Cost of a Management Failure: Organizational Downsizing at General Hospital*. Westport, CT: Quorum Books.

Argyris, Chris. 1982. *Reasoning, Learning, and Action*. San Francisco: Jossey-Bass.

Ashback, Charles, and Victor Schermer. 1987. *Object Relations, the Self, and the Group*. New York: Routledge & Kegan Paul.

Barry, David. 1991. "Managing the Bossless Team: Lessons in Distributed Leadership." *Organizational Dynamics*, 20 (1):31–47.

Baum, Howell. 1990. *Organizational Membership*. Albany: State University of New York Press.

———. 1987. *The Invisible Bureaucracy*. New York: Oxford University Press.

Bennis, Warren. 1989. *Why Leaders Can't Lead*. San Francisco: Jossey-Bass.

Bergquist, William. 1993. *The Postmodern Organization*. San Francisco: Jossey-Bass.

Bion, Wilfred. 1961. *Experiences in Groups*. London: Tavistock Publications.

Blau, Peter, and Marshall Meyer. 1956. *Bureaucracy in Modern Society*. New York: Random House.

Cartwright, Dorwin, and Alvin Zander, eds. 1969. *Group Dynamics: Research and Theory*. New York: Harper & Row.

Colman, Arthur, and Harold Bexton. 1975. *Group Relations Reader*. San Rafael, CA: Associates Printing and Publishing.

Covey, Stephen. 1989. *The Seven Habits of Highly Effective People*. New York: Fireside.

Czander, William. 1993. *The Psychodynamics of Work and Organizations*. New York: Guilford Press.

De Board, Robert. 1978. *The Psychoanalysis of Organizations*. London: Tavistock Publications.

Diamond, Michael. 1999. "Embracing Organized Disorder: The Future of Organizational Membership." *Administrative Theory & Praxis* 21 (4):433–440.

———. 1993. *The Unconscious Life of Organizations: Interpreting Organizational Identity*. Westport, CT: Quorum Books.

———. 1984. "Bureaucracy as Externalized Self-System." *Administration & Society* 16 (2):195–214.

Diamond, Michael, and Seth Allcorn. 1987. "The Psychodynamics of Regression in Work Groups." *Human Relations*, 40 (8):525–543.

Donaldson, Lex. *American Anti-Management Theories of Organizaton: A Critique of Paradigm Proliferation*. Cambridge University Press, 1995.

Downs, Anthony. 1967. *Inside Bureaucracy*. Boston: Little, Brown and Company.

Fayol, Henri. 1949. *General and Industrial Management*. London: Sir Isaac Pitman & Sons.

Gabriel, Yiannis. 1999. *Organizations in Depth*. London: Sage.

———. 1993. Organizational Nostalgia: Reflections on "The Golden Age." In Stephen Fineman, ed., *Emotions in Organizations*. London: Sage, pp. 118–141.

Greenberg, Jay, and Stephen Mitchell. 1983. *Object Relations in Psychoanalytic Theory*. Cambridge: Harvard University Press.

Hall, Jay. 1994. "Americans Know How to be Productive If Managers Will Let Them." *Organizational Dynamics*, 22 (3):33–46.

Hammer, Michael, and James Champy. 1993. *Reengineering the Corporation: A Manifesto for Business Revolution*. New York: Harper Business.

Horney, Karen. 1950. *Neurosis and Human Growth*. New York: W.W. Norton.

Howell, Jon, David Bowen, Peter Dorfman, Steven Kerr, and Philip Podsakoff. 1990. "Substitutes for Leadership: Effective Alternatives to Ineffective Leadership." *Organizational Dynamics*, 19 (1):21–38.

Hummel, Ralph. 1982. *The Bureaucratic Experience*. New York: St. Martin's Press.

Jacoby, Henry. 1977. *The Bureaucratization of the World*. Berkeley and Los Angeles: University of California Press.

Jaques, Elliott. 1990. "In Praise of Hierarchy." *Harvard Business Review*, 68 (1):127–133.

———. 1989. *Requisite Organization*. Arlington, VA: Cason Hall.

Kanter, Rosebeth. 1983. *The Change Masters*. New York: Touchstone Books.

Kernberg, Otto. 1979. "Regression in Organizational Leadership." *Psychiatry*, 42:24–39.

Kets de Vries, Manfred and Associates. 1991. *Organizations on the Couch*. San Francisco: Jossey-Bass.

Kets de Vries, Manfred, ed. 1984. *The Irrational Executive*. New York: International Universities Press.

Kets de Vries, Manfred, and Danny Miller. 1984. *The Neurotic Organization*. San Francisco: Jossey-Bass.

Kilmann, Ralph, and Ines Kilmann. 1994. *Managing Ego Energy: The Transformation of Personal Meaning into Organizational Success*. San Francisco: Jossey-Bass.

Kohut, Heinz. 1984. *How Does Analysis Cure?* Chicago: University of Chicago Press.

Lawler, Edward. 1988. "Substitutes for Hierarchy." *Organizational Dynamics*, 17 (1):5–15.

Levinson, Harry. 1972. *Organizational Diagnosis.* Cambridge: Harvard University Press.

———. 1968. *Executive: A Guide to Responsive Management.* Cambridge: Harvard University Press.

Mayo, Elton. 1945. *The Social Problems of an Industrial Civilization.* Boston: Division of Research, Graduate School of Business Administration, Harvard University.

McMaster, Michael. 1996. *The Intelligence Advantage.* Boston: Butterworth-Heinemann.

Merton, Robert, Ailsa Gray, Barbara Hockey, and Hanan Selvin, eds. 1952. *Reader in Bureaucracy.* New York: The Free Press.

Metcalf, Henry, and Lyndall Urwick, eds. 1941. *Dynamic Administration: The Collected Papers of Mary Parker Follett.* New York: Harper & Brothers.

Micklethwait, John, and Adrian Woolridge. 1996. *The Witch Doctors: Making Sense of Management Gurus.* New York: Times Books.

Morgan, Gareth. 1986. *Images of Organization.* London: Sage.

———. 1990. *The Matrix of the Mind.* Northvale, NJ: Jason Aronson.

Ogden, Thomas. 1989. *The Primitive Edge of Experience.* Northvale, NJ: Jason Aronson.

Peters, Thomas, and Nancy Austin. 1985. *A Passion for Excellence.* New York: Warner Books.

Peters, Thomas, and Robert Waterman Jr. 1982. *In Search of Excellence.* New York: Harper & Row.

Roethlisberger, Fritz, William Dickson, and Harold Wright. 1939. *Management and the Worker.* Cambridge: Harvard University Press.

Schein, Edgar. 1985. *Organizational Culture and Leadership.* San Francisco: Jossey-Bass.

Schwartz, Howard. 1990. *Narcissistic Process and Corporate Decay: The Theory of the Organizational Ideal.* New York: New York University Press.

Senge, Peter. 1990. *The Fifth Discipline.* New York: Doubleday.

Shapiro, Edward, and Adrian Carr. 1991. *Lost in Familiar Places.* New Haven: Yale University Press.

Stacey, Ralph. 1992. *Managing the Unknowable: Strategic Boundaries Between Order and Chaos.* San Francisco: Jossey-Bass.

Stein, Howard. 1994. *Listening Deeply.* San Francisco: Westview Press.

Taylor, Frederick. 1947. *Scientific Management.* New York: Harper & Brothers.

Taylor, Thomas, Donald Friedman, and Dennis Couture. 1987. "Operating Without Supervisors: An Experiment." *Organizational Dynamics,* 15 (3):26–38.

Vaill, Peter. 1989. *Managing as a Performing Art.* San Francisco: Jossey-Bass.

Waring, Stephen. 1991. *Taylorism Transformed.* Chapel Hill: University of North Carolina Press.

Weber, Max. 1947. *The Theory of Social and Economic Organization.* Edited by T. Parsons. New York: Free Press.

Winnicott, Donald. 1965. *The Maturational Processes and the Facilitating Environment.* New York: International Universities Press.

Wren, Daniel. 1979. *The History of Management Thought.* New York: John Wiley & Sons.

Zaleznik, Abraham. 1966. *Human Dilemmas of Leadership.* New York: Harper & Row.

Zander, Alvin. 1985. *The Purposes of Groups and Organizations.* San Francisco: Jossey-Bass.

Index

Aggression in the workplace, 52
Alienation, 25
Annihilation anxiety, 42, 45–46
Anxiety, 8, 24, 31–32, 46, 48, 53, 61, 63, 76, 82, 84, 89; containment of, 96; control of, 27, 29, 34–35, 66, 97–98, 140; expansive solution to, 50; freedom from, 31; in groups, 144; interpersonal, 143–4; intrapersonal, 141–3; limiting by managing organizational boundaries, 140–1; promotion of, 138–40; resigned solution to, 45; self-effacing solution to, 49; within ring organizations, 144–5
Attachment anxiety, 42

Balanced workplace experience, 54–57, 158; as a positive force, 54; consultation to, 105–6; facilitation of, 99–100; in a group, 31–33; stability of, 37–38; versus bureaucratic workplace experience, 75–78, versus chaotic workplace experience, 68–72. *See also* Psychodynamics of
Best practices, 3
Blame game, 94
Boundary management within ring organizations, 140–1
Bounded instability, 44–45
Building organizational theory: start with a theory and apply it to the workplace, 15; start with the workplace and build a theory, 16

Bureaucracy: absence of excessive control within, 129; constructive aspects of, 55–56; consultation to, 104; control within, 163; dysfunctions of, 48–49, role of human nature in, 48; facilitation of, 98; group experience within, 26–28; history of, 47; impact of human nature upon, 48; nonbureaucratic organizational design, 114; stability of, 83–85; work experience within, 47–50, 157. *See also* Psychodynamics of
Bureaucratic hierarchy, 26–28, 45, 47, 49, 72–77, 84–85, 109–115, 119–20, 137–8, 150; absence of, 129; as a paradigm, xvii, 119, 166–7; redesigned to create ring organization, 134
Bureaucratic workplace experience, 157; versus balanced workplace experience, 75–78; versus chaotic workplace experience, 62–65, versus charismatic workplace experience, 72–75

Case examples, xv–xvi, 20–21, 81–82
Change, organizational. *See* Organizational change
Change dynamics, 34–35
Chaos: at work, 23, 43–45; bounded instability of, 44–45; constructive aspects of, 54–55
Chaotic workplace experience, 43–46, 80–83, 157; consultation to, 103; facilitation of 96–98; stability of, 80–83;

ABOUT THE AUTHOR

SETH ALLCORN is a principal of DyAD, a consulting firm specializing in organizational development and management, in Asheville, NC. Author of eight books on management and organizational life and numerous articles, he holds an MBA and a doctorate in Higher and Adult Education. His most recent books include *Managing People During Stressful Times* (1997), *The Human Cost of a Management Failure* (1996), and *Anger in the Workplace* (1994).